FROM SORROW'S WELL

UNDER DISCUSSION
Marilyn Hacker amd Kazim Ali, General Editors
Donald Hall, Founding Editor

Volumes in the Under Discussion series collect reviews and essays about individual poets. The series is concerned with contemporary American and English poets about whom the consensus has not yet been formed and the final vote has not been taken. Titles in the series include:

From Sorrow's Well

The Poetry of Hayden Carruth

Shaun T. Griffin, Editor

THE UNIVERSITY OF MICHIGAN PRESS

Ann Arbor

First paperback edition 2015
Copyright © 2013 by Shaun T. Griffin
All rights reserved

Published in the United States of America by
The University of Michigan Press
Printed and bound by CPI Group (UK) Ltd, Croydon, CR0 4YY

2018   2017   2016   2015   5   4   3   2

A CIP catalog record for this book is available from the British Library.

Library of Congress Cataloging-in-Publication Data

From sorrows well : the poetry of Hayden Carruth / Shaun T. Griffin, editor.
    pages cm. — (Under Discussion)
    ISBN 978-0-472-11896-0 (cloth : acid-
    1. Carruth, Hayden, 1921–2008—Criticism and interpretation.   I. Griffin,
Shaun T. (Shaun Timothy), 1953– editor of compilation.
    PS3505.A77594Z63   2013
    811'.54—dc23   2013015599

ISBN 978-0-472-03632-5 (pbk. : alk. paper)
ISBN 978-0-472-12117-5 (e-book)

for Hayden
who started in darkness and wrote through dawn,
and for Joe-Anne, Martha, the Bo and Rose Marie—
from all of us

Whatever our personal weaknesses may be,
the nobility of our craft will always be rooted
in two commitments, difficult to maintain:
the refusal to lie about what one knows and
the resistance to oppression.

—ALBERT CAMUS, NOBEL ACCEPTANCE SPEECH,
DECEMBER 10, 1957

Acknowledgments

The editor would like to thank several people, without whom this book would not have been possible: Betty Glass, Special Collections Librarian, University of Nevada, Reno, who repeatedly found missing references that I simply could not; Cameron Sutherland, fearless proofreader; William Wilborn, poet and editor of my countless drafts; Baron Wormser for his steadfast belief in this project; Gary Short, who purchased and gave me Carruth's first book, *The Crow and the Heart,* his book of criticism, *Working Papers,* and several early reviews from the *Hudson Review,* which ultimately led me to undertake this book; my friend and spouse, Debby, who gave her heart and mind to mine so that I might finish this gathering; the late Bill Cowee, who remarked from his convalescent bed, "This is something worth putting down in one's life"; Robert Leonard Reid for his erstwhile support of my unleavened attempts at writing; Steven Nightingale for the use of his library, which contained the intralinear translations of Virgil; Hayden, who gave me the guts to try anyway; Wendell Berry, who stood by this book from the outset; Douglas Unger, whose magnanimous spirit kept me going; Marilyn Hacker for her unwavering insistence that I get it right; and so many more hands that were held out to make *From Sorrow's Well* possible.

Grateful acknowledgment is given to the following publishers for permission to reprint previously published material.

Berry, Wendell. "My Friend Hayden." *Imagination in Place.* Berkeley: Counterpoint Press, 2010, 55–72. Copyright 2010 by Wendell Berry. Reprinted by permission of the author and publisher.

Booth, Philip. "A Few Riffs for Hayden, Sitting in with His Horn." *Seneca Review* 20, no. 1 (1990): 14–15. Copyright 1990 by *Seneca Review.* Reprinted by permission of the Philip E. Booth Family Trust and *Seneca Review.*

Budbill, David. "When You Use Your Head, Your Ears Fall Off:

Contents

Introduction

> Severe labour overcame all *things,* and poverty in our severe
> circumstances.
> —VIRGIL, *The Georgics* I.145–46

A book will not measure the consequence of Hayden Carruth's artistry—and so it is a daunting task to set out to edit one. His poetic labor spanned six decades, and he worked closely with and among the finest poets of his generation—from Delmore Schwartz to Donald Hall. As the young editor of *Poetry,* Carruth vigorously defended Ezra Pound, and in his seventies he resolutely turned down President Clinton's invitation to the White House. He was an editor, critic, anthologist, jazz writer, poetic spokesman, and foremost, both a reader's and a poet's poet. His belief in self-sacrifice for the good of the community (particularly the rural Johnson, Vermont, farmers) and the value that derives from mutual hard work informed his lasting poems. When I think of him in the Vermont cowshed where he wrote and the landscape within which he carved the language, the rituals, and the saga of his neighbors—people for whom poetry was not *necessary*—I think of Virgil's "strong sense of the necessity and dignity of labour." This appealed to Carruth. He knew that toil was inextricably woven with the larger pulse of the community, the place in which he lived and contributed. That is why his poems from this period resonate far from Vermont. The pattern of a life must be earned, and Carruth understood this.

This book is organized around Carruth's four major poetic themes, themes that he used to define himself: the realist, the jazzman, the survivor, and the innovator. I am haunted by the knowledge that some, like Galway Kinnell, James Wright, John Haines, and James Laughlin, are missing from these pages, or are underrepresented, like Adrienne Rich and Denise Levertov and others who saw Carruth as central to the practice of poetry.

The first section of the book concerns the realist. For most of his life, Hayden Carruth lived in relative isolation. Nonetheless, his poetics were founded on the belief that poems should be read, that they should have a social utility. This went against the grain of his peers and the time in which he wrote. His most widely read poems come from the years he spent in Vermont cultivating a realist's voice, a poetry based on the values of shared labor, community, thrift, and hardship. Many readers feel these years of struggle sculpted the humanity that is emblematic of his poetry. This comes from his belief that in order for a poem to be authentic it must be based in experience, must be honest, and not derivative. He felt a poetic responsibility to others, a desire to account for a sensibility that imagined this world beyond its fragmented state. Against the lingering backdrop of the Cold War and the Vietnam War that followed, his poetry is suffused with personal and political skepticism grounded in concern for his fellow man. The essays and reviews in this section point to this fundamental characteristic of his work—which, sadly, made him a literary outsider.

This first section is followed by the jazzman. For Carruth, real freedom came in jazz because he could finally improvise on set harmonics—fixed rhythmic patterns in a line. His early poem "Freedom and Discipline" is about trying to stray from the metric structure of a poem to create the sonic quality of jazz. The irony is, like most of his art, he was a self-taught musician and yet his book of essays on jazz, *Sitting In,* is considered a standard in the field. Carruth heard the music, the beat in both jazz and blues and recognized how this could be imported to poetry. This was a seminal insight for the poet because it expanded his range of tonal qualities. It gave him permission to improvise like so many jazz riffs. His poems became meditations on sound. Whether those sounds were the colloquial speech of his Vermont neighbors or the worn tracks of city dwellers, he heard their rhythms as music, as a musician, and this proved to be an indelible quality of his poems and his jazz writing. This ability to hear jazz in spoken language freed him to create like a jazz musician—again making his poetry harmonically fluid, like speech put to music. This was a huge triumph for a self-taught clarinetist.

The third section of the book is the survivor. Carruth was never far from personal devastation. From the terrible fear of agoraphobia, from the anguish of realizing that hope and despair were literally one and the same, from the booze and the cigarettes to the joy and sorrow of loving, he wrote always and lived far from the center of the literary mainstream. If he had not been such a survivor, virtually none of the books would have surfaced. But he was determined "to annul the verdict" of so many. He made a room of his own, to paraphrase Virginia Woolf, in rural Vermont. The long winters, his mutual interdependence on "cowshit farmers," and his poverty contributed to his nightly output. After working all day he wrote poetry, sometimes until dawn, so that he might have something to show for his day. Due to the necessity of taking literary "hackwork," he became a formidable critic, a person who reviewed dozens of books every quarter. Now, in retrospect, his opinions were not only correct, but they were the defining moment in the careers of many poets. Reading his reviews is like peering into the future. It is a miracle he survived, but he did, and his art is a testimony to his undying will to create a record of that experience.

The final section of the book is the innovator. Strangely, boredom figured into the creation of Carruth's original poetic forms. As he moved from one location to the next, Carruth found the physical environment fresh, the language startling, the local habits and visitations all fodder for the new poetic forms—the Vermont narratives, the georgics (like Virgil's but in name only), the long, open-line poems of *Tell Me Again How the White Heron Rises and Flies Across the Nacreous River at Twilight Toward the Distant Islands,* and the "paragraph," a highly evolved fifteen-line sonnet. In some cases he used this form for his longer poems, *The Sleeping Beauty* and the sequence simply titled "Paragraphs" from *Brothers, I Loved You All.* These latter poems remain among his finest. But again, after writing in a particular form he grew tired of it and reinvented himself as an artist. This, too, accounts for his readership among his closest peers but a general misunderstanding of his poetry by critics. His poetry was varied and difficult to label. He wanted to create the most meaningful art he could—but within his strictures, not theirs. Consequently, literary people frequently overlooked him because he was not interested in their community. His primary reason for writing was the reader. That was an uncommon threshold with which to begin a poem. Eliot, Pound, and Stevens had broken the ground of the poem seemingly written unto itself. Carruth's forms were designed to let the reader in, to avoid separation between poet, poem, and reader. In most cases, he succeeded, and that frightened all but those who were secure enough in their own work to acknowledge such an accomplishment.

I hope this book will begin to answer the question that Judith Weissman raised in *Working Papers,* and was continued with the special edition of *Seneca Review* edited by David Weiss: where have Carruth's readers gone? These editors began a conversation that has lasted well into this century. The writers gathered here understood Carruth's unrelenting desire "To stake it all / On a flawed, soft, / Abused and unreliable, / Imperfect word: / Magnanimity," and brought their full attention to it. This luminous chorus is an invitation to return to Carruth's shelf of reflection and edification. And so, if I can, I welcome the reader to the portent of his lifework—from jazz to georgics, from Vermont to villanelles, from sonnets to haiku.

Read on that he may not die, that he may not disappear and become a poet that was regarded but not understood.

S.T.G.

1. *Realist—the social art of a solitary man*

realism: N. 3. Fidelity in art and literature to nature or to real life and to accurate representation without idealization.

We're realists,
And realism means place, and place means
where we are.

—HC, "Vermont"

Quadruple bypass: yes, he had it.
What happens next is anybody's guess.
After the surgeon's pre-op visit
he pulled the tubes and needles out, got dressed
and stalked outside to smoke a cigarette.
The surgeon threatened not to operate.
Old heart, old curmudgeon,
old genius, terrified old man
who more than anyone knows form
is one rampart of sanity,
your mind is ringing like a fire alarm
and you still smoke three packs a day.
Not lover, barely friend, from this distance
I break your rule and say,
stay in the present tense. Stay in the present tense.

—Marilyn Hacker, *Desesperanto: Poems 1999–2002,* 2003

DAVID WEISS

An Interview with Hayden Carruth

Carruth: . . . and I went into the Army during World War II and I
wrote some poetry while I was there, too. When I got out I had the
GI bill, and I went to graduate school at the University of Chicago
because I didn't want to go to work, and there suddenly everything
opened up, and I began to read Eliot and Pound and Williams and
Stevens and people like that whom I had never heard of before. And
also writers of that period, writers of my own age. There were a
couple or three good bookstores in Chicago at that time and I used
to go there and buy little magazines and things like that. And so I
began writing seriously. By then I was 25 years old. My first published poem was in 1946, I believe, and I wrote a lot then. I had
some poems accepted by *Poetry,* and I was invited downtown to
have lunch with the editors, and I became a member of the staff and
eventually became editor. So by that time I was stuck.

Weiss: By that time you had a sense of vocation?

Carruth: I had a sense of vocation. So I think of my early years
when I was living in the country in a little town and not getting a
very good education as a preparation. I think the desire to write
poetry was there. I was just terribly ignorant at the time. I didn't
really know what I was doing.

Weiss: What made your sense of vocation? What did you feel
poetry could do that made it worthy of a vocation?

Carruth: Well, I think the sense that we all had in the middle part
of the century was that the great poets of the modernist period had
made changes in our lives and in civilization in general. It wasn't
until later that we began to be concerned with what the solution
was. In 1935–1950 we felt that—I can remember Alan Tate saying
one time that what he and his generation had wanted to do, hoped
to do, was to move American education off the dead center it had
been on since Cambridge in 1870. And that, in fact, is what they did.
The modernist poets entered the curriculum in universities and
even in high schools and the terrific emphasis on Longfellow and
Whittier and Lowell was abated, settled. And we felt that that was

7

progress, we felt that something had happened, that poetry had made this happen, that people were consequently more aware not only of poetry but of life in general. I don't know that in the long run it made all that much difference, but that's the way we felt then, and I felt as a young poet that that was what I would aspire to do. I would write poems that would be good enough and strong enough to make people move, to change their minds.

Weiss: Do you still feel like a modernist?

Carruth: No. I got over the modernists a long time ago. In fact, I think I was one of the first who began criticizing the new critics and modernist writers in general back in the 50's, early 60's. There were a lot of things wrong with the modernists and in my prose writing, in my criticism, I was pretty clear about it. In my poetry I wasn't so clear. I really didn't know how to write poetry that wasn't modernist. All of the business I've associated with energy and function and form and so on that I picked up from Pound and Eliot became my working habits, and it's hard to find your way out of that. I'm not sure I ever did, but younger poets have now.

Weiss: You mean you gave up being a modernist in the sense that poetry has no efficacy in the world anymore?

Carruth: I was forced to give up that idea. The people who affected me the most when I was in my twenties and early thirties were the mid-century European existentialist writers, and they had this idea of engagement or responsibility that I believed in and still do believe in. One of the things that was wrong with the modernists was that they tried to get away from reality in the period between the two wars. Some of them were explicit about it, like Gottfried Benn in Germany and Wyndham Lewis in England, and others were not explicit but they were doing it anyway. They were trying to create some kind of imaginative world that would be saner and safer and more bearable than the actual one. Then came the death camps and all the terrorism in the late 30's and 40's. And people like Sartre said you don't create an imaginary world, you write about the real world. That's been the guideline of my work. I have never been a poet for poetry's sake. I never have been able to do that. I was raised in a family where my grandfather and my father were both newspapermen and professional writers, and always they insisted on the social utility of writing. I can remember sitting in my father's office, he was the editor of a daily newspaper, and when I was six or seven or eight years old, watching him at work pounding on his typewriter with three fingers the way he did and wearing a green eyeshade and sleeve guards, smoking a cigar; he was pounding away at the typewriter and he suddenly looked up at me and he said, "Don't ever take any job that isn't a service to the community." I can remember his saying that to me . . .

Weiss: Milan Kundera has said that in the West, God gave way to culture, and now culture has given way.

Carruth: That's a big, broad statement but I think that it certainly has a lot of truth in it. That's what the modernist movement tried to do: replace conventional faith with the imagination, and culture with works of art. It failed. Now I see a lot of struggling and exploring and experimenting among younger folks, my students, for example, and I don't see anybody that's got a clear vision of the right thing to do, but at least they are trying to find some other way.

Weiss: "North Winter" ends, "Winter is the vacancy that flowers in a glance wakening compassion and mercy and/ lovingkindness north is the aurora north is deliverance emancipation . . . / . . . north is nothing." All human and moral values seem to derive from this emptiness, this abyss. Has this remained true for you?

Carruth: Yes. Very clearly. When I was writing "North Winter" I was also writing a book about Albert Camus called *After the Stranger* and it was the first winter I spent in the North country, and I went out for a walk each day and by the time I came back I wrote down a little note, and then at the end of the winter I realized that these notes had some coherence so I edited them together and wrote that, the "Afterward," I think it's called; it comes at the end of the book. I was thinking a great deal about freedom and responsibility and the difficulty of the human being who has no faith, no support in a metaphysical sense. Life is absurd, yes. There is nothing, there is no underpinning, there is no over-intelligence: the human being makes his own way by resisting and by denying, by disacquiescence, and sustains himself as a human being with some kind of human dignity in spite of chaos and absurdity. So those are the things I was thinking about when I wrote that poem. And so they got into it. I think I still feel that way, basically. Many of my friends, it seems lately, have become religious people in one sense or another. I've had some discussions with them about it. I just don't see it. I don't like it.

Weiss: You think it has something to do with the exhaustion that comes with the continual work of self-creation?

Carruth: I think that has a lot to do with it. Also, the exhaustion of living in the nuclear age. All the terrors that we have all the time.

The end of the world is now a real possibility. People have been writing about it since the beginning of time and it has usually been a vision like some kind of terrific violence, recently atomic, but now it's just what's happening when you look out the window.

Weiss: "The Incorrigible Dirigible," the first poem in *Tell Me Again How the White Heron Rises and Flies Across the Nacreous River at Twilight Toward the Distant Islands,* ends with these lines, "such a magnificent, polychronogeneous idea, flight by craft that is lighter than air!/ I hope it will be revived." Do you think of this as a figure for the poem itself?

Carruth: I did at the time that I wrote that poem. Most of my concepts have sprung up spontaneously and in an impromptu way and many of them I throw away. I do believe in that quality of just taking anything, coming out of anywhere, out of any topic or any object and making it float, making it shape itself in such a way that it will go. That is what poets do in our time. That is necessarily a fragmentary process. We don't believe in masterpieces anymore and I don't think we should. We don't believe in the Great American Novel. We used to talk about it all the time when I was young. The Great American Novel is never going to be written or it's going to be a compendium of a hundred novels written by a hundred different people.

Weiss: In this notion we have come a long way from the 40's and its idea of the perfectly made gem.

Carruth: Yes, we have. I think we've had to get rid of that idea. That was the modernist hangover from the nineteenth century, I think. The idea that a poet like Yeats or Eliot could produce a work that would be self-enclosed, autonomous, and famous—kind of a monument—we had to give that up. It just didn't work. In a world of terrorism and war and all the rest of our problems that kind of poem was irrelevant. It's a museum piece and as working poets, as writers, we have to engage ourselves more in the chaotic situation we live in. A lot of things have happened. One of them is certainly the emphasis that the Theorists with a capital T put on the deconstructability of the text and the inability of the language to represent contemporary reality and so on. Ideas like that are very damaging to the modernists. But we live with them now all the time.

Weiss: "Before a man can create a poem," you once wrote, "he must create a poet." What did you have in mind?

Carruth: I don't remember writing that and I don't know really what I had in mind at the time. But, a poet has to be somebody who is sensitive and has some kind of a vision. Even a very amorphous vision. The reason that most of the kids that are coming along now are not poets is because they don't have that. They don't have any sense of goodness. To me, poetry and goodness are almost synonymous. They go together, so in order to be a poet, you have to have a vision at some point. As a product of the 20's and 30's, the depression and all that sort of thing, I have that. I also believe that the real poem, and I've said this many times, the real poem is not what's on the paper, it's what occurs in the poet's mind, in his imagination, before he starts messing around with language.

Weiss: So the creating of the poet is a prior activity?

Carruth: Frequently the imaginative process and the writing process go hand in hand and you don't conceive the whole poem until you've written it. But before you sit down to write, you have to have an imaginative field of knowledge and feeling of what you want the poem to be like. Usually you have some sense of timbre or texture, something like that. The relationship between imagination and reality is something that's important.

Weiss: Do poems begin with a hurt?

Carruth: I think poems begin with a concern. They may begin with a hurt. I think the concern is prior. You have to have that. If you are not concerned about something then your poem is going to be empty.

Weiss: You have always been concerned with philosophy. Is that a matter of idea or language? What is the distinction between poetry and philosophy?

Carruth: Well, it seems to me that in the most fundamental sense both the poet and the philosopher are aiming at the same thing. The poet works with his imagination, the philosopher works with his reason. That's very arbitrary and the fact of the matter is that poets work with reason and philosophers work with imagination. The extent to which I can write specifically on the topic of philosophy has varied from time to time. When I was writing the *Heron* poems, I was reading Schopenhauer and enjoying it a good deal. What Kant was trying to do when he wrote the *Critique of Pure Reason* was to explain something, explain how we function, who we are, and I think he did it very beautifully. It's out of date now, and no longer are we able to believe that he had his finger on truth with a capital T, no more than anyone else. But I think of it as a poem basically. Something I like to read for the way he orchestrated his ideas. In that sense philosophy has been very important to me.

Weiss: You say the following thing, and I wonder if it's similar to what you think is common to the philosopher and the poet. "The poet's task is to fashion a new image of man in his own time."

Carruth: Well, that was an idea that was common among the modernist poets and new critics. That certainly is part of what the poet does—give back an image to the reader to enable him to see himself in his own contemporary predicament, and that's part of what the philosopher does too.

Weiss: Does *Asphalt Georgics* provide such an image, satirically?

Carruth: Yes. I don't think of it as being satire very much.

Weiss: You think it's a kind of verisimilitude?

Carruth: I think it is, and I hope the poems in that book have a kind of sympathy. There's a certain sense in which I am making fun of the people in *Asphalt Georgics,* but I hope that the reader gets the idea, the feeling, that I'm making fun of myself just as much, that we're all in the same boat. Speech patterns have always interested me a lot. While I was writing those poems I intentionally carried a notebook around which I don't normally do. I copied down things that I overheard in diners and restaurants and bars and places like that and then I'd go home and work them into a poem. I wrote most of those poems fairly easily and I enjoyed writing them. From the very beginning I always liked to write against a relatively difficult, technical program of some kind. I invented those poems when I lived in Liverpool, N.Y., near Syracuse, in 1981 or 1982, because I felt I was in such a changed environment from anything I had lived in before, and I thought my poetry ought to change too. I had written syllabic poems before but never of this kind, and I sat down one day soon after I got there with a tablet of paper and I began writing down numbers and things like that and I came up with a simple, little syllabic stanza with perfect rhymes, and they seem to have evolved out of each other; one poem suggested the next one and then I exhausted it. That's what has happened to me many times in my life. I got tired of writing the syllabic lines. The sonnets (*Sonnets,* The Press of Appletree Alley, 1989) were written in a period of about a year and a few months and I wrote five or six a day sometimes; other times I went a couple of weeks without writing any. I came to the point where I didn't want to write any more sonnets. So I stopped. The long-lined poems in the *Heron* book were also written in a period of about a year and a half and I got tired of writing those also.

Weiss: How different are your "paragraphs" from the sonnets?

When you started writing sonnets why didn't they turn into fifteen liners? Is it purely the rightness of the arbitrary? Or is it a matter of structure?

Carruth: I think it's a question of my relationship to the tradition. When I wrote the sonnets I wanted to write a sonnet sequence based on sex and romance in the great Renaissance tradition. The fifteen liner, what I call a paragraph, is my own. I invented it and used it a number of different times. I used it for *The Sleeping Beauty* because I thought of it as my poem, my personal form. I suppose the reader doesn't notice much difference between the paragraph and the sonnet, one extra line and a slightly different rhyme scheme, but I do think that there's a difference. When I first invented the paragraph, I was influenced by a sonnet of Paul Goodman that I published in *Poetry* magazine when I was an editor in which he displaced the final couplet and put it in the middle after the octet and followed by a quatrain, and I like that. I thought it changed the sonnet, gave it a kind of a pivot in the middle. So when I invented the paragraph I put a rhymed couplet in the middle, a tetrameter couplet, and in a way the whole history of what I did with the paragraph was to get around that terrible barrier, that terrible problem I'd given myself, because having a rhymed couplet in the middle tends to break up the poem terribly and I had to find ways to flow through that.

Weiss: And you felt the necessity of retaining that difficulty?

Carruth: I'm stubborn as hell. I did it from the beginning.

Weiss: "Tradition is not convention. Tradition is always unexpected/ like the taste of the pomegranate, so sweet," you wrote in "My Father's Face."

Carruth: Well, I think that's true. I think that the tradition is alive and it is always surprising. When you run into it, it does have the quality of novelty. That seems to be paradoxical in a way because it is attached to things in the past. But as a person who is very interested in jazz music, I have always been fascinated by the problem of how you can tell that a record made in 1950 by a group of good musicians has the spontaneity and originality that a record made in 1960 by other musicians who are influenced by the first ones and who are imitating them, doesn't have. I have no solution to that problem. I don't know how to explain it, but I know; I can tell when the musicians on a record are doing something new and original and fresh and spontaneous and when they're not. Even though the imitation ten years later may be very, very good, it doesn't have the same quality. And that's the tradition, the tradition does that. I teach prosody to a certain extent. All kinds of prosody, not just conventional English prosody, but other kinds, too. It seems to me that the most important function of prosody, of meter, measure of any kind, is not to establish a rhythm for the sake of the rhythm itself, but to let the reader or the hearer anticipate what's coming, the next beat. And that kind of propulsiveness, that's the tradition. Meter serves the same function in a poem that tradition serves in literature in general. It is what allows us to see what's coming next, anticipate the next phrase, the next phase, the next evolution. I think that's a fair analogy.

Weiss: Would you use measure and meter interchangeably? It seems measure is something more—many of the lines in your poems which are not strictly syllabic, strictly accentual, strictly iambic, have measure. The sense of measure doesn't seem to have to do exactly with that.

Carruth: Well, I use the term in different ways, at different times, and that's part of the inconsistency. Fundamentally, though, I agree with you. My sense of measure is much bigger and it doesn't even apply to poetry to a certain extent. You know in Langue D'oc, the language of the south of France, *mesura* is the word for wisdom. Aristotle said the same thing: wisdom consists of a just perception of measure. But when I'm teaching prosody I use the term to indicate the meter, the beat, or the actual rhythm in that particular line.

Weiss: In one poem, Paul Goodman writes, "Through the brilliant curtain of July,/ I spy the way whereon we deviate,/ but do not err." Something about both deviating but not erring has to do with the large capacity within an ideal like measure.

Carruth: Deviation is what we invent. The way we get to where we go is the invention. And it needs limits. It needs the tradition. It needs something. Jazz musicians have discovered that you can improvise in infinitely extraordinary ways, but almost always it works best if it's based on a simple meter and a simple figure. A simple melodic structure. Musicians who have tried to improvise in what they call complete freedom without anything in their minds to control the way the improvisation goes have not been so successful. And I think it's the same in poetry. I have to have limits at any rate when I write, and that's one of the reasons why I sometimes write in syllabics. You can't hear syllabics in English. It's simply a compositional aid for me and I like that sense of working against a frame or a scaffold or whatever you want to call it. I think probably in most of the long-lined poems in *Heron* there is a certain consistency from line to line. Not a fixed number of beats by any means, but they are not extremely different. I'm not the kind of poet who writes long-lined poems with very short lines stuck in there. The rhythm in those poems is controlled by syntax, by the flow of ideas, by the mood I'm interested in. In very much of my poetry I am conscious of pace, the speeding up or the slowing down, keeping the beat but at the same time creating a tension against the beat through fast and slow passages. I think that's at work in the long-lined poems just as it is in all of the others.

Weiss: I think particularly for the long-lined poems the word *pace* is good because one feels a kind of gait that remains steady no matter the terrain you're passing over.

Carruth: I think that's true. As a person who has been a musician and very interested in music, I think for me, personally, the beat is the beat and as Count Basie said, "No cheating." Four to the measure and no cheating. Well, I feel that way. Obviously the analogy of poetry to music is a little dangerous, but for me the beat is the beat and I stick to it. If I create a long line that's got 9 or 11 beats in it, that's what determines the line breaks. The pacing of the line is determined by vowel sounds to a certain extent, by the difficulty or ease of the consonants, and especially by the placement of unaccented syllables. How many you have together in one place, how few you have and things like that. At Syracuse University, to the extent that I teach anything, I try to teach the—I don't like to use the word tradition and I don't like to use the word convention—I like to teach the young people something about what I call the company, the assembly of great artists: great poets, artists, and philosophers. Take Alexander Pope, for instance, a very important poet. When I was learning, when I was a kitten, I studied his versification, I tried to imitate it, but more than that I found him a person whom I admired tremendously and I still do. Here is a man who, before the Romantics ever came along, helped invent the first poetic persona in a way that had never been done before as far as I know. Here was a man whose life was absolutely miserable and crippled, no sex, nothing. So whatever life he had, had to be in his poetry. Between his early poems and his late poems he turned himself into a presence, a real presence in the poems. And that presence is as important to me, was as important to me as a young writer, as the actual poems themselves. The quality of his imagination flows out from the poems like an aura, and the energy, the love—these poems are written in love. Most people don't realize that and I think that is very important. Young poets can attach themselves to a dead poet in that way. I don't know how many of them do it, but it is possible.

Weiss: What you describe sounds like a relationship of apprenticeship.

Carruth: Very much. I remember when I first came to Syracuse and first went to work as a teacher, I had a conversation, as everybody has to, with the Dean. The Dean was a chemist and he said to me, "Well, what do you think about teaching?" And I said that I feel the way to teach would be to have the teacher or maybe two teachers or three teachers and a few students living together and running a farm. It would be similar to the apprentice/master relationship that existed in the studios of painters during the Renaissance, for instance. I got a surprising response from him. He said, "That's true. It's the same way with chemistry. The most learning takes place in the laboratory, not in the classroom, where the teacher and his assistants are equally engaged in a project of some kind. There is basically an apprentice/master relationship between them and it is informal. That's the way chemists learn the most." I thought that he was perceptive and I still think that. There's no way that anybody has figured out how to do this within the structure of the academy. But I try to push my workshops in that direction, if possible.

Weiss: How did you turn out to be such an inveterate neologizer? Whether it's prefixes or suffixes or a word like *bestowal* from the Brahms cigar poem or *furiosity* or *vanishment* or *verbigeration.* They all feel inspired, outlandish and, most of all, wonderfully appropriate at that instant.

Carruth: Well, the only thing I can say about that is that they come spontaneously and I think when I do that there's a little crisis. If you're a jazz musician and you are improvising, you're blowing along on your horn and you come to a point where something is just too difficult, you don't know what to do, so you just blow as hard as you can and make a sharp noise. Hope that it works.

Weiss: Well, that's a good explanation for it. It mostly does work. I think of it as a kind of witching stick; it's something that just shoots down to some improbable configuration of syllables.

Carruth: I think that poets of my age, basically, and older poets too of the twentieth century in America, have been lucky because the condition of the American language in the twentieth century has been similar to the condition of the English language during the Elizabethan Period and the Tudor Period. It's expanded. Neologisms are a part of the popular imagination. There's a lot of wonderful slang that's been invented during our time, which is necessary. It sticks; it fills a need. There weren't any words there to do it before. Technology and so on obviously was also pumping vocabulary into the language all the time, so that we have an inventive attitude toward language and I love that. I love to be on the street and listen to kids talking, especially if they're kids who are black or Puerto Rican, any group that has a subdialect that has at least a potentiality of replacing standard English. I've always felt that some of the best writing, a lot of the best writing, comes from the fringe. It doesn't come from Oxford or Cambridge, it doesn't come from Harvard. It comes from Ireland, it comes from Nigeria, it comes from the south in the United States, it comes from the edges where people feel a lack of language. The language is not rich enough for them and their conditions are changing so they've got to have new words and then give new meanings to old words, all kinds of things like that.

Weiss: A lot of your neologisms have a wonderfully archaic feel. I don't know if archaic is the right word, but they feel etymologically rich.

Carruth: I think I have always been interested in old language as long as it's lively and has something going there. I love to read seventeenth-century prose. I don't read very many sermons and I don't read political tracts, but there are a few books, prose books, from that period that I think are just wonderful. Things like Aubrey's *Brief Lives* and *Pepys's Diaries* and Bradford's *History of the Plymouth Plantation.* Those writers make up grammar, they make up syntax, and they make up their vocabulary as they go along.

Weiss: Robert Pinsky has written in his recent book *Poetry and the World:* "To imagine an American life, American poetry characteristically—maybe inevitably—begins by imagining, implicitly or explicitly, its own unrealized place in that life."

Carruth: I think that's an acute formulation of a problem that we all deal with all the time. I just finished writing a review for a magazine. One of those big quarterly round-up things, and most of the poets, all of the poets in the review except one, are living American poets. The other is Yannis Ritsos. A number of things stuck with me as I was reading that distinguish Ritsos from the American poets. One of the things, strangely, is that Ritsos is not influenced by Catallus as everybody else in Europe and America is. I don't think I would have noticed that if I hadn't also been reviewing a new translation of Catallus at the same time. More important, Rit-

sos so obviously lives in and has lived all of his life in a social, political, and cultural environment that was active and in which he
participated as an active agent, and it gets into his poems, even poems that don't have anything to do with politics. Every poem of his
has a kind of, what I call, applicability that our poems don't have in
this country. In our country we don't have that. Not just poets, but
most Americans live in a kind of political torpor. We feel helpless.
The kind of changes we know ought to be made are not being
made. In our poetry we tend to turn away. We all work in the
knowledge that we're not producing any effect on our civilization.
The politicians and the powerful people in our country conduct
their operations and their lives without any reference to art at all. In
other places, that's not true.

Weiss: At the close of "Paragraphs" you say you'd rather be a
"supernumerary/cockroach i'th'corner . . . / than be the Prazedint
of the Wurrurld." What would you do if you were "Prazedint of the
Wurrurld?"

Carruth: Well, I would put things right. God knows how. I think
people of good will and intelligence all over the world know what's
wrong, know that the evils in the world are basically derived from
greed and the desire for power. That kind of thing can be legislated
against. That's what I would do if I were a politician. I would legislate
against the greed. Legislate against people living off of other people.
There's nothing new about that. Aristotle said the same thing. Certainly not on the scale of the world or even of the nation, but communal enterprises at one time or another throughout history have
worked. Most people of intelligence and goodwill have been interested in it. Basically that was what Ezra Pound was interested in. He
was interested in a banking system which didn't have any usury. And
he wrote about the historical examples of that happening. There
weren't very many of them and he got to be cranky and kind of
crazy. We have here in Oneida a pretty good example of a nineteenth-
century utopian community, the Oneida Community. Organized
first, I think, after the Civil War, they believed in communal living to
a very large extent, even to the extent of communal marriages. Consequently they raised a lot of people's eyebrows. But they succeeded,
for a long time anyway, and they succeeded financially too because
they founded the Oneida Community Silverware Company, which
is still profitable. Things like that are hopeful.

Weiss: After legislating against power and greed, would you then
outlaw legislation itself?

Carruth: Well, I would. But I'm what you used to call a philosophical anarchist. I don't have any illusions that real anarchism is going to work on a large scale. I do believe, however, that freedom is the basic goal, and in political activity you try to move in that direction. I know that in my life, a sense of sympathy for suffering people began very, very early and where it came from I'm not certain. It may mean that I had been injured myself in my childhood. I can remember, though, when my family got the first radio that we had, which was perhaps 1927 or '28, being in tears because of things I heard on the radio that other people didn't pay much attention to. I remember especially a terrible, terrible program called *Major Bowe's Amateur Hour.* It was during some international fair in New York back around 1930. This was an ordinary amateur program where people came on and did their turn and if they weren't good enough the Major would bang a bell and interrupt them and chase them off. So they had an African guy from the fair who came and who couldn't speak any English and didn't know anything about American culture; I doubt if he even knew exactly where he was, but he was a fine drummer, a wonderful percussionist on the African instruments, and he began to play. He was doing what he did and the major laughed and the audience laughed and the major banged on the bell and this poor African guy got dragged off the stage, and I wept for hours after that. I just could not believe that anybody could be that cruel, that barbarous. That was in me. I don't know where it came from, it was in me. It's always been.

Weiss: I think of that section in *The Sleeping Beauty,* the 53rd, in which you're thinking about the Cuban revolution in relation to the poet Ernesto Cardenal, "who loves [the] revolution, the equalities,/ the courage, the beautiful new nation." But then you say, "Cardenal *saw* the camps, saw the oppression,/ Cardenal saw the State. . . ." You then call yourself, "still a boy-anarchist," and add, "They say: choose./ But Spirit he cannot, he can't. Then what shall he/ Do?/ Nothing./ He'll be. And he'll sing the blues." That's an awful yet necessary position to have to be in. In this poem, you are unable to affirm this change because of the suffering it has caused.

Carruth: Yes. That's true. I have always thought of myself as radical and a person who wants radical change. I still do, but the idea of suffering that has to go with it is more powerful in me than the desire to see that change, I guess, especially since so often the change is not a change but simply more of the same. But it is a tough question, and when I say that there is nothing to do but sing the blues

I'm saying, in effect, that the existential situation of the individual in the twentieth century is such that probably the only real outlet is in making something. It doesn't have to be a poem, it doesn't have to be music, but it has to be something imagined, something created.

Weiss: It was Camus who said that either you can be on the side of those who make history or on the side of those who are subjected to history, and a writer must be on the side of those who are subjected to the forces of history.

Carruth: In that sector, in the sector of political thought and feeling, he was more important in my life than anybody else—although I had read a lot of radical literature when I was young, including a lot of anarchist literature. What I say in the poem is true. I did become an anarchist to the extent that one can become anything at the age of fifteen, when I read an account of the meeting of the International, the First International in Brussels, I think, in 1870 or so, when Marx and Bakunin split over the question of the dictatorship of the proletariat and the takeover of the state. I still believe that. Basically I've gone through Lord knows how many changes and shifts in attitude and judgment since then, but basically I still think that the ideal is freedom, that both the community and the individual should be moving toward freedom even though they never can reach it.

Weiss: There's a passage at the end of *Sitting In* which in its visionary hope reminds me of Whitman. It's not a "Prazedint's" hope; clearly it's a poet's:

I don't know what a poet's dreams are worth—maybe not much. But I dream continually of a great session where race, or more properly speaking, ethnicity, has no significance at all, where "culture" is irrelevant, where every performer and listener participates freely and equally in the bodily and spiritually wrenching, exhilarating, purging experience of jazz-in-itself.

Carruth: Well, this is a prose statement that is very parallel to a section in *The Sleeping Beauty.* I don't think I have been influenced by Whitman much. But yes, I do think art in general has that capacity if it is recognized in its greatness. It's the source of freedom. There is no freedom as such in the real world, in existence. One has to transcend existence to find freedom, and one does that through the imagination, or at least it can be done through the imagination.

The individual becomes existentially free when he is using his imagination in some kind of transcendent moment. In the real world you are determined, you can't avoid it. You are determined biologically, you're determined historically, socially, politically, and economically, and every other way. When you are living within your imagination and your imagination is active, all of these determinants fall away and you become existentially free, and at the same time you come into some kind of sympathetic understanding with other imaginations which are also existentially free. How this happens exactly is something that is mysterious to me, but it does happen. That kind of freedom and that kind of imaginative activity is to me the richness that we are capable of as human beings and very, very important to me. I've written about it a lot, but this section from *The Sleeping Beauty* expresses it, I think, in one sense, the same as the end of *Sitting In* does:

In the mind's house of heaven, the great night never
Ends.
    All the brothers are there: Berrigan, Bechet,
Russell, Hawkins, Dickenson, Hodges,
And Mary Lou and Lady Day,
And so many others.
                  And oh they play, they
    jam forever,
Shades of strange souls nevertheless caught together
In eternity and the blues.
              No need
To cut anyone any more, no fatigue
From the straights out front or the repetitive changes,
But only expressiveness, warmth,
Each invention a purity, new without strangeness
In that session.
            Always they strained on earth
For this thing, skin and soul to merge, to disappear
In howling sound.
             God, but it would be worth
Dying, if it could be done,
    to be there with them and to hear,   *to hear.*

ADRIENNE RICH

A Tool or a Weapon
A review of *For You: Poems* and *The Clay Hill Anthology*

At a time when mere careers matter less and less, and poetry seems to matter finally as testimony, as one of the radical acts necessary for survival, Hayden Carruth is a distinguished figure. I mean that not in the sense that others have conferred distinctions upon him and thereby created his importance. I mean it in the sense that a single tree, or a mountain profile, is distinct through its separateness and integrity; distinguished by what it is, but also by its particular relation to the landscape. Though he has been living and working for many years apparently far out of the mainstream of letters, cities, the churn of careers, it would be ridiculous to call his reputation underground or obscure. There are few poets whose work has nourished so many magazines so steadily; and no criticism of poetry has been written in the last decade more extensive and searching than the reviews and essays Carruth has contributed to such publications as *Poetry,* the *Hudson Review,* the *Chicago Sun-Times, The Nation,* and the *New York Times Book Review.* Bound to no sect, member of no clique, vastly read in the poetry of his own time and of the past, Carruth has been through the force of his own gifts at the mainstream of our poetry when it was gathering its fullest momentum and achieving its richest variety.

The two books of his poetry most recently published stand, at least as far as external method is concerned, at two opposite reaches of his work. *For You* is a collection of long poems, dating from 1957 to 1968; it goes backward in time and represents a kind of poem for which Hayden Carruth has special strengths: meditative, poring, searching for a language and for images that shall be necessary to externalize an intensely inward experience. *The Clay Hill Anthology* is not an anthology but a collection of brief poems. Based on haiku, but very Occidental, these "jottings" possess an unmistakable continuity and are remarkable for their variety, tensility, toughness, and genuine music—the music of a real man's voice speaking his own language. There is nothing fragile or precious about these poems, which for all their brevity are addressed to large matters.

We still have to wait for the book which should accompany these two in any consideration of Carruth's poetry as a whole: the collected shorter poems of which two earlier volumes, *The Crow and the Heart* and *Nothing for Tigers* would comprise only a portion. These shorter poems, which have been appearing steadily in magazines for years, would surely reveal themselves as one of the long poems that the poet has been writing all his life.

But right now we have *For You,* a handsome volume, and *The Clay Hill Anthology,* one of the most attractively and sympathetically designed books I have recently seen from a small press. *For You* is a series of journeys from within the poet's self, beginning with a poem called "The Asylum" and ending with an elegy for his father. At first look the poems embody a very inward world, the passage of a man's spirit from psychic defeat into that confrontation with the real that Americans call pessimism. But the title, it seems to me, goes to the root of what this kind of poetry is really about: a man who uses language as a tool or weapon for his own survival, picks up that tool, honed and tempered by him, its handle stained with his sweat, and offers it to us, as if it might be of use to us, too. There is no brilliance of craft or aesthetic surface that can do this for us of itself; this is a quality of poetry that the poet conceives as functional, as a way of existing—first for oneself, then perhaps for others.

One of the striking things about the poems in this book is the way they trace the development of a poet's working language. "The Asylum" has always seemed to me a poem of courage, the poem of a proud man acknowledging humiliation and apparent failure, yet under no illusion that that acknowledgment offers him a reprieve. The poems' concerns are the collapse of an identity and the relation of that collapse to the society around the self. It should be remembered that poems out of Bedlam were not yet fashionable in 1957, and that illness of the mind was still seen as a form of individual failure to adjust to a presumably sane and sound society. It does seem to me, however, that the poet's sensitivity was protecting itself, in this poem, by a diction which, except at a few striking moments, clothes itself in literary costume. Ezra Pound is a figure in the poem, seen as both fellow sufferer and master, and the language reflects that aspect of Pound's influence which has always felt to me as sticky as candy: verbal nostalgia and hyper-musicality at the expense of naturalness—qualities into which Pound's imitators, including the best of them, have often fallen. Yet distinct and articulate images also appear:" . . . a twisted beech/ Whose nineteen leaves were glittering, each/ A tear in a rigid eye. . . ." And the final section breaks into a different mode:

> If love fails
> To soothe such pain and runs like the salt sea down
> The wounds of these particular halls
> Goodnight. Goodbye. Here's darkness and rain
> And a small wind in broken walls, dear walls.
> Here am I—drowned, living, loving, and insane.

In "Journey to a Known Place," a poem written two years later, the language becomes harsher, more brilliant and violent; there is almost no trace left of the inversions and archaisms that occur in "The Asylum." It is a language of verbs, a reaching-out into action, into movement, a bursting of the asylum walls and entering into regions where there is no asylum, no protection. Nevertheless, in this poem, it is only when Carruth deals in precise terms with the natural or the human world that his experience comes most sharply into focus. The mythology or "plot" of the poem seems rather a contrivance; I believe that its elaborated metaphors of air, earth, fire, and water are used as literary diction is used in "The Asylum"—out of a lack of trust. Where the images take on a life of their own, however, as in the undersea passage, "Aqua," they are nightmarish and powerful.

In 1963, Hayden Carruth, now living in a small village in northern Vermont, undertakes to write a long poem without using the pronoun "I." The result is "North Winter," first published by the Prairie Press, and, in that edition, now presumably a collector's item. The poem is a sequence of short, open-line poems tracing the onset and the experience of winter in the hills, and ending with the compelling description of two men—possibly Commander Peary and his black companion Matthew Henson—on their first trek to the Pole. In renouncing the personal pronoun, Carruth becomes more intensely than ever the persona and the soul of the poem: he is no longer recounting his own experience from one remove, looking back at himself; he becomes pure consciousness, the mind of a man, the mind of a poet, translucent, relentlessly selective, fixing the natural world in images and sounds that are precise and varied and wholly successful. In pretending to be simply a sequence of images of winter, the poem creates a context in which the reader is left to make the unsaid connections between the visible object and the conditions of our being. Carruth here is using materials so close to him in every sense, and which he is so gifted at observing and understanding, that the words appear on the page as if they had always been there; it is hard to imagine the poem as something *made*. One is looking through Carruth's eyes, yet hardly aware of his presence.

In "Contra Mortem," dated three years later, the materials of this immediate landscape—Vermont woods, stream, meadows, village, wife, child, sky, night, dawn—are the personae of a thirty-part poem. It almost seems that this is the poem Carruth was trying to write in the final section of "Journey to a Known Place." The celestial city of the earlier poem has become a Vermont village; the mythic landscape has become one far more familiar—though still at times and places possessing an ecstatic quality. Carruth, now moving among the actual facts of his existence, is in contact with the poetry of that existence as never before. And the poem is an attempt to use poetry, to use the body of the visible world, against the little deaths and the great death which thread their way through this and each of the earlier long poems. The fact that the core of nothingness, seen in each other's eyes by the two explorers at the end of "North Winter," exists also in "the socket/ Of the candlestick or in that/ of the shotglass look in the empty gauntlet or look/ in the clamshell . . . look the fear"—this fact, this "place where nothing is" is also the core of the poem. Written out of the most acute, unswerving, unhysterical perception of absurdity, that poem's great beauty and paradox is how lovingly and intensely it evokes, nevertheless, the physical, sensuous world.

The final "little death" in this book is the death of Carruth's own father, and the breaking—by the son, of his own will—of "the net that holds/ everything together." A sensation of release at such a time not uncommon, but Carruth's vision of the release in "My Father's Face" is an act of choice:

How easy! I wonder why
I took so long, learning
that to destroy

what could never be either right or wrong,
this net, this mere order
or any order,

is no real destruction—
look, I walk as I have always walked,
one foot in front of the other foot.

The rocks and birches take so warmly
to the purity of their restoration. I see this.
I have done it with one gesture, like that.

I walk in the tact of the ultimate rebel
graduated from conspiracy,
free, truly free, in the wonder of uncreation.

There is in all of Carruth's poetry a tension between this rebel-
lion, this uncreation, and longing for a time when tradition and
convention (which he sees as very different) were more congruent,
when song was more harmonious, when absurdity was as yet unrealized. Carruth's temperament is genuinely radical in its need for
roots, and its hatred of the rootless shifting opportunism and greed
and dishonor which are wasting our country as well as Southeast
Asia and other parts of the world. I think there is no poetry being
written now in which anger and pity for the wasting of man by
man are more melded with love for the possibilities, for the earth
and man upon it. The move from self-doubt and self-hatred to
"leaning to my limp/ learning,/ Swinging/ at last on my wound,"
to an expanded sense of the woundedness of others, and a greater
mercifulness toward them and one's self, is a history which will have
to be sweated out over and over by those who come after us, not to
mention ourselves. This, finally, is why these poems matter.

DAVID RIVARD

A Meaning of Hayden Carruth

The self, that quaint "fiction" supposedly put to death by the oligarchs of critical theory, still seems to bedevil American poetry, thirty-five years or so after the LANGUAGE poets drove a stake through its heart. Disdain for the "autobiographical" looks more and more like a form of wishful thinking—as if by removing one set of mannerisms and replacing them with another, one could solve a "problem" bound up with being, with contingency and necessity. We will not be rescued from meaning. How to write with clarity out of the truest parts of one's being then? And how to make it more than an occasion for the manifestation of personality, more than simple self-obsession?

The affectation of sincerity is not the way, as Hayden Carruth knew. The attractions of this kind of tonal authority are strong; its creation often a matter of props. In his essay, "A Meaning of Robert Lowell," Carruth describes Lowell's defect as "the temptation to mere appearance, to effects, trappings—to the extraneous." The "I" in Lowell's poems (especially after *Life Studies*) rests on this impulse, claims Carruth. In another essay, he calls for poetry that contains "the whole individual subjectivity, the spirit-body-soul." For Carruth, this subjectivity equates with neither individuality nor surface personality. It is not based on an autobiographical "I." The voice creates itself out of a responsibility to life. "The work of the poet," he says, "is self-transcendence."

In Carruth's view, Lowell's "too-great concentration of effort upon the verbal surface" (in *Near The Ocean* and other work) produces a distorted brilliance-for-brilliance-sake. He argues that these excesses of rhetoric, syntax, and figurative language become Lowell's persona, his tone, his "meaning," and that they actually obscure the poet and his life (despite Lowell's allegiance to autobiography). Although it feels exaggerated to me, paying only cursory attention to Lowell's often tremendous originality of vision, it's still a criticism with no small validity. In fact, sometimes the effect of Lowell's writing is unintentionally comic, as in this couplet from "No Hearing":"I watch the muddy breakers bleach to beerfroth,/our steamer, THE STATE OF MAINE, an iceberg at drydock." In other instances, what seems inspired turns out to be merely confused, as in this description of a house:

> Tonight, though, I see it shine
> in the Azores of my open window.
> Its manly, old-fashioned lines
> are gorgeously rectilinear.
> It's like some firework to be fired
> at the end of the garden party,
> some Spanish *casa,* luminous
> with heraldry and murder,
> marooned in New York.
>
> (from "The Opposite House")

This passage moves, undeniably, with a wonderful economy and precision; yet, what does it add up to? A series of questions. Why is the view an "Azores"? How exactly is the building "like some firework"? And why does it shift shape to become the "*casa*"? The context provided by the poem offers no answers. While aiming at imaginative objective description, perhaps these figures only really define the speaker's state of mind, or the mind as personality. And even the great bravery and technical accomplishment of Lowell's best work is sometimes undermined by an isolating self-drama, one which goes unresisted:"I hear/my ill-spirit sob in each blood cell,/ as if my hand were at its throat. . . . /I myself am hell;/nobody's here. . . ." Lowell's illness was very real, his struggles with it often deeply moving, but a passage like this offers us only a steel cage disguised as a confrontation with the self.

Carruth's poetry largely avoided the emphasis on a direct and unmediated autobiography, the creation of a recognizable persona, all the while undermining the notion of hyper-sensitivity (verging on the neurotic) as heroic. In "Simple," for example, a poem which ritualizes the memory of a separation and loss in quatrains composed of varying 2–3 beat lines, he gives shape through mythmaking to the experience of madness:

> how we made a pier, a jetty
>   of lights, a brightness
> in that fantastic dark,
>   down which we took our way

to the vessel that lay in the
shadows. . . .

The pier and jetty lights seem to echo an image which occurs in a
passage of *The Bloomingdale Papers,* Carruth's book of poems written thirty years earlier and detailing his institutionalization for psychiatric disorders. There, he remembers sitting "at the end of the
long curving jetty/whose base is attached to the city of Chicago."
Here the place becomes one of leave-taking from an unknown
person. After which, Carruth says, " . . . I turned/back into the
knowledge of going/crazy from loneliness."
But the poem doesn't want simply to follow his descent into illness; there's a resistance to the potential bathos of the situation, and
that resistance feeds itself on *imagination.* "Looking/back," he writes,
"I imagine":

> how I retired to a room
>   I built, perhaps
>
> a kiva lit by reflections
>   of the moon, where I
> celebrated over and over
>   the trembling mysteries
>
> of loss. I became a living
>   brain in an effigy
> of reeds and cloth and paint,
>   completely insane.

The drama of the self is deflected into an imagined space, quite
literally a room that becomes a kiva, a structure used by the Pueblo
Indians for ceremonials, often underground. Against the self-
destructive tendencies of the mind ("a living/brain in an effigy/of
reeds and cloth and paint") he pits the freedom of the self to create,
to transform and redeem the experience of feeling oneself made
nothing by madness. The space of the poem, the poem as a "kiva,"
allows him this freedom. The architecture of the final stanza, with
its pattern of slant end-rhyme and its perfectly iambic penultimate
line, clearly argues for it. Just as the words themselves argue not for
an ennobling of madness, or a self-pity, but for a kind of sorrowful
wonder at it after all this time.
    If one thinks of Robert Lowell's poems about his own institu-

tionalizations, the contrast is immediate and instructive. For example, the ending and especially the final couplet of Lowell's "Waking in the Blue" ("We are all old timers,/each of us holds a locked razor"), seems, ultimately, stagy or postured, its ironic realism a merely aesthetic resolution—neither as terrifying as the "effigy" made in Carruth's poem, nor as absolutely and understatedly factual as his final line's "completely insane." Instead, Carruth's poem has a freshness to it, a liveliness of music inseparable from vision, part its refusal to romanticize suffering.

The feel of music I'm talking about here is what Carruth calls "spontaneous improvisation within a fixed and simple form," the heart of jazz, one of his great influences. Improvisation, as a value, might be opposed to the artifice and "shapedness" seen in Lowell, the emphasis on aesthetic product. In an essay titled "Some Influences: The Formal Idea of Jazz," he makes this proposal:

> What happens, subjectively and spiritually, when a musician improvises freely? He transcends the objective world, including the objectively conditioned ego, and becomes a free, undetermined sensibility in communion with others. . . .

Communion. This is what marked the difference between Carruth and Lowell. A life, Carruth writes, is created by "a series of successive imaginative acts." For him, this power can only be fulfilled through a responsibility to others. In his essay on Lowell, he comes at the issue by claiming that self-creation must move outside the self, toward the other, for the reader's sake. Otherwise it is of no use, it concocts a stick-figure, mere personality; and, as in the case of Lowell, it may lead to the evolving of a style "too much like a shell, a carapace, an extraneity."

For Carruth, improvisation is achieved through "the disciplines of the instrumental imagination." Metaphor is one of these disciplines. In his poems it is largely a way to get at our essential relatedness, an entrance into, as he says in "The Ravine," "the relationship between things." That poem recognizes and weaves such relationships:

> Stone, brown tufted grass, but no water,
> it is dry to the bottom. A seedy eye
> of orange hawkweed blinks in sunlight
> stupidly, a mink bumbles away,

a ringnecked snake among stones lifts its head
like a spark, a dead young woodcock—
long dead, the mink will not touch it—
sprawls in the hatchment of its soft plumage
and clutches emptiness with drawn talons.
This is the ravine today. But in spring it
cascaded, in winter it filled with snow
until it lay hidden completely. In time,
geologic time, it will melt away
or deepen beyond recognition, a huge
gorge. These are what I remember and foresee.
These are what I see here every day,
not things but relationships of things,
quick changes and slow. These are my sorrow,
for unlike my bright admonitory friends
I see relationships, I do not see things.
These, such as they are, every day, every
unique day, the first in time and the last,
are my thoughts, the sequences of my mind.
I wonder what they mean. Every day,
day after day, I wonder what they mean.

There are many wonderful things about this poem. The hawkweed
blinking "stupidly," the mink that "bumbles" away (verb and adverb
perhaps also describing the speaker's mind?)—brief moments of
comedy in the landscape that give way to the horror of the dead
woodcock. The woodcock, which becomes a Zen-like emblem
both of non-fulfillment and courage. The contradiction of starting
this poem about "relationships," about process, with a beautifully
rendered catalog of things. And the more meditative passage that
follows it, reminding me a little of Stevens, the Stevens, say, of "Es-
thetique du Mal"—a music of grave, pivoting phrases running inside the lineaments of argument, the construct of avowal, repetition,
and conjunction. The music itself seeking to replicate the feel of
relationship as an activity in which one partakes, and outside of
which one also remains.

But what I love about "The Ravine" is the leap Carruth takes
toward the end: "These . . . are my thoughts, the sequences of my
mind." With a precise ambiguity, "these" is made to refer back to
"relationships," and the mind—the self here—is metaphorically
transformed into the process it has been describing. All distance collapses in the speaker's identification, "every/unique day, the first in

time and the last." For Carruth, this is a sort of *ars poetica*. The more so because its final two lines, characteristically, blend together curiosity, humility, awe, horror, and acceptance.

In an essay called "Found in Translation: On a Social History of the Moral Imagination," the anthropologist Clifford Geertz describes one condition of mind and its process of imaginatively giving shape to the world in a way similar to Carruth in the "The Ravine." Referring to Faulkner, he points to

> how what happens, recountings of what happens, and metaphoric transfigurations of these recountings into general visions, pile, one on top of the next, to produce a state of mind at once more knowing, more uncertain, and more unbalanced.

A state which makes, as in Carruth's case, for an openness toward life, an essential inquisitiveness—a hunger for connection.

The voice of Carruth's poetry is always aware of its relatedness, of community, of sympathy. Much of the time, it is a poetry of people in specific locales: the rural scene in particular, the life of small farms in the Vermont hills—one of difficult, constant work—and other places, upstate New York, the small city turned fast-food strip and mall, the psychiatric hospital, small-town Connecticut, as well as remote stretches of history. He wrote of these places with the wisdom and humor and horror that belong to their people, and especially to his family and friends. Not only their lives, but their very voices were brought into his work. And he did the same with nature, so that we see ourselves as one species among many. All this while at the same time writing both movingly and directly about himself, his joys and pain.

It's easy to feel Carruth's spontaneity, his inquiring empathy, as a form of wonder. It makes even the most despairing of his poems seem vibrant. Probably, it's the reason why many of his best poems are about work, especially farm work, where communal relations, the necessity of helping others, the interdependence of lives, are always a felt presence, as strong as the natural landscape.

Empathy locates itself in what we most have in common. If work is one, suffering is another. And the two often coincide in Carruth's poetry, as in "Emergency Haying." At the opening of this poem, the descriptive plainness of riding home on a wagon, exhausted and cut up after haying all day, gives way to a crucifixion image, not an identification with the suffering of Christ but a sympathy with it (a risky distinction, which I think he pulls off by undercutting it slightly with the ironic aside: "Well, I change grip and the image/fades"). "It's been an unlucky summer," he writes, and the brief catalog of difficulties that follows is as trenchantly and plainly stated as the explanation it ends with: "and Marshall needs help."

> We mow, rake, bale and draw the bales
> to the barn, these late, half-green,
> improperly cured bales: some weigh 100 pounds
>
> or more, yet must be lugged by the twine
> across the field, tossed on the load, and then
> at the barn unloaded on the conveyor
>
> and distributed in the loft. I help—
> I, the desk-servant, word-worker—
> and hold up my end pretty well too; but God,
>
> the close of day, how I fall down then. My hands
> are sore, they flinch when I light my pipe.
> I think of those who have done slave labor,
>
> less able and less well-prepared than I.

In the meditation on oppression and torture that follows, Carruth is careful not to appropriate that suffering or to glorify it for his own sake. It's why, in the passage I just quoted, he is honest enough to see himself as both different from and the same as Marshall, as "the desk-servant, word-worker." The distinction is real and necessary; though I love the way it and the loose pentameter of the poem is cut against by the colloquial assertion, "I help . . . and hold up my end pretty well too."

When Carruth emerges from his cataloging of "clerks and housekeepers/herded to the gaunt fields of torture," he looks around to the surrounding hills, the trees just coming into fall color. And it feels as if the inspiration of the New England landscape (an inspiration come to a little ironically: "I look beyond/our famous hayfields to our famous hills"), the movement into it, is what takes him to the uprising—and another kind of acknowledgement of Christ—which ends the poem:

> . . . . It must be so. My strength
> is legion. And I stand up high
> on the wagon tongue in my whole bones to say

woe to you, watch out
you sons of bitches who would drive men and women
to the fields where they can only die.

Though it feels self-conscious, and intentionally inflated in its gesture, the pentameter breaking down in the anger, its effort and passage out of the self moves me.

Marshall, the neighbor Carruth mentions in "Emergency Haying," is the subject of one of the remarkable series of character studies and dramatic monologues published in *Brothers, I Loved You All* (as well as in *If You Call This Cry a Song* and *Asphalt Georgics*). "Marshall Washer" is an essay/meditation, through the character of Marshall, on the life of farms in northern New England and on the nature of friendship. Moving, in sections, from the general and archetypal to the particular and personal, Carruth's aim doesn't seem so much the realistic delineation of character or psychology as the rendering of a moral sensibility: "the remnant of human worth/to admire in this world, and I think to envy."

The idea of fate figures strongly in this poem, as well as in the others like it. They are a little reminiscent of Robinson in this, or of Frost (the locale is familiar enough, so is the colloquial blank verse). But there's little of the distance, the view from tragic heights, that one feels in either Frost or Robinson. Carruth's sympathetic nature probably wouldn't allow it. In the strongest (and most terrifying) of these pieces, "Marvin McCabe," he sets up, initially, the conditions of the life—the cruel father who is a rural laborer, escape into alcohol and cars, the pregnant girlfriend, and war service—until he arrives at the auto accident that robs McCabe, the speaker of this interior monologue, of his motor functions, most seriously of speech. "The usual story here in the mountains," says Carruth through McCabe. It has more than a touch of melodrama, or would if it weren't undercut by the weird and homely humor present in McCabe's voice:

                . . . . The talk machine's busted,
    that's all. Connections all screwed up. Have you ever
    wondered how it would be to have your thought
    that's clear and shiny inside your head come out
    like a mouthful of mud? As for simple things,
    I say, "Ahwan ahg' abah'"—what does it mean?
    I say it five times, "Awhan ahg' abah',"
    grimacing and smiling, *pleading,* and no one

hears me say I want to go to the bathroom.
I have to take a leak, for Christ's sake!

Or, this, a little later:

....What
I'm thinking now—and most of the time—is how
I wish whoever invented beer had been stuffed
back and smothered in his mother's womb.

What would it be like to lose the ability to talk, and how possible
is it, really, to speak for someone else? Or for ourselves, for that matter. The joke, it turns out, is on all of us. The speaker gestures toward
Carruth, who "knows not only what I'm saying but what/I mean
to say. . . ." But even that acknowledgement is over-ridden late in
the poem:

....But the hardest
of all was always this feeling that my thoughts
were shut inside me, that all I could do was smile.
I knew the words but couldn't say them—do you
know what that means? No one knew who I was.
It was like those people who believe your soul
can pass into another body when you die.
I was in the wrong body, but I hadn't died.
Can jail be worse than that? I wanted to die.
I would have if wanting could do it. But then
I came to see it doesn't make any difference.
If I spoke, what would it do?—my thoughts mean nothing,
my life means nothing, my death means nothing.
And everything means nothing.

It has an appalling and blasted feel, this passage. It reminds me,
too, of the somewhat more gentle ending of one of Randall Jarrell's
best poems, "Next Day," another persona poem:

How young I seem; I *am* exceptional;
I think of all I have.
But really no one is exceptional,
No one has anything, I'm anybody,
I stand beside my grave
Confused with my life, that is commonplace and solitary.

The Rilkean undertones of Jarrell's writing, the mention of the "grave" with the communal associations and consolation of the burial ceremony, tend to mitigate the message in ways that are impossible in "Marvin McCabe." In Carruth's poem, we witness an understanding that collapses into existential nothingness. But, paradoxically, when that nothingness is taken inside, it levels all boundaries between self and other. It's no real consolation, except that it teaches us a bravery which we didn't know we were capable of, the bravery of our humanness:

> . . . . This body is wrong, a misery,
> a misrepresentation, but hell, would talking make
> any difference? The reason nobody knows me
> is because I don't exist. And neither do you.

I think it is as frightening an epiphany as I know of in the poetry of the last fifty years, made only more so by the sly jocularity of "a misrepresentation." But its courage and severe lucidity feel like a challenge—by Carruth, to himself and to us—a dare to make meaning out of meaninglessness. And it is more compelling for having been rendered in the speech of the everyday.

The tragic finds its music in the everyday, common speech being only one form of it. Jazz—as I've already mentioned, one of Carruth's primary influences—is another, and it can move us beyond the tragic. The influence arises from his twinned need for "freedom and discipline," by which means he has "interfused thematic improvisation and . . . metrical predictability." Jazz embodies his understanding of how, as he writes,

> in its moments of transcendent freedom the self is, in fact, a communion with the other, though how to define that other still escapes me. I think it may be the transcendent selves of all human imaginations not irreparably maimed by the life of machines in the objective world. I call it love.
> (Introduction to *Effluences from the Sacred Caves*)

In a poem like "Bears at Raspberry Time" this aspect of love is visible in the way in which the self is not quite speaking for itself but being spoken for by the life that surrounds it. This is the beginning of the poem:

Fear. Three bears
are not fear, mother
and cubs come berrying
in our neighborhood

like any other family.
I want to see them, or any
distraction. Flashlight
poking across the brook

in briary darkness,
but they have gone,
noisily. I go to bed.
Fear. Unwritten books

already titled. Some
idiot will shoot the bears
soon, it always happens,
they'll be strung up by the paws

in someone's frontyard
maple to be admired and
measured, and I'll be paid
for work yet to be done—

with a broken imagination.

An effect similar to call-and-response sets itself up here, in the shut-
tling back and forth between the speaker's woes and the bears, in
the torsion between the sentence fragments and shorter clauses and
phrasings and the unwinding of the longer sentences. You catch the
feel of it too in the fourth and fifth stanzas, in the movement from
"some" to "soon," which is echoed at "strung" and "someone," then
slurs down to "done" and "imagination." This is song as a tracking
through consciousness. "Is middle age what makes/even dreams
factual?" asks Carruth. The answer comes in the return of the bears
later in the evening. That is, the bears *seem* to come back, he can't
"be sure." But the wish for their presence is a mark of Carruth's affection for them, for life, and it carries him beyond the repetitions
of "fear."

Carrying the motion outward: the transmission of energy, located in love. In "Sometimes When Lovers Lie Quietly Together,

Unexpectedly One of Them Will Feel the Other's Pulse" (a somewhat comically prolix title), from *Lighter Than Air Craft,* Carruth finds the pulse of the two lovers quite literally in a pair of power lines swinging rhythmically in noonday sun:

> Above the street at heavy opalescent noontime two electrical
> cables, strung from pole to pole,
> Hung in relationship to one another such that the lower swung in
> and out of the shadow of the one above it,
> And as it did so the sunlight reflected from it was sprung gleaming
> outward and inward along its length,
> A steady expansion and contraction. And for a while I was taken
> away from my discontents
> By this rhythm of the truth of the world, so fundamental, so
> simple, so clear.

The unfolding of syntax hugs the visual in these long lines—lines probably more influenced by Ovid than Whitman. It comes to rest, wonderfully lulled, in his being "taken away from my discontents/By this rhythm of the truth of the world." I think this rootedness in love, and the way love is carried into the world, is what has always moved me in Carruth's work. Even though it is the habit of the self to turn away and in, even though, as he says in section 9 of the long poem "Paragraphs," it was his "custom" to "be silent,/to think the song inwardly":

> Yet sometimes two
> heard it, two separately together. It could come
> nearby in the shadow of a pine bough
> on the snow, or high in the orchestral lights,
> or maybe (this was our miracle) it would have no
> intermediary—
> > a suddenness,
> > > indivisible, unvoiced.

This "suddenness" is the singing of transcendence. It rests on the deepest understanding of how, in Simone Weil's words, "shifting fortune and necessity hold in subject every human spirit. . . ." Yet, the possibility of achieving this understanding is, as she wrote, "fraught with temptations to falsehood, temptations that are positively enhanced by pride, by shame, by hatred, contempt, indifference, by the will to oblivion or ignorance." These are the temptations that Hayden Carruth sang himself past. And for taking us with him, I'm grateful.

STEPHEN KUUSISTO

Elegiac Locales
The Anarchy of Hayden Carruth

I.

Poets have always read nature as a text for transcendence, but following World War II, the natural world was no longer a "de profundis" muse. The poet's relationship to landscape had changed: henceforth it would have to be defined and enacted in the context of post-atomic industry. Poets as diverse as Kenneth Rexroth, Yvor Winters, and Gary Snyder created locales in which a careful enumeration of geographies and human actions furnished a primer or blueprint for merely living—an aesthetic realpolitik which has roots in nineteenth-century anarchist principles.

Many anarchists were surveyors and mapmakers. Kropotkin was a geographer. His encounters with rural people who faced adversity through cooperative efforts furnished proof that nature might still be our school. Reading *Mutual Aid,* one sees that work and community are the means by which human beings *create* human nature: the farmer, the builder, even the doctor—all confirm through their work that value derives from serving the land and the community. Every human action thereby reflects the dignity of work. No idea was more crucial to the American communalist tradition, which tried to build a new Eden. Anarchy depended on the belief that human beings are part of an organic community and that the proper aim of culture is to live in a creative, non-exploitative relationship with our neighbors and the environment. The key to this lay in our working lives.

The aesthetic and political impact of these concerns have influenced recent American poetry in diverse ways. Robert Bly settled on a farm in Minnesota and wrote *Silence in the Snowy Fields,* a book which celebrates rural solitude. In Gary Snyder's *Earth House Hold,* working in the mountains or in the merchant marine is only partly an aesthetic experience: labor is often a paradigm for human fran-

chise. Workers become citizens, freethinkers, and "Dharma Bums."
Their exertions in the service of ecology are also exercises in meditation. In this way "culture" is restored to its earliest meaning. Snyder's essay "The Yogin and the Philosopher" argues that caring for
the environment has been the nucleus of our ancestors' labors.
Robert Bly, Galway Kinnell, Thomas McGrath, Hayden Carruth,
and Wendell Berry have all written poems and essays which link
farming and conservation with the craft of writing.

II.

Hayden Carruth's rural narratives make connections between landscape and individual character. Farming is hard, talking is hard, the
erosions of traditional ways of life are insurmountable. The farms
Carruth knows and works are small, marginal, almost worn out. The
acreage won't sustain much capital investment in machinery or labor. By enumerating the passing of small Yankee farms, Carruth's
poems record the disappearance of essential knowledge and, in a
sense, become elegies to the kind of life that Kropotkin once envi-
sioned in *Mutual Aid*. The passing of a cooperative, rural, social, and
economic order is contiguous with the despoiling of the environment: the people who know the land and tend it have been bought
out or foreclosed. *Brothers, I Loved You All* contains a series of meditations on these themes.

In "Marshall Washer" Carruth presents the works and days of a
struggling, solitary northern Vermont farmer who is also the poet's
neighbor and friend. The work "breaks the farmers' backs./ It makes
their land./ It is the link eternal, binding man and beast/ and earth."
This is Carruth's appreciation for a man who knows the land and
tends it, and the poem provides a glimpse of labor as a locus or
point of connection between mind, life, and nature. Farming is the
act of *making:*

>   I see a man in bib overalls
> and rubber boots kneeling in cowshit to smear
> ointment on a sore teat, a man with a hayfork,
> a dungfork, an axe, a 20-pound maul
> for driving posts, a canthook, a grease gun.
> I see a man notching a cedar post
> with a double-bladed axe, rolling the post
> under his foot in the grass: quick strokes and there

is a ringed groove one inch across, as clean
as if cut with the router blade down at the mill.

In "Marshall Washer" craftsmanship is synonymous with assiduousness and spirit. Marshall's handicraft reflects his engagement with trials and tests. In a sense, Marshall's work may be understood as an essay, and the poem's theme is in the relationship between farmer and poet. Carruth has been Marshall's neighbor and friend, as well as his student. By becoming his historian he articulates the unwritten essay of Marshall's life. In turn, the poem becomes an essay on work, cooperation, landscape, and poetry:

> I have written
> of Marshall often, for his presence is in my poems
> as in my life, so familiar that it is not named;
> yet I have named him sometimes too, in writing
> as in life, gratefully. We are friends. Our friendship
> began when I came here years ago, seeking
> what I had once known in southern New England,
> now destroyed. I found it in Marshall, among others.
> He is friend and neighbor both, an important
> distinction. His farm is one-hundred-eighty acres
> (plus a separate woodlot of forty more), and one
> of the best looking farms I know, sloping smooth
> pastures, elm-shaded knolls, a brook, a pond,
> his woods of spruce and pine, with maples and oaks
> along the road—not a showplace, not by any means,
> but a working farm with fences of old barbed wire;
> no pickets, no post-and-rail. His cows are Jerseys.
> My place, no farm at all, is a country laborer's
> holding, fourteen acres "more or less" (as the deed
> says), but we adjoin. We have no fence. Marshall's
> cows graze in my pasture; I cut my fuel
> in his woods. That's neighborliness. And when
> I came here Marshall taught me . . . I don't know,
> it seems like everything: how to run a barn,
> make hay, build a wall, make maple syrup
> without a trace of bitterness, a thousand things.
> (Though I thought I wasn't ignorant when I came,
> and I wasn't—just three-quarters informed.
> You know how good a calf is, born three-legged.)
> In fact half my life now, I mean literally half,
> is spent in actions I could not perform without

his teaching. Yet it wasn't teaching; he *showed* me.
Which is what makes all the difference. In return
I gave a hand, helped in the fields, started
frozen engines, mended fence, searched for lost calves,
picked apples for the cider mill, and so on.
And Marshall, alone now, often shared my table.
This too is neighborliness.

The poem assays neighborliness, sorrow, age, and loss—the intangibles from which lives are achieved. The knowledge Carruth acquires from Marshall is functional, but his awareness that there are distinctions to be made between "neighbor" and "friend" alerts the reader that the poem is engaged in an intricate "weighing" of values. To "name" Marshall is to conjure his presence as a figure who works side by side with the poet: together they tend the land and share what's in common. Writing about Marshall becomes an exercise in discrimination: the precise values of words and actions must be arrived at. Carruth aims for exactitude—literal meanings—and the poem seeks to establish whatever distinctions can be made between terms like "neighbor" and "friend" because in naming Marshall, Carruth is hoping to preserve the propriety and right-mindedness of a man whose world is on the verge of extinction.

Accordingly, we learn that friendship can be built from silence, or it can persist when conversation is provisional. For Carruth, whose "art" is contingent upon the spoken and written word, Marshall's silence provides a lesson in "reading" a man. It's a curious, ascetic's world that Carruth explores, and the poem's language works toward similitude in its precise accounting of both Marshall's vernacular and his silence. The accuracy of Marshall's language and Carruth's curiosity about its etymology makes this a memorable tribute to a friend:

I see a man who studied by lamplight, the journals
and bulletins, new methods, struggling to buy
equipment, forty years to make his farm
a good one; alone now, his farm the last
on Clay Hill, where I myself remember ten.
He says "I didn't mind it" for "I didn't notice it,"
"dreened" for "drained," "climb" (pronounced climm)
for "climbed," "stanchel" for "stanchion,"
and many other unfamiliar locutions; but I
have looked them up, they are in the dictionary,

standard speech of lost times. He is rooted
in history as in the land, the only man I know
who lives in the house where he was born. I see
a man alone walking his fields and woods,
knowing every useful thing about them, moving
in a texture of memory that sustains his lifetime
and his father's lifetime. I see a man
falling asleep at night with thoughts and dreams
I could not infer—and would not if I could—
in his chair in front of his television.

Marshall's language is accurate: his "texture of memory" makes
him a guide—a person who informs the poet by example. Carruth
trusts Marshall's silence and, as a consequence, learns to make distinctions between "talk" and "articulation." The latter is a junction:
a marriage, a concurrence, and people who use words sparingly
may possess it. The former is profuse and digressive, something the
poet learns to distrust:

> Marshall and I
> worked ten years together, and more than once
> in hardship. I remember the late January
> when his main gave out and we carried water,
> hundreds and thousands of gallons, to the heifers
> in the upper barn (the one that burned next summer),
> then worked inside the well to clear the line
> in temperatures that rose to ten below
> at noonday. We knew such times. Yet never
> did Marshall say the thought that was closest to him.
> Privacy is what this is; not reticence, not
> minding one's own business, but a positive sense
> of the secret inner man, the sacred identity.
> A man is his totem, the animal of his mind.
> Yet I was angered sometimes. How could friendship
> share a base so small of mutual substance?
> Unconsciously I had taken friendship's measure
> from artists everywhere who had been close to me,
> people living for the minutest public dissection
> of emotion and belief. But more warmth was
> and is, in Marshall's quiet "hello" than in all
> those others and their wordiest protestations,
> more warmth and far less vanity.

I'm reminded here of Santayana's notion of "animal-faith"—human instinct, that "animal" of the mind, is a kind of forbearance against the quotidian. By rejecting silence as dismissal or unconcern, Carruth also rejects language which is overtly designing, the glib chatter of our age, and insists that knowing another human being depends on reception, harmony, and cooperation. Making the distinction between privacy and reticence allows Carruth to more accurately estimate the nature of friendship. It's no coincidence that in defining this he also underscores ecological values: the sacred identity, the man as totem is properly "in" the world.

In a very real sense, the poem is much more than a tribute to a teacher. Carruth's precise estimation of Marshall allows for a reciprocal interaction between the subject of the poem and the making of a poem. Marshall is the inspiring muse of the poem as well as the figure being "assayed." This becomes an essay on human cooperation, the value of friendship, and the importance of deliberation and judgment in our dealings with our fellows and the environment.

III.

The "elegiac" character of *Brothers, I Loved You All* is in the poems' careful listings of the many extinctions that have happened in our time. Carruth writes: "This/ has been the time of the finishing off of the animals./ They are going away—their fur and their wild eyes,/ their voices." Elsewhere he says with a laconic twist: "The weak/ have conquered and the valley is their domain." The farms and the topography of Vermont have been sold to "predatory" developers. Carruth describes "bulldozers, at least of the imagination":

> The hilltop farms are going.
> Bottomland farms, mechanized, are all that survive.
> As more and more developers take over
> northern Vermont, values of land increase,
> taxes increase, farming is an obsolete vocation—
> while half the world goes hungry. Marshall walks
> his fields and woods, knowing every useful thing
> about them, and knowing his knowledge is useless.
> Bulldozers, at least of the imagination,
> are poised to level every knoll, to strip bare
> every pasture. Or maybe a rich man will buy it

for a summer place. Either way the link
of the manure, that had seemed eternal, is broken.
Marshall is not young now. And though I am only
six or seven years his junior, I wish somehow
I could buy the place, merely to assure him
that for these few added years it might continue—
drought, flood, or depression. But I am too
ignorant, in spite of his teaching. This is more
than a technocratic question. I cannot smile
his quick sly Yankee smile in sorrow,
nor harden my eyes with the true granitic resistance
that shaped this land. How can I learn the things
that are not transmissible? Marshall knows them.
He possesses them, the remnant of human worth
to admire in this world, and I think to envy.

In the end, all knowledge is particular, its acquisition comes in bits
and pieces, and it can't be hurried. Marshall's "granitic resistance"
and taciturnity represent both concealment and revelation: the signs
of a life shaped by work and weather. Carruth explores the complex
relationship between the making of a farm and the "texture of
memory that sustains [Marshall's] lifetime/ and his father's lifetime."
The poet reads that texture and deciphers it. The effect of Carruth's
writing is perhaps reflected in Carlyle's assertion that "In Symbol
there is concealment and yet revelation: here therefore, by Silence
and by Speech acting together, comes a double significance." These
poems lament the passing of something more intangible than the
farms. The "remnant of human worth" is recorded in the poem's
description of lost trades and vanished skills:

> He sows
> his millet broadcast, swinging left to right,
> a half-acre for the cows' "fall tonic" before
> they go in the barn for good: an easy motion,
> slow swinging, in a slow dance in the field, and just
> the opposite, right to left, for the scythe
> or the brush hook. Yes, I have seen such dancing
> by a man alone in the slant of the afternoon.
> At his anvil with his big smith's hammer
> he can pound shape back in a wagon iron, or tap
> a butternut so it just lies open.

When Carruth enumerates the ways of knowing that have vanished he's as precise as Hardy, as direct as any Yankee. We see the farms broken up and their owners driven off even as we're hearing the local speech. In this locale there is a life-supporting relationship between language, landscape, and character.

DOUGLAS UNGER

On Hayden Carruth
The Poetics of Social Utility

Hayden Carruth is one of the first poets I confessed to about making a possibly illicit use of poetry. While writing prose, when I'm struggling for an appropriate language figure or pattern in a sentence, I often reach for books of poems. I page through them, scanning lines the way a mechanic in his shop might sort through jars of screws, nuts, and engine parts to keep going with a repair. Poetry can fix things, get prose back on the road.

Hayden gave me his hearty approval to use poems in this way. He insisted poetry should be *of use,* that, above all, poetry should *make sense,* both common and uncommon sense. Writers should make use of each other and be available to other writers. Together, we can find strength against a world that in the main is hostile to poets and writers and seeks our destruction.

What Hayden encouraged is a sense of writerly community, in part based on a conviction that *it's us against them.* He put it just this way. And I don't believe he meant the "us" to be any elitist club of poets and writers or anything of that ilk, the "poetocracy"—as he called it—which he detested. He meant Humanists in the traditional sense, as in *persons of letters.* We should form a literary community allied against the forces that seek our obliteration. This is an intensely political stance, and the force of his politics runs through Hayden's writing.

Hayden Carruth refers to himself as an "anarchist" and cites Bakunin in his poems. He frequently recalls his family's Socialist roots. The example of his life is one of a perpetual self-exile from engagement with organized politics and as much as possible from mainstream consumerist society. For much of his life, he withdrew from large groups of people, not only to restore his sanity and achieve clarity of mind amid the harsh, wintry solitude of Johnson, Vermont, or of Munnsville, New York, but all the better to embrace the endangered Yankee values of thrift, hard work, appreciation of life, and concrete achievement through struggles and trials. This becomes a paradox of Hayden's life—his personal isolation as if all the more intensely to express community and political values in his writing. In his autobiographical fragments, Hayden advises young writers, "You need difficulty, you need necessity." Life dealt Hayden necessity. He also sought it out. His poems that I reach for continually are the activist political statements born of necessity, filled with protests and outrages at current political leaders and topical events. This is the kind of political force that I find lacking, a vacuous failure, in so much of contemporary American poetry.

Carruth's political poetry anchors itself not so much in the topical as the more general, though in quite a number of lines he invokes the names of sitting politicians and references current events. The poet positions political statement as thematically generalized, transcending the specific, and is exemplified in an early poem, "My Father's Face," that works through family and political conflicts that once contributed to driving the poet to a nervous breakdown:

but the power of money has bought the power of heart
monopoly eats the word, eats thought, desire,
your old companions now in the thick of it, eating

is that betrayal? They fatten, but for my part
old hatred deepens,
deepening as monopoly deepens,

until my socialism has driven me to the sociality
of trees, snow, rocks, the north—solitude.

This poem expresses the Carruthian paradox: a political voice is cultivated in solitude; aesthetics arise from toil, compost, chainsaws; a poet-lover's gift is a day in hell; a community is found in exile and asylum; wise statement, or useful assertion more than wordplay, can make beautiful poems. Read together over fifty years of his work, the many diverse voices in Carruth's poetry combine into a stern working-class critique of American values:

We forget sometimes that a shattered person
Twists and cries and dies like a dog or a woodchuck

Flesh ripped apart, ragged, bloody. Violent sex
is what war is and what the warriors are.

(from "Bosnia")

49

. . .Yes, old men now must tell
our young world how these bigots and these retired
Bankers of Arizona are ringing the death-knell

For all of us, how ideologies compel
Children to violence. Artifice acquired
For its own sake is war . . .

                              (from "Saturday at the Border")

        . . .Well, o.k. But
to me the climate's basic. Change
that and you're done for. What

could do it but the system?

                              (from *Asphalt Georgics,* "Names")

II.

In her book, *21st Century Modernism: The "New" Poetics* (2002), critic
Marjorie Perloff complains about "the unfulfilled promise of the
revolutionary poetic impulse in so much of what passes for poetry
today—a poetry singularly unambitious in its attitude to the materiality of the text" (5–6). And in her signature work, *The Poetics of
Indeterminacy,* the poet's subjective voice, and the poet's *persona* or
poetic self as a representation, are criticized by Perloff as if no longer
deserving of a relevant artistic claim in the aftermath of Modernism. She rejects narrative and formalist poetry as being romantic or
reactionary. Perloff advocates a poetics based in large part on self-
conscious language experimentation, poems that point emphati-
cally at their own language and at their own "materiality" as texts.

Nowhere in Perloff is there much space made for the poetics of
statement. Perhaps her stance can be justified as a reaction to the
canonical establishment of narrative poets and of their poet-
personalities in the previous generation, best exemplified by the
table of contents of Donald Hall's *Remembering Poets,* or by years of
Robert Lowell then Galway Kinnell writing essays for the *New York
Review of Books.* After all, every vanguard produces an opposing
avant-garde, and Perloff's voice becomes one of its strongest advocates.

There is no doubt great critical value in Perloff's books and essays, still, what are we to make of her divisiveness? In her relentless

advocacy, the poets and poetry of political relevance, of social utility, are harshly dismissed, not least among them the poetry of Hayden Carruth.

Through the 1970s and 1980s in American poetry, the postmodern wave of so-called *language poets* (if this term even applies anymore), exemplified for Perloff by John Ashbery, Charles Bernstein, Susan Howe, Lyn Hejinian, and others, directly opposed in their aesthetic Hayden Carruth's *poetry of use*—his political poetry, his insistence on social utility. As a result of the rising popularity or dominance in the "poetocracy" by these postmodern poets and their critics, Hayden suffered years of rejection and marginalization. No doubt that some of this rejection resulted from personal vendettas and reactions to Hayden's own tough, uncompromising editorial and critical stances when he served as editor of *Poetry,* and in numerous reviews and essays. By the late 1980s, Carruth found himself so marginalized that almost all of his books fell out of print, and he despaired of a world that seemed to have turned its back on traditional poetic forms and the poetry of social utility. He kept writing, though never confident that he could; and his poems as though in response to his rejection became even more grounded in his reach for wise statement and political relevance.

In Hayden's later works—in so many diversely voiced poems in *Scrambled Eggs & Whiskey,* in *Doctor Jazz,* in *Asphalt Georgics,* in *Letters to Jane*—he reaches for wise statement. Seeking for truth enters his arguments, and post-structuralism be damned, *meaning* is intended. In "voiced" poems that represent not so much the poet as the speaking voices of many exemplary, working class American characters, Carruth reaches for social and political relevance. As Philip Booth states, "In the poet's consciousness of his relationship to the actual, what's ordinary becomes extraordinary as it is raised by the power of a voice, however quiet. . . ."

Wendell Berry confirms this reading: "The thing we notice immediately is that the poem comes to us in the sound of a voice speaking. . . . Hayden Carruth is the master in poetry of the speaking voice—the result of technical skill so perfect and assured that it does not pause to admire itself, and therefore calls little attention to itself . . ."

In Carruth's rendering of "ordinary" voices, all the language experiments any reader could desire can be discovered, in cleverly composed word collages, musical notes and half-tones, subtle rhyme schemes, unusual line breaks and enjambments, crafted techniques often made less obvious on first reading because of the overwhelming power of the poem's statements. Formal music and poetic devices can be masked by political relevance:

> . . . Then the first wire broke,
> and the second, and the garage collapsed
>
> sideways like a fat senator loaded with scotch
> on the state house lawn. . . .
>
> (from "Surrealism")

> —How the hell
> can he come home at night and look
>   at you and the kids af-
> ter messing all day with them bombs?
>
> (from "Phone")

> Most of the starving children die peacefully
> in their weakness, lying passive and still.
> They themselves are as unaware of their
> passing away as everyone else. But a few . . .
>
> (from "The Camps")

III.

In the 1980s and '90s, the practice by the National Book Foundation to give out the National Book Award was to invite the nominees in the categories to a gala and ceremony in New York at which the writers in each category were asked to sit together on a stage and wait for the announcement of the winner. In this fashion, for what amounts to an elaborate social affair for the literary elite, writers were put on display for an audience composed mainly of publishers, editors, and booksellers. A name was announced in each category. The winner rose to accept the award and be applauded, with the four or five runners-up writers sitting by, acting as a living backdrop for the winners.

When Hayden Carruth's *Collected Shorter Poems* was nominated for a National Book Award in 1992, he discovered himself subjected to this ceremony, forced to sit by mutely as Mary Oliver won the award. Hayden found this way of doing things ridiculous, and worse, he felt humiliated. It wasn't that he couldn't take not winning the prize—he was used to not winning prizes; and he was gracious and congratulatory to Mary Oliver, whose work he appreciated. Still, the whole thing pissed him off. We talked about this afterwards, about the physical effort of the trip, plus the added costs to get to New York only to find himself sitting onstage, feeling stripped naked before a publishing world he felt had long ignored his work and the work of most poets in favor of an increasingly cynical marketplace commercialism. And to be put on display as a loser in front of *them*—Hayden didn't feel it was right to put *any* writer through such a rude ordeal, and certainly not for philistines. He told Bruce Berlind—the esteemed poet, translator, and Professor Emeritus of Colgate University, and an old friend and neighbor—the same story.

In 1996, a new collection of Hayden's poems, *Scrambled Eggs & Whiskey*, was nominated for the National Book Award. Instead of making the trip to New York, the evening of the ceremony, Bruce Berlind and his wife invited W. S. Merwin, his wife, and Hayden and his wife, Joe-Anne McLaughlin, over for a wine-filled dinner spent talking of just about everything but the award ceremony. They shared a wonderful time, even as simultaneously, at the gala in New York, Janie Wilson, of Copper Canyon Press, uneasily accepted the prize on Hayden's behalf, expressing his critical sentiments: "Like most poets, Hayden writes out of a passionate commitment to his art, and he is disinclined toward competition in the practice of his poetry. . . . Five years ago, Hayden's books were largely unavailable and out of print, and Copper Canyon published his *Collected Shorter Poems*, which was also nominated for a National Book Award and didn't win."

Meanwhile, Hayden and Joe-Anne were getting happily drunk at Bruce Berlind's place. No one remembers how anyone got home. The next morning, Bruce received a phone call about Hayden winning the award. He and Bill Merwin drove to Hayden and Joe-Anne's farmhouse near Munnsville to wake them up for a cheery, hung-over breakfast celebration.

Hayden is proud of the stance he took in not attending that award ceremony. Generally, he stayed away from other such affairs, reinforcing the high value he placed on the poet's public presence by pointedly refusing to appear. He turned down President Bill Clinton and First Lady Hillary Clinton's invitation to the White House two years later, his curt R.S.V.P. airing acidly on National Public Radio:

. . . Thank you for thinking of me. However, it would seem the greatest hypocrisy for an honest American poet to be present on such an occasion at the seat of power which has not only neglected but abused the interests of poets and their readers continually, to say nothing of many other administratively dispensable segments of the population. Consequently, I must decline.
—Hayden Carruth.

Two years before this, in Washington's "National Airport"—Hayden refused ever to refer to it by its re-named "Ronald Reagan Airport" in any form—he expressed his revulsion to the politicians in Washington, D.C., in a letter to Jane Kenyon written while waiting for a flight. The letter included a poem penned that morning in a Holiday Inn coffee shop:

Meanwhile rich and famous men are pursuing their lifestyles two
    blocks away
In four-story Federal brick houses with porticoes and flagstone
    steps.
Fucking each other's wives in dens and laundry rooms and
    pantries.
This is called a party. Some are Democrats, some Republicans, all
    are fuckers.
They are emboldened by bourbon and vodka and the anticipation
    of power.
Tomorrow they will arise hungover and wield the resources of the
    nation.

                                        (from "In Georgetown")

Throughout his life, Hayden Carruth believed that poets and writers should be willing to put themselves *on the line,* as it were, put even their well-beings *out there* with their words by taking public stances in support of what they believe in, even at the possible risk of their livelihoods and reputations. In an early interview with David Weiss, Hayden Carruth outlines the origins for this aspect of his poetics of social relevance, his *poetry of use:*

The people who affected me most when I was in my twenties and early thirties were the mid-century European existentialist writers, and they had the idea of engagement and responsibility that I believed in and still believe in. . . . I have never been a poet for poetry's sake. I never have been able to do that. I was raised in a family where my grandfather and my father were both newspapermen and professional writers, and always they insisted on the social utility of writing . . .

Carruth struggled to balance this sense of social utility against the distressing cultural vacuity of American culture and its market-place disenfranchisement of poets and literary writers from playing impactful political roles in society. My overall sense from his poems and letters is that Hayden consistently believed (as he also stated in the same early interview with David Weiss) that the cause for this marginalization of artists is a larger malaise that affects American society relative to others in the world, and one that marks in significant measure its ever deepening social crisis and decline:

. . . Americans live in a kind of political torpor. We feel helpless. The kind of changes we know ought to be made are not being made. In our poetry we tend to turn away. We all work in the knowledge that we're not producing any effect on our civilization. The politicians and the powerful people in our country conduct their operations and their lives without any reference to art at all. In other places, that's not true.

IV.

That my own personal relationship should play a strong role in this essay on Hayden Carruth's poetry might seem out of place. Little to be done about this, as I read his writing in the context of our friendship, with emotions and memories of how deeply he affected my life and the lives of my family. Also, I must believe that politics is grounded in personal experience, and a poetics of social utility expands from the personal to achieve more general relevance and express significant truths.

In late February 1988, my wife, Amy Burk, and I, sat together at Hayden's bedside in an intensive care unit of a hospital near Oneida, New York. We took turns holding his hand, by turns also talking to him, hoping he might take comfort in our familiar voices as he was gradually returning to consciousness and clarity after a very nearly successful suicide attempt. Hayden was hoarse, hardly able to speak.

His lips were stained black from granulated charcoal the doctors had pumped into him to absorb the cocktail of deadly medications he had swallowed.

Why did he do this? The most immediate and available reason we talked about was that he had fallen into despair over a lost love relationship. But I'll always believe that this suicide attempt also resulted from a more existential impasse with life and its significance rising from a crisis brought on by his doubts about what he perceived to be the value of his writing and its reception. In the late 1980s, the publishing culture, and the "poetocracy" that seemed so dominated by such divisive figures as Marjorie Perloff and Helen Vendler, had turned its back on Hayden and his work. This was at the end of a period when many of his books with commercial publishers and even smaller presses went out of print. That winter we had conversed frequently about and complained of this sad state, and Hayden had been steadily sinking more deeply into depression.

It was a hard, cold winter. We were all also concerned and downcast by Ray Carver's lung cancer, Hayden extremely pessimistic about Ray's chances. My wife, Amy, had just come out of an especially violent, public psychotic break caused by the manic-depressive illness that afflicted her all her life, during which she had streaked naked through the snow and ice of Campus Avenue at Syracuse University and had to be tackled to the ground by university police. Hayden had helped Amy through her recovery, visiting her frequently in the hospital, essential to bucking up her self-esteem once more, the two of them sharing, often with sly laughter, their lifelong experiences fighting off insanity and madness. He called her naked winter sprint her "constitutional run." He kept reminding her what good company she was in now, Syracuse University the place where Delmore Schwartz had suffered a similar, legendary breakdown. We all talked together a great deal about the world, and more—as in his poem "Mother," which Amy had memorized—those "long years of my private wrecked language, when my mind shook in the/ tempests of fear."

After his suicide attempt, Amy and I visited Hayden faithfully in a psychiatric ward, where he was committed for the following month. The talks we shared are difficult to describe, since we exchanged so much by a shared dumb forbearance expressed mainly in grunts, gestures, and numerous shared cigarettes. We "kissed the wall" together at the push-button electric lighter to kindle them, like a car lighter set into a little wire cage near the door, as he described later in his essay "Suicide," a prose masterpiece which makes an astonishing turn of the drive to kill himself into an uplifting, at times even comical meditation on happiness and spirituality. When he got out of the "hatch," as he called it, we met regularly for dinner. Hayden was riding an upswing by then, looking spry and energized by an emerging spring. Hayden got busy again teaching, and putting together poems for *Tell Me Again How the White Heron Rises and Flies Across the Nacreous River at Twilight Toward the Distant Islands*. He spent a lot of time staying in Syracuse, often at Stephen and Isabel Dobyns' big hospitable home, embraced into the warmth of their bustling family, an atmosphere always full of the high energy of children, our students, and visiting writers.

We all became closer friends because of him, because of our caring for him. That summer, Hayden fell in love with Joe-Anne McLaughlin, sometimes meeting with her and courting her at our home, where she stayed for a time. We observed the poet with a spring in his step, gripping a bunch of wildflowers and his new book of verses, dressed in his best houndstooth jacket—he was a smitten suitor, ringing our doorbell to call out his lady love to play.

Ray Carver died that August. We were together in this, too, with eulogies and functions that kept going, for years. Hayden proved steadfast in his emotional and professional support for Tess Gallagher, who was devastated, as were we all. Ray Carver had introduced me to Hayden Carruth six years before, always one to link friends with friends and at the same time pass on their books. And together, at a big country party on a farm that felt like a scene painted by Jan Brueghel the Elder, sun shining with precisely those tones and qualities of northern light, Ray and Hayden had welcomed me into my first full-time teaching job, and into their literary community. At that party, I mentioned the quality of light as in a Brueghel, then sat, astonished, as Hayden and Ray started trading off lines from William Carlos Williams, between them reciting the whole poem.

This memory is all the more valued and poignant now, as full as it is of the very tough emotions of grief and loss, recalling Ray Carver's death, and Hayden's, missing now such good friends. More difficult still is remembering my late wife, Amy, who died of lung cancer in 2003, though it still feels like last week. She was far more intriguing, loquacious, and interesting than I could be, and closer to Hayden—sly poet—who signed his books first to Amy then to me. Hayden, Amy, and I kept up a correspondence for two decades, with Amy writing far more letters than I did, and Hayden always faithful to answer, his letters typed on the blank sides of partial draft pages of new poems, which we would just as eagerly read.

Just hours before she died, Hayden and Joe-Anne spoke to Amy over the phone. I stood by her bed, passed the phone to her, then she passed it back to me, in a tiny cottage overlooking a blue lake that reflected a shimmering panorama of evergreen forest in the Pacific Northwest. Our four voices—Hayden's, Joe-Anne's, Amy's, mine—combined into a kind of staggered, family conversation. We didn't talk about Amy's death, which we all knew would be mere hours away. Instead, we traded endearments, those small but significant indulgences expressing our love. We shared the happy news about Joe-Anne's book, *Jam,* just out from BOA Editions, Ltd. Then our conversation turned to current events, sharing outrage about the despicable politics and tyranny of that president Hayden called "Shrub." Amy made quick references to Hayden's *Doctor Jazz,* which I had been reading to her in the evenings. The short poems titled "Faxes to William" had felt like faxes to Amy, making her laugh, even on her deathbed, and she could recite some of the lines.

That summer, a problem plagued the lake Amy's tiny cottage looked out over—Canada geese were too numerous, and they had fouled the water with intestinal parasites so that swimmers would break out in rashes, or worse, unless they used earplugs and showered as soon as possible when they got out of the water. These geese came up in the conversation. Amy recited from *Doctor Jazz:* " . . . Why must we be reminded/ that Nature can be as corrupt as Congress?"

We all laughed. It was a fine moment. Then suddenly, Amy felt too tired, seized by a grip of her exhaustion. "I'll sign off now," she said. We all said good-bye.

When I think of Amy's death, then Hayden's, what comes to mind are the love poems born of his romance with Joe-Anne, so many of them political. In "Testament," the poet meditates on what he might possibly leave behind, then he despairs of making provisions for the woman he loves in the alienating language of economics:

                    . . . Now
I am almost entirely love. I have been
to the banker, the broker, those strange
people, to talk about unit trusts,

annuities, CDS, IRAS, trying
to leave you whatever I can after
I die. . . .

(from "Testament)

And so it must be, in a country in which it is *us against them,* where what a poet customarily earns, as measured by the values of consumerism, is "at best a pittance in our civilization,/ a widow's mite . . ." What then follows in the poem is a defiant list of the poet's genuine will, what he really values in this world that he leaves to his wife, which includes tulips, and trilliums, and: "our red-bellied/ woodpeckers who have given us so/ much pleasure," . . . Then the kisses, embraces and love-makings—"millions"—and more, all held out as the poet's true bequest, which becomes limitless.

Voices in poems by Hayden Carruth argue for their own worth, offering a system of countervailing values to the obscene culture of American consumerism. His poetics of social utility intends to make moral statements, and he seeks a politics based on Humanism. This stance toward poetry should increase in relevance as consumerist culture crumbles around itself in the new century. His poetry will last because it insists on being of use.

GEOFFREY GARDNER

The Real and Only Sanity, an Essay-Review of *Brothers, I Loved You All*

We live in the way of such a constantly drenching flood of new poetry—those of us who try to keep up with it at all—and so much of it "good," that I worry our responses grow soggy, and we fail to recognize what is more than good. Hayden Carruth's new book, *Brothers, I Loved You All (Poems 1969–1977)*, is at every step at least a shade beyond all the current categories of praise, categories for coping with the last ten years' welter of poetry.[1] And I find myself frightened that its arrival will go unnoticed and unremarked.

I don't mean to suggest that Carruth is, in any sense, unknown or his work neglected beyond what it would be fitting to expect for a poet who has always chosen to make his stand just aside from any of the presently conflicting mainstreams. In fact, since the late forties, Carruth has been active as an editor for many well-known literary periodicals and publishers, written much telling criticism, and been a tough and omnivorous reviewer of new poetry. *Brothers, I Loved You All* is the thirteenth book of his poetry to appear since *The Crow and the Heart,* his first, was published in 1959.

I think *Brothers, I Loved You All* is Carruth's best book to date. Certainly it's the richest for the scope of its materials and the overwhelming mastery of its huge variety of forms and styles. It's also that rarest of things, not just a collection of poems, but a whole book, and in that lies its greatest excellence. Not every poem here is equally a gem. But taken all together in its sequence and unity, *Brothers, I Loved You All* gives full rein of expression to the whole experience of a poet of deep imagination and clear intelligence. And it insists powerfully on the utter continuity of life—in its widest range—and art. Reading a book like this, I sometimes become furious that for years and years and years, longer than I can remember, our poetry has been read by virtually no one but poets and college students and their teachers.

More than twenty-five years ago, in his Harvard lectures, *The*

Estate of Poetry, Edwin Muir, speaking in surpassingly assured and gentle tones, tried to understand this gap between poetry and its audience as a function of poetry's loss of contact with its popular origins: song, ballad, myth, and the world of primary creatures and happenings. Muir was trying to encourage the return of poetry to a common language, however heightened, and the re-founding of our view of poets as—whatever else they might be—public people with public responsibilities. We all know very well what stands between and what such an attitude is up against. Wordsworth's formulation of it is quickest and, perhaps, still best, provided we magnify for ourselves its intensity to make up for all that's passed in the nearly two hundred years since he wrote it:

> The most effective . . . causes are the great national events which are daily taking place, and the increasing accumulation of men in cities, where the uniformity of their occupations produces a craving for extraordinary incident, which the rapid communication of intelligence hourly gratifies.

All I'll add to Wordsworth's list is a reminder of the all but unavoidable and dinning presence in our lives of the centralized "mass media," the debasement of our language by public men whose perpetual lies are the outward sign of the futility of their acts and institutions, and the endless styles of academic criticism that have disturbed communication by twisting all the arts, and especially poems, back in on themselves, often with the gleeful consent of artists hungry for acknowledgment. But the last three decades have also brought a revival in poetry of what *is* urgent, common, primary, and public. And some of our best poets—Rexroth, Levertov, Kinnell, Ginsberg, Snyder, Berry, Adrienne Rich, John Haines, and Paul Goodman, to name just an obvious few—have long been writing as if in response to Muir's quiet challenge or in recognition of the universal situation behind it. It is important that not one of these people writes at all like another. It is also within this frame of reference that Carruth's work, especially *Brothers, I Loved You All,* needs to be read.

There is a saying of Herakleitos that "eyes are better informers than ears." I for one doubt the truth of it. But certainly many, if not most, poets now working write as if it were so. We've grown accustomed in our poetry to exhaustless chains of images that follow too quick, and often too arbitrarily, on one another, so that we lose ourselves and can't take them in. And this image spinning, more often than not, is set in a syntax and to a music that are lax and unaffecting and frequently deadening. What we get from much of our poetry is very little more than a momentary *petit frisson,* clothing mere remarks about the world and our lives in it. For the reader, they are hearsay. And that, perhaps, is what Herakleitos meant by his dictum: only what we know directly can inform us; what we have by hearsay leaves us cold.

Reading Carruth's new book, I've thought often of Herakleitos. Not because there's anything oracular or esoteric about these poems—far from it!—but in part because in them "the vision is cold chaos." One phase of this world is endless, ungraspable flux and change. But even endless change is not necessarily betrayal. For Carruth, the chaotic world of destructive flux is also the very body of value, at times beautiful and encouraging of fidelity and love. How can this be? Herakleitos also says that embedded in flux, as its principle and meaning, there is Logos, which

 . . . is eternal
but men have not heard it
and men have heard it and not understood.

I've got no idea what Carruth thinks of Herakleitos or whether he even reads the fragments or has taken them into account. In any event, there is a more than fortuitous coincidence between Herakleitos' feel for the nature of things and Carruth's.

But what matters most is that Carruth measures his experience in the world with an ear that is as responsive as his eye is discriminating and acute. And his ear also listens to what the poems say, measuring and shaping them so that they can come across to us as far more than hearsay. Over and over in the lyrical philosophic and elegiac poems that fill more than a third of *Brothers, I Loved You All,* it is something heard—often as a voice—that starts a poem or becomes the hinge point or resolution of a poem: "The oven door creaks/ in the night in the silent/ house, like all old things," " . . . the earth too cried out for justice,/ justice!," "The brook talks. The night listens." And there are human voices as well: a Pueblo woman, applying fresh mud to the wall of her adobe house, the voice of a black urban guerrilla come over the mountains from the city to Carruth's imagining ear. Frequently his ear picks out and names what cannot be heard, as when, writing an elegy on the proliferation of dead animal elegies in our times, he ends by saying:

                                        . . . I don't know
if the animals are capable of reproach.
But clearly they do not bother to say good-bye.

But let me give a larger example. In "The Joy and Agony of Improvisation," Carruth and his wife have listened to the wind in the pines as though "in the midst of voices in some/ obscure contention." Then later the wind changes, and Carruth wakes to hear:

                                    . . . how the voices
have turned to song. Hear
it rising, rising, then breaking, then
rising again, and breaking again. Oh, something
is unutterable, the song cannot reach it.
Yet we know it, know what we cannot
hear—out on the night's great circle,
the circle of consciousness with its far rim always
hidden, there where suffering and joy
meet and combine,
the inexpressible. How the song is striving
and how beautifully failing—the measure
of beauty, beyond plentitude,
never but always enough . . .
. . . it is the gathering of our love
into all love, into that suffering and joy.

How close this is to the ungraspable Logos! But there are other times when Carruth manages to hear its music and directly translates it, as when he gives us this "little song" of the wind high in the trees and its whispered meaning, while he sits at a fire in the forest with his son:

Sweet Bo I know thee
              thou art ten
and knowest now thy father is
five times more again
              and more
and most gone out of rhymes
sweet Bo
       for thou dost know me.

And thou old spruce above us

                many are they of comrade and kin
                who love us
                            so that their loving proveth
                everything
                            although their way hath not
                the same compassion
                                as thy nonloving.

I have passed many hours under similar trees across the Connecticut
River just into New Hampshire, not seventy miles from Carruth's
forest, and that *is* the song the wind makes in them. And when I'm
lucky, it does intimate something very much like that.

By talking so long about Carruth's ultimate sense of the order of
things, I hope I haven't given the impression that these poems are
abstractly philosophical or cold. On the contrary, they are all poems
about very daily affairs: things seen and heard, the loneliness of
missing friends absent or dead, the alternations of love for and es-
trangement from those present, the experiences of a man frequently
alone with the nonhuman which all too often bears the damaging
marks of careless human intrusion. Courage, human fidelity, and
love as well as their failures, loyalty to the nonhuman—these are the
obvious subjects Carruth writes about in these poems. But the underlying drama of what passes and what abides, of what is hidden
and what is revealed is never very far from their surface. They are
also exemplary of what Carruth says he learned to hear in the music of "that beautiful hot old man Sidney Bechet": "that tone, phrasing, and free play/ of feeling mean more than originality." In all
their variegation and intensity, these lyrics have much in common
with the "wavering music" of the loon's song, which occurs in the
first of them as though it "came from inside the long wilderness/
of my life" and "seemed/ the real and only sanity to me."

If these lyrics were all of this book, it would be worth reading
and reading again. But there's far more. Carruth's long poem "Vermont" was one of the very few bicentennial poems to come from a
poet of serious intention. I also think it is the best. Surely, for all its
gravity, it is the funniest.

    We need a new crop, something that will grow
    on hillsides, and on granite hillsides at that . . .
    My own idea that I've been working on
    is a neat machine that will exactly crack
    butternuts so the meat will come out whole.

Oh, there's a market for them. Rose Marie
knows eighteen recipes. But cracking them
the butternuts, that is, though Rose Marie's
handwriting can be pretty near as hard—
takes hammer and anvil, and generally it means
bloody fingers and nutshells in your cookies
and a visit to the dentist. Who needs that?
Well, all I need is *half* a hundred grand.
That's all; no more. Think what the state would save . . .
Then what? Easy. I'd make all Butternut Mountain
one huge farm and then hire half of the town
at harvest time, which would just nicely fill
that slack, fidgety season after the cider
has been put down to work and everyone
is sitting around uptight, waiting to test it.

"Vermont" is both a parody and expansion of Frost's "New
Hampshire." Carruth's faultless ear allows him the assumption of a
Yankee—more specifically Vermont—speech that is wholly authentic and natural to him, wholly assimilated to his own voice. To
my taste, the exquisite skill with which the vernacular rhythms and
inflections are laid against the blank verse far outdoes Frost at his
best. "Vermont" is an investigation of the history, prehistory, and
character—both human and natural—of its place. It also serves as a
detailed study in the grim and absurd relations of Americans to
nature, place, speech, poetry, and each other. The poem moves along
on a progression of epithets. Vermont is "a land of passage" whose
people are "passing on" and whose (official) business, quite regardless of people, is business above all. The special virtue of the Vermonter is "curiosity," which Carruth also insists was the virtue
shared by "those two old enemies," Frost and Pound, who "had
more between them, I expect, than either/ would have been willing
to allow." By character the Vermonter is a "son-of-a-bitch" who
takes "the directest way in everything but speech." Politically he is a
"Republican," which (here) is to say an "anarchist" and a "forlorn
believer," traveling by himself "or with a dog" through "Vermont's
protracted gloom/ our end-of-winter desolation." At its core the
poem is an overwhelming protest against grinding poverty and the
destruction of farming and native character that are the consequences of development and tourism, the famous ski slopes and
poster pictures of quaint barns that in fact are going irrevocably all
to hell. Carruth comes to the politics of all this with a vengeance

and avoids absolutely anything like the foolishness of Frost's persona of official public sage.

"Vermont" is Carruth's conscious extension of characteristic attitudes and poetic practice to regional materials of political and historical urgency. Not that he's "applied" any of it to the subject; it's rather that in "Vermont" he's hit on a form and style that have allowed him to advance his habitual equipment to meet new materials and give them shape. He does something similar in four other longish poems that follow "Vermont." How to describe them? I don't know anything else quite like them. At the least they are character portraits of particular Vermonters, written with an extreme compulsion to render the native speech as accurately as possible. But more than that, two of them, "Johnny Spain's White Heifer" and "Lady," are really masterful short stories in which only the most essential details are given and under the greatest possible compression. The other two, "John Dryden" and "Marshall Washer," are more like short novels in their scope, though the method of selection and intense compression is the same. All four are attempts to show the effects on individual souls of life in a difficult region, especially as it has come to be under the extraordinarily corrosive influence of an overpowering economic and industrial style that explicitly takes everything small and direct for its victim. Taken together the four poems are also a masterpiece of human sympathy.

I won't quote from these poems. Each is too much of a piece with itself, and quotation would be a violation. Three are full of weirdly hilarious gravity. The fourth, "Marshall Washer," is just utterly grave. They all bear strong public witness against the wastes and shames of our culture that are destroying human value with a will in a world where values are already hard enough to maintain, in a universe where they are always difficult to discover. Carruth does not express much anger in these poems. Yet one feels that an enormous energy of rage has forced them to be.

What is most outstanding in these poems is Carruth's uncanny fidelity to the speech of the people in them. It's not just that he's gotten it all down so accurately, or even that it comes up off the page at you as it does. Rather it's that through all the accuracy and life of this talk one can still hear so clearly Carruth's own voice as pedal point. That, I take it, is the embodiment of compassion. It's a kind of unawares participation, and it can't be chosen. Carruth knows this.

              . . . but have you noticed
I can't talk *about* him without talking *like* him?
That's my trouble. Somehow I always seem
to turn into the other guy . . .

What's the "trouble?" The trouble is that if one refuses nostalgia and
the picturesque and at the same time acknowledges that the chances
for amelioration and reform—especially in any direct way through
poems—is at best a forlorn hope, then compassion itself becomes a
heavy burden.

   How then to continue honestly to resist? What are the sources, if
any, of hope or, at least, endurance? What are the springs of joy?
These are the questions Carruth faces in "Paragraphs," the most
ambitious piece of work in the book, and for me the most successful and the most moving. In "Paragraphs," with magnificent energy
and compactness, Carruth gathers all the elements of his previous
concerns and allows them their fullest scope. Once more the poem
focuses on the difficulty and destructiveness of oblivious natural
forces and the superadded destruction of human exploitation. The
poem begins in Vermont, the scene again of the ravages of development, the intrusion of "the national mean taking over. Or/ the
mean nationals." It ends at a jazz recording session in New York,
February 12, 1944. In between, woven with these events, are scenes
and episodes of a vast range: Siva on Kailas, Dante, the partition of
Verdun, Thoreau at Walden Pond, the Ulster Troubles, Puerto Rico,
Vietnam, even a long, splendid and dead accurate direct quotation
from Bakunin on the meaning of liberty, perhaps the very best
piece of writing ever to come from that particular pen. And again it
is Carruth's uncannily faithful ear that extends to the most remote
of these sections and unifies the whole.

   In its general outlines, "Paragraphs" owes much to the methods
of Pound. It is true to Pound's ideals of clarity and hardness of detail
and the avoidance of sentimentality. But Carruth's language itself, its
cadences and feeling, owes nothing to Pound. Unlike so much
Pound inspired work, this is no imitation. And even though the
poem combines and intercuts immediate events and historical and
cultural concerns, public questions and personal attitudes in a manner close to *The Cantos,* there are none of Pound's fragmentary
loose ends or lapses of coherence.

   There is anguish here and horror and enraged accusation. But

there are also long moments of contemplative power. In paragraph
11 there is a kind of ritual communion, a catalog of the names of
jazz musicians, ending "Brothers I loved you all." And there is this
intimation of love itself:

It was the custom of my tribe to be silent
to think the song inwardly, tune and word
so beautiful they could only be held,
in quietness . . .
. . . and always we were alone.
Yet sometimes two
heard it, two separately together. It could come
nearby in the shadow of a pine bough
on the snow, or high in the orchestral lights,
or maybe (this was our miracle) it would have no
intermediary—
            a suddenness,
                indivisible, unvoiced.

All these are the sources of joy and persistence. And at last, at that
recording session there is the transcendence of an art which does
not close in on itself, which never leaves the world, but starts there
and returns the world to us and us to it—purified, enlivened, and
both whole again.

    . . . for they had come

                28
high above themselves. Above everything, flux, ooze,
loss, need, shame, improbability/ the awfulness
of gut-wrong,   sex-wrack,   horse & booze,
the whole goddamn mess,
And Gabler said "We'll press it"   and it was
    "Bottom Blues"
BOTTOM BLUES   five men knowing it well   blacks
    & jews
yet music, music   high
in the celebration of fear, strange joy
of pain: blown out, beaten out
                    a moment ecstatic
in the history
of creative mind *and* heart/   not singular, not the rarity
we think, but real and a glory
our human shining, shekinah . . .   Ah,

                    holy spirit, ninefold
    I druther've bin a-settin there, supernumerary
    cockroach i' th' corner, a-listenin, a-listenin,,,,,,
                            than be the Prazedint of the Wurrurld.

There again are the sources and the song that is "the real and only
sanity."

I've heard that Carruth is working on a new long poem. We've
got much to look forward to.

NOTE

1. A considerably fuller version of this essay was published in *American
Poetry Review* 10, January/February 1981: 19–22.

JUDITH WEISSMAN

From the Introduction to
Working Papers
Selected Essays and Reviews

It is difficult to write an introduction to the works of any living author, and it is particularly difficult to write about this selection of Hayden Carruth's essays and reviews. His work is awesomely rich, full, complete—thirty years of essays that begin with Pound and end with numerous younger poets in mid-flight. But the appearance of completeness is illusory, for these essays are no more than a tenth of those Carruth has written. I am particularly sorry not to include a review of a group of critical books on Spenser and three notes on Pope, to whom Carruth brings the same sense of joyful discovery that he brings to poets whom he is actually reading for the first time. But some principles of selection were necessary, and one was that I would try to present, through these essays, a history of the last thirty years of literature. (Occasional departures from even this principle were made, as in the inclusion of the review of Casanova's memoirs. I included that review because it was thematically so well connected with others on love and aristocracy.) This selection concludes with a review that points toward the future, on what poets may do in the 1980s, because this volume should not appear to be nicely and neatly *finished*. Plenty of people are still writing, and Carruth is still reviewing them.

The title, *Working Papers,* modest as it is, was chosen by Carruth years ago, when he first planned to publish a collection of his essays. It is still appropriate now: it is modesty that characterizes these essays, and Carruth's poems, and Carruth himself. In addition, the subtle pun of the title, the several meanings of the phrase, are too important to abandon. It is true that this book is sketchy, a draft, in a way, of the polished book of literary criticism that Carruth might have written in another life. Most of these essays were written as real *work*—which, in our society, means labor performed in exchange for money. The reviews, particularly, were the work Carruth did instead of being part of a university—they got him out of school, like the working papers of sixteen-year-old boys in the 1930s.

In need of money, Carruth has taken review assignments as they came, on books which he did not choose. The few long, fully developed essays here—like those on Robert Lowell and on "Poetry and Personality"—make me wish he had been able to write more of them, rather than being driven by necessity into doing so many brief reviews. But there is no reason to mourn over what he has done, or to treat this volume as one of promise rather than fulfillment, of frustration rather than realization. How many people in the privileged world of academia have written anything as good as this collection of reviews? Their genesis as work, as daily labor, has given them life. Carruth wrote them, not for the audience of scholarly journals, but often for newspapers or political magazines like *The Nation* or the *New Republic*. (Some, of course, were for more literary journals, though not academic ones, like *Poetry* and the *Hudson Review*.)

Some of the humanity of these essays and reviews also springs from Carruth's knowledge that he could help to determine the success of other people's books and affect how much money they made. The importance of reviewing, and of Carruth's reviewing in particular, became strikingly clear to me one evening when we attended a reading by a middle-aged poet who will never be rich or famous. He was amazed and delighted that Hayden Carruth had driven thirty miles to hear him, and after the reading, in private talk, recalled Carruth's review, many years earlier, of one of his books. "My marriage was falling apart, I was cracking up. I had written what I knew was my best book, and no one would review it. Except you. You knew it was good. Man, you saved my life." The man was not joking.

A well-known reviewer has a lot of power. He can give outrageously high praise to his friends, who will then of course return the favor; he can put down rivals and newcomers who are potential rivals, and anyone who has dared to insult him; above all, he can advertise himself. Carruth never does any of this. The unspoken values of these essays and reviews—humility, modesty, generosity, self-effacement—are the most important values of all. Carruth occasionally acknowledges the flawed, human self which, like everyone else, he certainly has—as in the essay on Robert Lowell, when he says that he envies Lowell's wealth and privilege, and easy success and fame as a poet—but how miraculously free from the bitterness of self these essays and reviews are! How encouraging to the young, how respectful to the old and out of fashion, how sincerely interested in the work of other writers.

Everyone who has read Carruth's poems knows some of the troubles of his life and can figure out that he wrote those lucid and kind reviews under some of the most difficult of human circumstances. The tone and texture are so even, strong, almost imperturbable, that it is an effort to remember that Carruth's daily intercourse with the human world has been unusually painful and difficult, and that he lived most of the last twenty years in northern Vermont, an especially poor man in a place where nearly everyone was poor. These reviews do not have the feeling of loneliness, which always does harm, though it sometimes also does good. They are so friendly, social, communicative. They could not be more different from the cranky soliloquies that we might expect from someone who has lived Carruth's life.

That life is not entirely absent here, however. The changes in the essays reflect Carruth's own life as well as his participation in a general cultural life. Most important is a change in his language. At the beginning, he sounds like what he was, an ambitious young editor of a prestigious urban magazine, *Poetry*, located in a big city, Chicago. By the end, we can hear Vermont in his voice. He is looser, more colloquial, more concerned with everyday life, nature, agriculture. One sentence, from the last review, will be sufficient illustration: "Dullness sprang up in the fertile soil of American poetry during the seventies like colorless saprophytes in a damp pine forest." This is not the talk of a Vermont farmer. It is the talk of an extraordinarily intelligent and observant man who knows both the world of poetry and culture and the plants of the Vermont woods, and understands both well enough to make use of one as an exceedingly precise metaphor for the other. A cultural tragedy is implied in this, a tragedy that informs Carruth's sense of the world. No one would bother to remark that Shakespeare or Milton or Wordsworth knew both culture and nature, but in our country the division has been growing deeper and deeper between the country and the city, agriculture and learning, the small community and the larger world. Carruth's life is extraordinary because he has known all of these possibilities so fully, and it has also been extraordinarily sad because he has known the pain of losing each of them.

Carruth's personal history is of less importance here than the other histories he writes about. The events of the world, as excluded from the New Criticism as the personalities of the poet and critic, are very much in evidence here. World War II, the Holocaust (before it became a fashionable topic), atomic weapons, racism in the United States (do other critics remember George Jackson?), and always, the suffering of the poor under the innumerable oppressions of government and bureaucracy. We hear occasionally about the problems of artists, too; but thank God we never hear that their sufferings are greater than those of the rest of the world. Justice and injustice, happiness and suffering, good and evil—yes, good and evil—and their consequences for the human race as a whole—those are always the final terms by which Carruth tests literature. These essays are not crudely utilitarian in any way; Carruth never says that some piece of writing is good simply because it contains some particular social idea or value. The utilitarianism (an unjustly disparaged philosophy in any case) is subtle and indirect. It lies in Carruth's refusal to let us forget that the ultimate context for art is the world—and that the world has been a very ugly place in the last thirty years. He has seen horror as clearly as anyone can, but has resisted the temptation to believe that an artist has the right to isolate and protect himself. He has held onto his vision of the sufferings of the world tenaciously, grimly, and above all, without cynicism.

The book, however, is primarily about neither Carruth nor the fall of the West. It is about literature and literary criticism. Carruth's interest in the literary criticism of the last thirty years has been more limited than his interest in poetry. He has not bothered with the bizarre explosion of academic criticism in the last few years, and we do not yet know what he has to say about the likes of Lacan and Derrida. Here he has written mainly about the New Criticism and some reactions to it, in his reviews of Karl Shapiro, Northrop Frye, Paul Elmer More, Joseph Frank, Martin Price, Eliseo Vivas, John Hall Wheelock, Edmund Wilson, George Steiner. Carruth shows the same respect and generosity toward other critics as he does to other poets; he admires intelligence, learning, scholarship, and love for the tradition of literature, in others. He deplores readings that include no glance at the outside world or that rest on esthetic values alone.

Carruth's own criticism is always on the verge of becoming philosophy. And he writes comfortably, surely more comfortably than most poets would, about philosophical and historical prose. Camus,

Sartre (on Genet), Genet, de Rougemont, Eliot, Eliot on Bradley, Casanova, Yevtushenko, Irving Singer, Gottfried Benn, Wyndham Lewis—a rather odd collection here, which, we must remember, Carruth did not choose. Such a disparate group does, oddly, belong together, for Carruth has unified them with two recurrent themes, the difficulties of human love, and the relation of art to the world. The European existentialists are among the heroes of this book, and surely its villains (I do not choose the word lightly) are Benn and Lewis. They are the primary examples of the evil to which men can come when they decide that they have the right to choose art over life. Carruth does not simply label them fascists and let them go, as a less conscientious critic might have done. He gives them the same intelligent care in reading that he gives to the others, and even praises them when they deserve praise. But he never allows their virtues—intelligence, skill, style—to obliterate his knowledge of the wickedness of what they believe. He cannot pardon them for writing well when what they say is evil.

Poetry is the subject of most of these essays, which constitute a perpetual reproach to the joylessness of academic criticism. There is joy in them. Read them—and remember what it was like to read for the first time Pound, Williams, Auden, Stevens, Muir, Ferlinghetti, Levertov, Aiken, Rukeyser, Duncan, Eliot, Perse, Lowell, Schwartz, Jarrell, Berryman, Zukofsky, Berry. Carruth is a graceful master of the myriad techniques of literary criticism, using them with ease to range widely, in lucid analysis of individual poems or poets, or the psychological development of a poet's work, or the poet's connection with a tradition which Carruth knows and reveres (a tradition which includes John Clare and William Barnes along with Shakespeare and Wordsworth). Though Carruth calls only a few human failings evil—cruelty, selfishness, fakery—he finds goodness in many places.

> *Paterson* . . . is a poem intense, complicated, and absorbing, one of the best examples of concision of poetry that I know.

> The love poems [of MacLeish], and there are many, written during every phase of the poet's career and under every aspect of feeling, are often splendid, composed with a restraint and exactness of language that is songlike, reproducing the sensuousness of ideas very evocatively, the basic eroticism of human thought.

Opulence—it is the quality most of us would ascribe to the poetry of Wallace Stevens before all others; profusion, exotic luxuriance.

This is hard substance, and the poems [of Muir] have about them, beyond their verbal utilitarianism, a kind of obduracy of spirit that we associate with the Scotch Presbyterian sensibility.

Force, directness, affection for the separate word and the various parts of speech (especially participles), knowledge of cadence and syntax, as components of meaning rather than vicissitudes of fabrication—there can be no doubt that Miss Rukeyser can write good poetry.

Perse writes a kind of pure poem of sensibility, an analytic of the heart, a conceptualizing poem. Without meter, without any rhythm except the self-sustaining verbal flow, his poetic principle, as one would expect in so abstract a composition, is pure grammar.

He has resolved to accept reality, all reality, and to take its fragments indiscriminately as they come, forging from them this indissoluble locus of metaphorical connections that is known as Robert Lowell.

In his war poems Randall Jarrell did rise, as if in spite of himself and at the command of a classical force outside himself, to his moment of tragic vision.

They all derive from his [Wendell Berry's] experience as a subsistence farmer, and they celebrate the earth and the strength a man gains from contact with the soil, water, stone, and seed. Make no mistake, these are poems in praise of Aphrodite of the Hot Furrow, full of generative force, even though their manner is seldom rhapsodic.

What word can describe Carruth's way of reading? *Pleasure* and *joy* have become debased—perhaps the word I am searching for is *celebration*.

Finally, Carruth has written a few, late, precious essays on the general subject of poetry—"The Writer's Situation," "Seriousness and the Inner Poem," "The Question of Poetic Form," "The Act of Love: Poetry and Personality"—which I would not attempt to summarize. They are rich and graceful and lucid, and unashamedly intelligent. And so I return to Carruth's history—not, this time, the change from the city to the country or from privilege to chosen poverty—but the history of growth into simultaneous modesty and confidence, seriousness and humor, humanity and wisdom. Again, I look for a word: can *adult* or *mature* still mean anything good when they have come to mean "pornographic"? I cannot think of one word with which to express my recognition that all these qualities could not belong to a young man. The complementary qualities of these late essays are highlighted in two sentences in "The Question of Poetic Form":

> Well, it seems to me that Plato made a very shrewd observation of human psychology when he conceived his ideals—if he was the one who actually conceived them (I am ignorant of pre-Socratic philosophy). . . .
> . . . I believe the closed pentameter couplet was natural to Pope, "organic," if you like, and if his poems are not as well unified *poetically* as any others of a similar kind and scope, if the best of them are not *poems* in exactly the same sense we mean today, then I don't know how to read poetry. (But I do.)

He feels free to offer an interpretation of Plato and also admits the limitations of his knowledge—an admission which itself establishes a breadth of knowledge which exceeds that of most current critics, who do not mention the fact that pre-Socratic philosophy exists. A younger and more anxious critic might have written a pompous little aside on where the interested reader might check up on pre-Socratic philosophy. Carruth can let it go. And he can also assert himself as a younger person could not, and say, in a biting parenthetical clause, that of course he knows how to read poetry. How good it is to read the work of someone whose knowledge and experience are so deep that he can make judgments without arrogance and without defensiveness.

But it would be wrong to make Carruth sound too much like the wise, good-hearted elder sage. There is always a more mysterious power in his writing, a power generated by the simultaneous existence of another pair of paradoxical qualities. I will use his own words, first on Lowell, second on Leroi Jones, to define those qualities: "this is tough, this is homely, this is American" and "our Shelley." Most of what I have praised in the essays belongs to the homely, American side of Carruth, to his affinity with Twain and Whitman, who never call people stupid or ugly, but only cruel or hypocritical or self-righteous, who value sanity and love, the natural world and common man. Shelley is here too, in the combination of rage and spirituality, visions of horror and visions of ethereal beauty, and fury at the sight of wrong that can only be felt by someone who wants perfection. Parts of the first essay in the book, Carruth's defense of Pound, sound almost as if they were copied from Shelley's "Defense of Poetry."

Poetry is the reason for all things humanly true and beautiful, and the product of them—wisdom, scholarship, love, teaching, celebration. Love of poetry is the habit and need of wise men wherever they are, and when for some reason of social or personal disadjustment they are deprived of it, they will be taxed in spirit and will do unaccountable things. Great men will turn instinctively to the poetic labor of their time, because it is the most honorable and useful, as it is the most difficult, human endeavor. Every spiritual faculty of man is a poetic one, and in poetry is that working of the spirit which engages man and his world in an intelligible existence. Only in poetry is man knowable to himself.

In the late essays the language is compressed, the tone, sober—but Shelley is still here, for example, in "The Act of Love: Poetry and Personality":

It follows that poetry is social, though not in any sense of the term used by sociologists. It follows that poetry is political, leaving the political scientists far behind. Maybe it even follows that if the substance of a poem, or part of it, is expressly though broadly social or political, this fact will reinforce the subjective communalism of the poet's intention in his transcendent act; but that is a question—the interrelationship of substance and the vision of form, or of moral and aesthetic feeling—to which twenty-five years of attention have given me no answer. Yet many, a great many, of our finest poems, especially as we read backward toward the evolutionary roots of poetry, seem to suggest such a hypothesis, and in any event we know that political substance is not, and in itself cannot be, inimical to poetry. Finally it follows that the politics of the poet, in his spirituality, will be a politics of love. For me this means nonviolent anarchism, at least as a means; I know no end.

Carruth has none of the qualities that alienate some people from Shelley—frothy poetic excess, squeamish disdain for earthly life—but the two are alike in their deep, pessimistic, undying spirituality. Despite his personal suffering, Carruth's spirituality has endured, as Shelley's might not have. Carruth never writes with the weary ease that often comes with self-confident skill and assured success. The late essays are less joyful than the early ones but just as loving; they are less hopeful but more dogged in their vitality. Carruth has endured without settling into stoicism because he has refused to cease either suffering or hoping. His progress has taken him continuously deeper into the knowledge of his own humanity, and of the humanity of literature.

2. *Jazzman—a lifetime of devotion to jazz, blues, and improvisation in his poetry and essays*

jazz, N. Possibly from Creole patois *jass*, sexual term applied to the African dances at Congo Square in New Orleans in the 1800s.

Why I went to verse-making

is unknowable, this
grubbing art. Trying,

Harmony, to fix your beat
in things that have none

and want none—absurdity!

—HC, "Freedom and Discipline"

BLUES SESTINA FOR HAYDEN CARRUTH

Red house, red barn, mailbox. I'm not late
but I am, in most ways, unprepared to meet you,
lost in your own smoke beside the wood
stove. Slow rise, gentle hand. You brew
coffee. I set up the tiny tape recorder.
Your wife gives your shoulders a "Be good"
kind of squeeze, and then she's good
enough to let us be.
I'm worried the percolator
will hiss-out the interview, that I'll only record
the ambience of your home and lose you
to the LP in the study, "Drunken Hearted Man" blues—

*My father died and left me
    my poor mother done the best she could.
My father died and left me
    my poor mother done the best she could.
Every man likes that game you call love
    but it don't mean no man no good—*

those thirteen cuts from Johnson's blues
sessions in Dallas, '37, late
June—

*Tell me, milk cow
    what on earth is wrong with you?
Your calf is hungry—*

                                    the recordings
of "Hell Hound," "Love in Vain," the final recordings
of his life.

    I begin with the obvious: "Could
you talk about freedom in poetry and jazz?" and you,
as if the question or answer could do any good:
"I have always tried to emulate
the improvisation that occurs, say, within a twelve-bar blues."

And when I ask you more about the blues
you walk me to your wall of records,
the stereo covered in cat hair. I follow a slate
path out the pipe-smoked window that could

lead to Robert Johnson or God
knows where:

> *Tell me, milk cow*
> *what on earth is wrong with you?*
> *Oooooooo, milk cow,*
> *what on earth is wrong with you?*
> *Now, you have a little calf,*
> *and your milk is turnin' blue.*

I persist: "You once wrote about really good
jazz musicians"—Carruth puts on a record—
"'it would be worth/ Dying, if it could
be done,/ to be there with them.'"
                    But by now it's late
afternoon, and you're gone, your mind recording
the '40s, all those blues clubs where you could
punish grief just by arriving good and late.
                    —Sascha Feinstein, from *Ajanta's Ledge,* 2012

MATT MILLER

A Love Supreme
Jazz and the Poetry of Hayden Carruth

Now and then a poet comes along whose work ranges across wide
and diverse territories of form, attitude, and emotion—yet with the
necessary intelligence that belies a deep, lifelong engagement with
tradition—so that variance never seems mere experimentation or
digression, but improvisation. Hayden Carruth is such an artist,
finding in his sonnets, haikus, and georgics, his organic-form poems
and his self-invented "paragraphs," a voice empowered and spontaneous enough to allow, as Wendell Berry puts it, "heart and mind to
speak as one." One listens ultimately in a good Carruth poem, not
for formal or technical mastery, but for how closely, in its moments
of relaxed and lucid transparency, his art can approach truth. And
with his ecstatic, jazz-inspired poetic vision, Carruth finds ways to
succeed. One thinks of John Coltrane, another great protean spirit,
and his passionate, hard-won vision, his "love supreme."

Carruth is a poet whose clear intentions have resisted critical
analysis. He has always been candid about his influences; and his
poems, in their clarity and their refusal to dress up in clever wordplay or private symbolism, seldom beg the presence of scholarly
input. Yet with his twenty-two volumes of poetry, his work as editor
at *Harper's* and *Poetry,* and his prolific, omnivorous book reviewing,
year by year Carruth contributed more to our literary heritage than
he has received either in the form of popular readership or critical
acclaim. While such a discriminating reader as James Wright describes "the powerfully spare and precise lyricism of his songs; his
almost spooky sensitivity to the voices of the people in his idylls . . .
and everywhere, gathering the other powers, the clear mind, Lucre-
tian in its exact intelligence," or while Adrienne Rich praises the
"heartbreaking powers" of his truest poems, Carruth is nevertheless
consistently omitted from the important anthologies, and so cor-
respondingly ignored by the academy. The cliché here is unavoidable: Carruth has thus far been "a poet's poet."

Some of our lag in responding to Carruth's achievement is probably a direct result of the impact of jazz music on his style. How does one convey the elusive qualities of good jazz improvisation? It is a pleasure apprehended on a level above (or below) conceptual discourse—again, resisting interpretation. There are, however, other factors that have led to Carruth's relative neglect. For years he chose to live among and write about rural farmers in northern Vermont—not a good position for self-promotion. He accepted a teaching position at Syracuse only after twenty years of steady publishing. While his influential anthology, *The Voice That Is Great within Us,* was published by Bantam, his own poetry has been offered by respected, though mostly out-of-the-way presses such as Prairie Press, Sheep Meadow, and Tamarack. So lists the material factors leading to the respectful but relatively sparse reading public of Carruth's poems. And beneath this logic, explaining it and tying it together, lies the vision Carruth expresses repeatedly in his writing: his sense of cultural responsibility informed by anarchist politics and its emphasis on working-class identity and responsibility, a fierce Yankee disdain for showiness and charlatanry, and the necessity for poetry to "give" and "bestow" and never to "demand":

A poem is not an expression, nor is it an object. Yet it somewhat
    partakes of both. What a poem is
Is never to be known, for which I have learned to be grateful. But
    the aspect in which I see my own
Is as the act of love. The poem is a gift, a bestowal.
The poem is for us what instinct is for animals, a continuing and
    chiefly unthought corroboration of essence
(Though thought, ours and the animals', is still useful).
                    (from "The Impossible Indispensability
                        of the Ars Poetica")

Carruth's emphasis on "instinct" and "unthought . . . essence" in this excerpt is telling; for in the exploratory openness toward which improvisationalists strive, "instinct" becomes the ultimate virtue; and "unthought corroboration of essence" seems as apt a way as any to describe jazz that really smolders and swings.

Carruth's relationship to jazz music has been lifelong, and it has expressed itself on many different levels in his work. In his essay "Influences: The Formal Idea of Jazz," Carruth describes his personal ideas on how jazz has influenced his writing. He discusses the "limitations and absurdities" of tracking influences to one's direct literary predecessors, acknowledging that when he first set about writing the poets he read were Ben Johnson, William Yeats, and Ezra Pound, but describing how "the statement is true but meaningless" because "the real question is not by whom I was influenced, but how."

For Carruth, never a purist in regard to the forms his improvisations will take on, the question of influence becomes especially complex. To discuss it, we might examine how from Wendell Berry, Carruth seems to have developed some of his sense of poetic citizenry, his integratedness with the country people with whom he has lived most of his life. We might analyze how "the peculiar and lovely syntax," as Carruth puts it, of poet Paul Goodman affected Carruth—or how Carruth, like Adrienne Rich, emphasizes the necessity for writers to "locate themselves" in their writing. And none of this would account for Carruth's reactive influences: the poets who exerted their influence by Carruth's rejection of their stance.

The truth is that Carruth's writing has taken such a variety of forms, ranging without concern across nominally hostile movements—the raw and the cooked of the sixties, the "smart and the sincere" of today—and adopting such a cornucopia of different attitudes—erotic Petrarchan lover, political spokesperson, friend to poets, and ornery Yankee backwoodsman, to name a few—that it is bewildering in the extreme to attempt to pull together any kind of a cogent picture of the *literary* factors that have influenced his writing. In tune with his vision of art as improvisation, his poems borrow freely from whatever sources they need to. Carruth reads a book of Ginsberg's poetry, then unselfconsciously sits down and writes "Thaw," a poem Carruth dedicates to Ginsberg and which intentionally expresses itself in Ginsberg's long, sweeping, incantatory lines:

> fuzzed snow browning in last year's haystubble, the pasture's
> winter-starved moss
> lionskin flung rumpled, moist, eaten, crushed eyes in the mange-
> fur
> old leaves, world-flakes, eddy and sparrow-dance, get up they
> whimper . . .

And so on. Or borrowing in a different way, Carruth spells his words phonetically to intimate the voice inflections of Yankee northeasterners:

"Whut do you spose thet thing is," Oi said. "Whut?"
she said. "Whoi, thet there annymule on thet
yaller diamon-shape soign back there set
boi the soid of the rouad," Oi said . . .

("Sonnet")

Whether structural or lingual, the important thing is not the formal
input, but the animating spirit that infuses Carruth's language and
makes whatever form it takes on uniquely his own.

Perhaps this accounts for how Carruth's progress over the years
has so closely paralleled that of a musician. Among musicians, it's
usually true that an early classical training in form is necessary before an artist can expect to play well in more spontaneous styles.
The discipline must precede the rejection of discipline. So it was
with Carruth—as his poetry demonstrates and as Carruth makes
clear himself in his many essays in *Sitting In: Selected Writings on Jazz,
Blues, and Related Topics*. All the while he was imitating Pound and
Yeats in his first books, in his secret heart he heard the music of
Coleman Hawkins, Sidney Bechet, and Pee Wee Russell; and he
longed to write with a similar instinct for spontaneity and exploration. The instinct was there; but in his earliest writing, Carruth was
not yet practiced enough to respond to it.

Consider these, the first few lines of a poem from Carruth's first
book:

Couplings buckled, cracked, collapsed,
And all reared, wheels and steel
Pawing and leaping above the plain,

And fell down totally, a crash
Deep in the rising surf of dust,
As temples into their cellars crash.

Dust flattened across the silence
That follows the end of anything,
Drifted into cracks of wreckage.

("The Wreck of the Circus Train")

The stately and carefully regulated movement of the poem shows
the poet's metrical influence by a more formal poetry, though the
music in the poem, compared to the impassioned strains of his later
work, remains muted and self-conscious. And the images of the

poem seem disembodied in the language: the poet expresses no relationship to those images personally. Similarly, the kinetic sense of an apprentice musician will often seem static until he or she is more practiced; and the internal gestures, until the musician improvises personal, auditory figures of thought, will by necessity be derived from the musician's masters (just as the primary gesture of this piece echoes Yeats's great "Circus Animals' Desertion").

Carruth's poetic development did not take long. While his first two books, *The Crow and the Heart* and *The Norfolk Poems of Hayden Carruth,* are exceptional in moments only, by his third full-length collection (he published two long poems in chapbook form in the meanwhile), we see Carruth coming into his own. *Nothing for Tigers* is a transitional book of sorts. Many of the poems here resemble those of his earlier collections: finely tempered mixes of stress, sound, and objectified imagery, which, though often technically adept and impressive, are seldom jazzy, seldom swing. In several of the pieces in this collection, however, we witness something quite different beginning to transpire. We see, in a poem like "Essay on Marriage," Carruth loosening his hold on the language and becoming casual, intimate, more himself:

> Snow came to us in the week of Thanksgiving.
> I was studying Dr. Williams on the "variable foot"
> And Hölderlin on the necessity
> For writing one more poem,
>
> And my wife and I had been married twenty-two days.
> Not long, but considering the nature of
> Joy it was long enough.

No longer are we distracted by Carruth's formal classical apprenticeship; this poem possesses the urgency of a life deeply lived and pressing toward speech.

Even more indicative of Carruth's breakthrough are the poems in this collection specifically about his jazz heroes, the most passionate of which is his great poem "Freedom and Discipline"—a personal testimony of Carruth's commitment to jazz and ecstatic art. In this poem, Carruth himself makes clear the transition he has undergone, describing his enchantment first with the classical Rachmaninoff, and then his second love, Coleman Hawkins, with whom he "leapt to the new touch,/ up and over the diminished/

in a full-voiced authority/ of blue-gold blues," describing how "Catlett/ drove the beat without/ harming it . . . / how Monk reconstructed/ a broken chord to make/ my knuckles rattle." The music of the poem continues to soar until it reaches its rapturous peak where Carruth can assert:

> Freedom and discipline concur
> only in ecstasy, all else
>
> is shoveling out the muck.
> Give me my old hot horn.

Except for a brief stint writing haikus while editing *The Voice That Is Great within Us,* almost all of Carruth's poems written after "Freedom and Discipline" follow this paradigmatic expression of his beliefs about creativity.

For Carruth, poetic improvisation does not mean the abandonment of form or rhyme, nor does it limit itself to any particular attitude or emotion. A quiet inward mood can be as "ecstatic" as a more public one. What improvisation ultimately amounts to is structure becoming a function of feeling, whatever that feeling may be. In classicism, a given piece of art formally determined *a priori* to its emotional content. The early romantics of the eighteenth and nineteenth centuries embody non-classical values in terms of content, but they are still a long way from the formal improvisation of a Coltrane or a Carruth.

Carruth produced several fine collections in this mode in the seventies, reaching one of his great creative peaks with the release of *Brothers, I Loved You All. Brothers, I Loved You All* represents another kind of development, an advance in Carruth's writing. What it expresses is not only a more rounded mastery of form, but a deepening of vision. By this time, Carruth's strategy of poetic improvisation had already reached mature form. No longer is Carruth struggling for his sense of voice or to expand on his technical mastery. In *Brothers,* Carruth is able to marshal all of the powers he has developed—his mastery of multiple forms, his spontaneity, his precise lyricism—and set them free in service of a poetic vision larger and more inclusive than any towards which he has yet aspired. The things he writes about here are never abstract or "metaphysical" in and of themselves. They are the tangible, concrete experiences which any of us might have. Carruth goes for a walk with his wife in the woods of Vermont to listen to the wind. At first the wind seems "shifting, directionless . . . voices in some obscure contention," but then later Carruth and his wife waken to hear:

> . . . how the voices
> have turned to song. Hear
> it rising, rising, then breaking, then
> rising again, and breaking again. Oh, something
> is unutterable, the song cannot reach it.
> Yet we know it, know what we cannot
> hear—out on the night's great circle,
> the circle of consciousness with its far rim always
> hidden, there where suffering and joy
> meet and combine,
> the inexpressible. How the song is striving
> and how beautifully failing—the measure
> of beauty, beyond plentitude,
> . . . it is the gathering of our love
> into all love, into that suffering and joy.
>
> ("The Joy and Agony of Improvisation")

Striving and beautifully failing indeed: for in the pure realm of transcendent subjectivity, where there can be "unthought corroboration of essence," all song must by necessity fail in its struggle towards the absolute. How much different this is from the "cold eye" Yeats asks us to cast on life; and yet in Carruth, this celebration is not mere romantic reversion. In its balance of order and disorder, in its vulnerability and spontaneity, Carruth's passionate, unadorned vision at its best seems more like realism than romanticism.

Brothers, I Loved You All could, I suppose, be divided into four types of poems. His "songs" are generally lyrical in organization and range in tone from the haiku-inspired sparseness of "My Hut" to the lovely, generous singing of "The Little Fire in the Woods," a poem for Carruth's son, David ("Bo"). His "essays" are just that: inductive, ruminative essays expressed with the brevity and precision of poems. A third mode for Carruth is his longer, open-form monologues about Vermont and Vermonters, a style rangy and flexible enough to suit Carruth's aim to sketch out the life of another human being. In "Marshall Washer," for example, Carruth evinces a sustained act of compassion the maturity and concentration of which leave the beholder breathless and shaken. So transparent is his language that only after we are finished do we realize that what we have been reading is *a poem*. A fourth mode, unique to Carruth, is expressed in the book's long, concluding poem, "Paragraphs," an intensely focused sequence of improvisations which bring into full scope the themes explored throughout the book: ecstatic love, song, community, and the threat of their extinction at the hands of capitalist exploitation.

Carruth's "paragraphs" are a fifteen-line verse form which Carruth invented back in 1955 and which he began working with as early as his first book in another long poem, "The Asylum." Rhymed complexly and consistently in an intricate rhyme (ABABAACCD-EDEFEF) and metrical scheme (554355445354555), the paragraph employs the irregular formalism of a Renaissance ode or elegy (Milton's "Lycidas," for example, could well be regarded as a formal antecedent). In "The Asylum," the form is employed quite strictly, using only the variations allowed in traditional English prosody: inverted first feet, cataleptic lines, etc. By the time Carruth wrote "Paragraphs," he had loosened up the form a good deal—with narrative interludes, staggered line breaks, and sentences that carry on without pause from one paragraph into the next. The pliancy of the later form of the paragraph reflects the improvisationalist's simultaneous need for a backdrop of order and his resentment of the mechanical repetition such an order traditionally implies. In "Paragraphs," the rules are there, but they are open for play and reinterpretation as the occasion demands. In this paragraph, Carruth is "playing":

Another hard, hard morning with a hard snow
Falling small and fast. It is eight below.
Yet the ash pail brims. I must go
Out to the garden and sow
This remnant of value where the beans will grow
Next summer maybe. The goddamned gods bestow
And men . . .
                         are at best a paradigm
Sowing and reaping in the void of time.
Or say that one must do what one does as though
It might mean something, so—
Broadcasting ashes, swinging my shovel low,
Spreading this color that I don't know,
Dirty lavender, dirty pearl, row upon row,

Death upon death, "sowing the ashes," to and fro,
A *tour de force* in an abandoned studio.

("23")

The most distinctive feature of the paragraph—and the "rule" to
which it most consistently pays tribute—is the couplet which is
always internalized in the middle of each section. Placing a couplet
in the middle rather than the end of each set negates the conclusive,
mnemonic effect which end-couplets commonly create in sonnets,
and so makes the form well suited to longer sequences intended to
flow together and capitalize on accumulating energies. Rather than
a continual "stop and start, stop and start" effect as becomes the rule
with sonnets, the internal couplet becomes the fulcrum point for
the attack and decline of each section as it fits within the whole.

The "paragraph" seems to be Carruth's preferred vehicle when
he is feeling most thematically ambitious. In *The Sleeping Beauty,*
Carruth's major book-length contribution, Carruth returns to the
form with a vigor and produces a hundred and twenty-four of
them in service of no less a task than mapping out a logos of love
and tragedy that defines a mythopoetic matrix for our time. He
includes paragraphs on the bomb, on Hitler, on anarchism and the
idea of freedom; he writes about rape and the crucifixion of value;
on music, psychology, existentialism, courtship, the blurring of sexuality, our quixotic, doomed longing for an ideal absolute: and everywhere, uniting the fragments, the anima and animus of our eternal duality as expressed in the paradigm of romantic love. If there is
a "philosophy of Hayden Carruth," this is the book to which one
should turn to find it. In it, Carruth sets in motion a world that is
immediately recognizable because it is the historical world Americans and Europeans all share.

In the late eighties, Carruth published two books completely in
form, one, quoted from earlier, *Sonnets,* and his *Asphalt Georgics,*
georgics that express no *formal* relation to the traditional georgic at
all, and are instead another of Carruth's self-invented formal modes.
"Georgics" employ a strict syllabic meter (8686) with exactly
rhymed end words in the second and fourth lines, i.e., so exact that
"the" and "a" are rhymed (because that's the way they're pronounced). Against this strictness Carruth casts a loose and mostly
very colloquial language, using phrases he overheard on the strip in
a commercial/industrial suburb in Syracuse where he was living at
the time he wrote them. Carruth's georgics extend his experimen-

tation with narrative poetry, which reaches its first mature form in several of the best poems from *Brothers, I Loved You All* (1979), and upon his still-developing style of ruminative, "metaphysical" poetry, a mode Carruth shows an inclination for even in his earliest pieces. In general, all of his poems written following the publication of *After the Stranger: Imaginary Dialogues with Camus* in 1965, Carruth's half-autobiographical, half-critical exploration of the permutations of existentialism, show the fruits of Carruth's study, and are written with greater flexibility and cogency than his earlier philosophical poems. Those in *Asphalt Georgics* are no exception:

> Many paths in the woods have chos-
> en me, many a time,
> and I wonder often what this
> choosing is: a sublime
>
> intimation from far outside
> my consciousness (or for
> that matter from far inside) or
> maybe some train of mor-
>
> tality set in motion at
> my birth (if our instru-
> ments of observation were fine
> and precise enough to
>
> trace it)
>
> ("Lost")

In the end, this poem takes the long, elliptical path towards affirmation (if only affirmation of mutability); but along the way Carruth will digress along any number of possibilities, testing their potential.

In his sonnets, georgics, and paragraphs, Carruth uses the external structure of a fixed poetic form to lend order to his improvisations. With these, as in a four-bar blues song, the structural principle is simple and easy to identify because it supports the exposition of the poem in a fixed and measured way: a kind of frame or scaffolding. The deployment of a relatively simple structural groundwork for improvisation is a tried and true technique in jazz (any lover of jazz could offer a favorite example, Miles Davis's collaboration *Kind of Blue* being a famous one). At first glance, the flowing, mostly long-lined poems in Carruth's collection, *Tell Me Again How the*

White Heron Rises and Flies Across the Nacreous River at Twilight Toward the Distant Islands, might, as the title suggests, seem formless—an anomaly to Carruth's assertion that "freedom and discipline concur/ only in ecstasy." With these poems however, structure is not imposed externally, but internally, in rhythm and pace. The "discipline" in these poems is less obvious visually, but it is present—in a more malleable form—as Carruth creates and discovers it line by line:

> My true friend's poem about aging and death held my mind as in
>   a sea-surge
> this afternoon, for they are true poems, and good ones,
> and I myself feel weakened much of the time now from the nights
>   of death-laden
>   insomnia,
> which no weakness cures.
>
> (from "No Supervening Thought of Grace")

With no significant rhythm of stress or rhyme, syntax and line breaks become the units of rhythm. They become active agents allowing Carruth to better capitalize on the epigrammatic density of a phrase like "which no weakness cures" by juxtaposing it in a short line against the more sweeping rhythm of the three preceding longer ones. Lacking an outside scaffold for poetic order, Carruth finds a "beat" to create one internally.

Carruth produced a total of five full-length collections in the eighties, two of which, *The Oldest Killed Lake in North America* and *If You Call This Cry a Song,* are full expressions of Carruth's talents, written in modes similar to those in *Brothers.* Aside from an occasional sonnet, Carruth's late poetry follows the pattern of *Oldest Killed Lake* and finds its structure internally rather than in an external frame of conventional form. Many of these poems show the mark of the aging virtuoso who has given up all tricks and artifice for the pure expression of meaning and emotion. Several of the best of them are elegies, and several, such as his marvelous poem titled simply, "Sex," are erotic poems, though with a difference, since they are written by a seventy-year-old man:

> . . . Aging men
> suffer two kinds of impotence, the ordinary
> kind that everyone makes jokes about, and then
>   the deeper psychic failure when they are full

of eros but it is hidden, too remote
to evoke the wonder of lust in their partners . . .

This type of vulnerability, characteristic not only of his late poetry but of so much of his best work, is one of the most persuasive elements in Carruth's work. A long career filled with many prestigious positions and prizes will not reduce him to posturing or defensiveness. After achieving mastery of technique, Carruth abandons technique for simplicity. After a long life filled with much extraordinary circumstance, Carruth will not revert to nostalgia but instead describes his present sorrow. These qualities—attributes of character as much as artistry—reflect the integration of life and poetry which Carruth's improvisation allows him to achieve.

So we approach a poet whose career is still being assessed. I find Carruth's body of work more distinguished from his peers for its cogency, its truth value, and its formal relationship to jazz and poetic traditions. And I use the word *truth* keeping in mind the complex philological burden which today this word is forced to bear. The truth for which Carruth strives, and, I believe, often achieves, is not the truth of the ego in narcissistic reverie, nor is it the presumption of objective truth handed down from the twin mountains of religious and intellectual tradition. It is the truth of impassioned subjectivity: the truth of self, yes, but of the self peopled by relationships with other human beings: the fluid truth of the self that responds not in solipsism, but in community: the truth of the individual perhaps, but including, as Carruth puts it in another essay, "the whole individual subjectivity, the spirit-body-soul." This means acknowledging, as Carruth so often does, the great instability of self-identity, the dynamic process by which we continually realign ourselves to changing relationships with people and ideas; but it does not mean succumbing to that instability and creating an art which tries to find value in meaning's absence. Carruth's is the truth of the jazzman who finds meaning in the artistic moment, spontaneously, ecstatically, and understanding that meaning is something apprehended through individual vision—but understanding also the need for that vision to include other individuals: its audience. On that note, I give Hayden the last word:

> . . . if I do not know which poem of mine
> Was my earliest gift to you,
> Except that it had to be written about someone else,

Nevertheless it was the gesture accruing value to you, your
　　essence, while you were still a child, and thereafter
Across all these years. And see how much
Has come from that first sonnet after our loving began, the one
That was a kiss, a gift, a bestowal. This is the paradigm of
　　fecundity. I think the poem is not
Transparent, as some have said, nor a looking glass, as some
　　have also said,
Yet it has almost the quality of disappearance
In its cage of visibility. It disperses among the words. It is a
　　fluidity, a vapor, of love.
This, the instinctual, is what caused me to write "Do you see?"
　　instead of "Don't you see?" in the first line
Of this poem, this loving treatise, which is what gives away
　　the poem
And gives it all to you.

DAVID BUDBILL

When You Use Your Head, Your Ears Fall Off

My Twenty Years of Listening to Music with the Supernumerary Cockroach

I.

Again and again when I go to somebody's house they say, "Hey! I got this great new album I want you to hear." So they put the record on and not eight bars into the first tune they start talking and then everybody starts talking and the party is on. And, once again, the music becomes what it almost always is in our lives, background something for that jawing noise we make with our mouths. When the record is over somebody *might* say, "Man, isn't that great?" And somebody else might say, "Oh, yeah, that was fantastic." Although usually nobody says anything, they just keep talking because nobody has even noticed that the music stopped.

In the world of music when somebody says you have "good ears" it means you play well by ear, you articulate on your instrument what you hear being played, either outside yourself by others or, more mysteriously, inside yourself, by those inner musicians, inner voices, who/which are always calling to any artist from the other side.

Over the music stand in the corner of my writing room where I practice my saxophone, I have a sign, a little piece of advice I made up to give myself, which says:

> When You Use Your Head
>   Your Eears Fall Off.
>   Don't Think:
>   Listen

In other words, if I try to *think* my way through the chord changes on which a particular tune is constructed, if I try to *think up* my musical poem, I can't play. However, if I relax and *listen* carefully and accurately enough to that other melody, the one I can hear being played inside me, then I can play, and it is likely to sound pretty good. If I put thinking in the place of listening, my "good ears" fall off.

II.

For the past twenty years Hayden Carruth has been for me a hawkeyed critic and a steadfast friend. Over those years together we have been through myriad personal traumas in both our lives, shared many mutual loves and hates, pleasures and consternations. And through all this we have spent almost all of our time together not talking about literature or gossiping about fellow writers, in fact, not talking at all but listening instead to music. What we have shared most and most deeply over the years is our mutual love for the music invented by African Americans, the music some people call jazz.

When Hayden and I listen to music together, although it seems almost ridiculous to have to say it, we listen. We don't talk while the music is playing; we talk after the music stops. Music is a conversation in another language; it is someone speaking directly to you, and, as your mother must have told you, it is impolite to talk while someone else is speaking.

We've spent twenty years listening together and when we are not together, which is most of the time, we send tapes back and forth and then talk and write to each other about what we hear. I want to remember here four specific times out of those twenty years of listening together.

First. Twenty years ago. I was just getting to know Hayden. I was at his little house on Clay Hill in Johnson, Vermont. We were in his tiny living/dining room. Hayden said, "Listen to this." and he put on to his old and rickety portable record player a cut from a record made live at the 1959 Belgium World's Fair Jazz Festival. The players were Sidney Bechet on soprano sax, Buck Clayton on trumpet, Vic Dickenson on trombone, and a rhythm section neither one of us can remember.

It was a blues, called simply, "Society Blues," one of those names thought up in a second and stuck onto a tune to give it a name for the album, an impromptu blues of numerous choruses over basic changes, a chance for each soloist to have his say. And when it came

Vic Dickenson's turn, he had plenty to say! He launched into his solo and proceeded to utter one of the most scathing bits of social commentary I have ever heard. He played the ugliest, nastiest, meanest, most sarcastic, most biting, most hilarious series of . . . let Hayden say it as he said it of another time when Vic Dickenson let loose:

> smears, brays—Christ
> the dirtiest noise imaginable
> > belches, farts
> > *curses*
> but it was music

In other words, how else is a Black man lost in a racist society to have his say and still keep his neck the length it is supposed to be? Defiance. Defiance. Vic Dickenson had articulated an essential element in the music of blues and jazz: defiance.

Last year I had a conversation with saxophonist David Murray in which we were both bemoaning the state of lifelessness and conservatism that has swept through not only poetry and jazz but all the arts. I remember at one point Murray saying, "When I was coming up we just naturally felt it was important to defy."

Second. Ten years ago. This time we were at my house. I had just gotten a new record: "Improvisations," a piano duet with Ran Blake and Jaki Byard. Hayden and I sat on the couch and did what we do: we listened.

Putting Ran Blake, the atonal, nonmelodic, arhythmic, analytic player together with Jaki Byard, the swinging, soulful, hard-driving, emotional player, is like trying to mix oil and water. This encounter between Third Stream Guru and Master of Charles Mingus Transmogrified Blues Roots was an instruction in the nature and necessity of voice.

Duke Ellington said, "A man's sound is his total personality."

If the reed instruments are the easiest instruments on which to produce your own personal sound, the piano has got to be the most difficult, yet even on an instrument so unyielding to individual sound as a piano, these two men spoke clearly and distinctly, and separately, as they spoke together out of their vastly different sensibilities and voices. You can't be who you ain't. To quote Thelonious Monk, "How could I be anything other than who I am. A man is a genius just for looking like himself."

One of the ways a musician expresses his or her unique voice is the way in which he or she approaches rhythm. Hayden found somewhere years ago a quote from Max Roach saying, "Every change in the history of jazz has been a rhythmic change." One of the general threads running through all our twenty years of listening together has been our attention to rhythm, cadence, location of the beat, listening for and talking about the rhythmic complexity and subtlety that any African-based music always has. One of the things that creates a distinctive, individual sound, a voice, is how a particular player approaches the beat, and one of the great sources of surprise and delight in all of jazz is listening for that approach, how he or she will attack the beat, lay back from it, get in ahead of it, shy away from it, steer it, be steered by it, overpower it, give in to it.

Third. Five years ago. Hayden was headed east from Syracuse to do a reading at New England College in Henniker, New Hampshire, where our mutual friend Joel Oppenheimer was teaching. On his way south, Hayden stopped by my place and picked me up so that I could travel with him to the reading. It would be nice, we'd have a few days together with not much to do but hang out, visit Joel and the vivacious and beautiful Teresa, and do what we always do when we get together: listen to music.

We got on Interstate 89 in Montpelier and headed for southern New Hampshire, then promptly got off the interstate at the first exit—both of us being well sick of years of high-speed, interstate driving—and slowed the trip down to a leisurely toddle. And as we drove in that insular privacy a car in motion affords, we listened to music.

First that day we listened to Hayden's beloved Sidney Bechet. Hayden had introduced me to Bechet years before. In my early days of listening to Bechet I did not appreciate him. I came to musical consciousness during that time in the mid-1950s when BeBop was in full bloom, and to my BeBop ear Bechet's music sounded too much like the Dixieland I had already learned to hate for its clichéd phrases and pat emotions. On closer examination, however, and in the care of someone with the depth of knowledge and concern Hayden has for music, I had come to see how Bechet and his friends were anything but pat or clichéd. I began to be able to hear the hard-driving passion of Bechet's playing, his relentless emotional intensity.

Then Hayden played an album by Odetta, who I'm sure just

about everybody thinks of as a folk singer. On this album, however, Odetta sings the blues. And again here was a musician fairly exploding with emotional intensity and drive. Odetta's verbal and rhythmic articulation is so sharp and cutting it is almost menacing. Her songs are full of the painful openness of the blues:

> Ain't it hard to stumble
> when you got no place to fall.
> I said, ain't it hard to stumble
> when you got no place to fall.
>> Stranger here, stranger everywhere
>> I would go home, but, Honey, I'm a stranger there.

But full also of political content:

> Oh, Mr. Rich Man, Rich Man
> Open up your heart and mind.
> Mr. Rich Man, Rich Man
> Open up your heart and mind.
>> Give the poor man a chance.
>> Help stop these hard hard times.
> While you're livin' in your mansion
> You don't know what hard times mean.
> While you livin' in your mansion
> You don't know what hard times mean.
>> Poor man's wife is starvin'
> Your wife a'livin' like a queen.

And we drove on toward Henniker and toward Joel and Teresa, listening and then talking and then listening some more.

Fourth. A couple of months ago. Hayden was in Vermont for a few days and we had only a short afternoon together. Charles Simic had given Hayden a videotape of a Danish program about saxophonist Ben Webster. If there is any one black musician who has joined Hayden and me together over the years, bridged our sometimes quite different tastes, and stood for our common understanding of the place and meaning of black American classical music in American life, and the meaning of being an artist in America, it is Ben Webster.

After nearly twenty years of the two of us listening intently to Webster in all his moods and manifestations, it was a delight to sit down and actually watch the man move through the world, and to see, and not only hear, him play his horn. I was struck, for example, with how often he took a breath and therefore how brief his phrases were. This was a surprise to me since his playing is so liquid and seamless. It was also interesting to see this "old" way of breathing now in a time when practically all reed players can circular breathe and therefore can play one, uninterrupted phrase literally for hours. It was exciting to see this great master use his breathing to "break the lines of his poem" so to speak.

There has never been a player in the history of jazz more willing to express direct, intense, and unabashed emotion than Ben Webster. He was never stuck in that sophisticated idea that the expression of emotion is—unsophisticated. And there has never been in the history of the tenor saxophone a player more capable of coaxing out of his horn a broader range of sounds, and I am not forgetting the innovations of John Coltrane, Albert Ayler, and David Murray to name only three. In short, nobody more than Ben Webster has produced a more human sound.

As Gil Evans put it, "All great music has to have a cry somewhere; all players and all music—they have to have that cry." No one cried more completely or included in his repertoire a greater range of cries—cries of anguish, sadness, silly joy, sexual ecstasy, hatred, sarcasm, rage, grief—than Ben Webster. In the richness and variety of his tone Webster was able to express, as Ellington said a player must, his total personality, and I would add the full range of human emotion.

III.

What has struck me in writing these memories of listening to music with Hayden is how much talking about the music we listen to is like talking about Hayden's poetry.

First, the kind of lovingly detailed observation of our world and ourselves and the infinite variety of moods and situations we and the world find ourselves in that is so clear in all of Hayden's work comes from an ability to focus upon the object, mood, emotion, and give it a kind of Zen-like attention. This ability to listen to the world both outside and inside the self and then attempt to articulate what you hear is rife throughout Hayden's work.

Second, Hayden has great ears. Where else among American poets is there a writer with a better pair? Whether it be the patois of northern Vermont, in one of Hayden's monologue poems, or the banter of people trapped in the strip developed suburbs surrounding Syracuse, wherever Hayden goes he takes his good ears with him.

Third, throughout all of Hayden's work lives an existential and life-giving *defiance,* a resistance, that is healing. But perhaps Hayden's greatest act of defiance is the simple and dogged avowal to keep singing no matter what.

Fourth, Hayden's voice is as distinctive and individual as any writer alive. Who else ever writes remotely like him? This individuality of tone whether it be regarding Ben Webster and his saxophone or Hayden Carruth and his poetry cannot be illustrated or explained. Yet through it all we know it is there, and just as somebody "with ears" can tell you in the second bar of the tune whether or not the player is Ben Webster, so also we can tell Hayden's tone instantly.

Fifth, rhythmically. In a time when too many white poets are still trapped—after all these years when they could have learned something from the Black writers and musicians all around them!—still trapped in their tight-ass, up and down cadences in the world's most boring 4/4, Hayden's work is as complex, various, and interesting as the best African American music.

Sixth, since the very beginning Hayden, like any good jazz or blues singer, has been incapable of separating art and politics. And the political is always and forever in the context of the personal. And furthermore, in the face of all this engagement and protesting, Hayden maintains his usual refusal to engage in false hope or pie-eyed dreaming. At the end of "On Being Asked to Write a Poem Against the War in Vietnam" and after making a list of all the wars he's protested he says:

> and not one
> breath was restored
> to one.

In a time in which not only do Councils on the Arts and Senators censor artists, but artists shamelessly censor themselves by declaring in one way or another that art and politics don't mix, it is informative and necessary to attend to the political commitment in

Hayden's work. And it is important and necessary to remember, or begin to notice, that everywhere else in the world art and politics are inextricably linked.

Seventh, in all of Hayden's work there is an unsurpassed and unabashed freedom to be openly and expressively, intensely emotional. Here is something Mercer Ellington said about his father that I think applies to Hayden's poetry. "Ellington sought a sensuality in the way his music was expressed; there was an *emotion* attached to the sound. . . . He was always very conscious of the need to make the listener *feel* experiences with sound." In short, as with our friend Ben Webster, nobody more than Hayden has produced a richer human sound, redolent of all its many moods and timbres.

And finally, eighth, it should be clear in Hayden's work that his poems come to him, he hears them and then writes them down, and clear also that what he hears comes into his ear and goes straight to his heart. In other words he does not make the mistake of using his head so much that his ears fall off.

IV.

Finally, in a piece about Hayden's and my years together listening to music, it seems only right for Hayden to have the last word.

This is from the last of the "Paragraphs": it is February 12th, 1944, New York City, the W.O.R. Recording Studios, a session to record *Bottom Blues* and "five men knowing it well blacks & jews" swing into the tune. And where is Hayden?

> Ah,
>   holy spirit, ninefold
> I druther've bin a-settin there, supernumerary
> cockroach i' th' corner, a-listenin, a-listenin, , , , , , ,
>   than be the Prazedint of the Wurrurld.

SASCHA FEINSTEIN

Those Upward Leaps
An Interview with Hayden Carruth

When I first contacted Hayden Carruth to request an interview, he declined. "I've done so many interviews over the years," he said, "that, frankly, I just don't see the point. I've said pretty much every-thing I want to say."

Without much thinking, I played what seemed to be my only card:

"I appreciate what you're saying. But let me ask you this: Has anyone ever talked to you about Vic Dickenson?"

Carruth paused. "No. Not that I can recall."

"I had hoped to focus the interview on Dickenson and his influ-ence on your work."

He paused again. "Yes," he said. And then, with still more enthu-siasm, "Yes—let's do it."

What inspired my suggested focus on Vic Dickenson? Initially, it was Carruth's tribute, "What a Wonder Among the Instruments Is the Walloping Tramboone!" which had surprised me, since I knew Carruth's horn was the clarinet. The poem made me pay more at-tention to his other trombone-related pieces, particularly those in-spired by Dickenson.

We agreed to meet at his home in Munnsville, New York. (Ac-cording to a census reading the year of my visit, the village of Munnsville has a square footage of less than one mile and a popula-tion of 437 people—roughly 400 more than I would have guessed.) In his home, built-in bookshelves lined the walls and wrapped around corners. Carruth sat in the center near a wood stove. With sweeping white hair and an expansive beard, he looked like one of Tolkien's wisest characters.

His wife, Joe-Anne, had made a fabulous carrot cake and a pot of coffee, and we sat across from each other in their small kitchen. At first, Carruth seemed a bit guarded—the way, I suspect, he feels around any stranger—but as the afternoon progressed, he seemed to enjoy the conversation more and more. Before I left, I asked him to inscribe some of his books, and in my copy of *Sitting In,* he wrote: "This was a damn fine session."

Feinstein: I want to talk about the trombonist Vic Dickenson and his influence on your work, but perhaps we can lay some groundwork. Who introduced you to jazz—or did you do that on your own?

Carruth: Almost on my own. The first jazz record I heard was in 1933, I think—somewhere around then. At that time I lived in a very small agricultural town in New England and never heard any jazz. But there was a rich kid in town (the only rich kid in town) and he went to a private school and came back with a couple of early records by the Goodman band. I used to think that the first jazz record I heard was *Stompin' at the Savoy,* but Goodman didn't record that until '36. Maybe I heard the Chick Webb version somewhere. It doesn't matter: from that point on I was hooked.

We moved, fortunately (for my interest in jazz anyway), to the suburbs in Westchester County, and I was able to hear more jazz on the radio. As I got a little older, I was able to go down to the City and visit the Commodore shop, and, eventually, go to Nick's and places like that on 52nd Street. And it went on from there.

Ever since I was a little kid I've played a tin whistle, what we used to call a ten cent Woolworth tin whistle. Six hole upright flageolet. [Laughs.] I still play it. And I studied the violin when I was a kid but I was not a good violinist. I was too tense and couldn't relax enough to play it. But I learned to read music, and after the [Second World] War—I was in my twenties—a friend of mine in Chicago loaned me an old Albert system clarinet, and I started messing around with that.

Feinstein: Albert system clarinet—that's a tough horn.

Carruth: Well, if you start on it it's not tough. The tough part is when you start on an Albert and switch to a Boehm—[laughs]—as I did. Most of the old-timers played the Albert system. Sidney Bechet—

Feinstein: George Lewis—

Carruth: All those guys. I loved the clarinet, and I became a pretty good clarinetist, although I was ill, and living in seclusion I hardly ever played with other people. Of course, I never even thought about performing professionally.

Feinstein: I find it interesting that you've written more about trombonists than clarinetists.

Carruth: I just love the trombone. If I had the right teeth and the right temperament and the right everything else, I'd have rather been a trombonist than anything else in the world. I love the sound, I love the range, I love all the textures and tones you can get on the damn thing. As I wrote in a poem at one time, I think it's a proper instrument. It's not a machine, like a tenor saxophone, or something like that. It's a basic tube which you slide on. I love that! [Laughs.] But I'd have been glad to play anything.

Feinstein: Unlike most poets who address jazz, you tend to focus on earlier players.

Carruth: That's because I'm seventy-seven years old, and that's what I heard when I was growing up. I suppose the early music you hear in your life is the one that sticks with you the most. I was listening to jazz very actively from, say, 1935 to 1980. The period since then I have not listened so much. I'm not sufficiently trained to appreciate the work that's being done by the workshop musicians and all those guys, and frankly it doesn't appeal to me so much. I'm an old time jazz guy. I like jazz that swings. I like jazz that's raucous and ripe.

Feinstein: That reminds me of those great lines in your poem "Freedom and Discipline" [from *Nothing for Tigers,* 1965]: "Freedom and discipline concur / only in ecstasy, all else / is shoveling out the muck. / Give me my old hot horn." [Carruth chuckles.] Could you talk a bit more about the difference in freedom between music and poetry? It sounds as though jazz has the edge.

Carruth: Jazz has the edge over poetry for me. It's more expressive, it's what I would have liked to do if I had been able to, but I don't remember if that's what I had in mind when I wrote those lines—which was a helluva long time ago. I think the combination of discipline and freedom in the arts is very well exemplified by a jazz musician who's playing a twelve bar blues. The form is absolutely fixed—as fixed as a triolet in poetry, or any other artificial form—and yet it provides him or her with almost limitless freedom to do what he or she wants to do in the way of harmonic and rhythmic invention. In my writing of poetry, I have always tried to emulate the improvisation that occurs within a fixed and sure and recognizable form. I like that. I think the analogy between music and poetry can be pushed only so far—but it can be pushed that far.

Feinstein: Is that the central influence that jazz has had on your poetry?

Carruth: Well, jazz is the sexiest music there ever was, and I hope some of my poetry is the sexiest poetry there ever was. [Both laugh.]

Feinstein: One of my favorite books of yours remains *Brothers, I Loved You All,* which concludes with the long poem "Paragraphs"— twenty-eight sections, each with fifteen lines—

Carruth: I invented that form, called it a "paragraph" (for no very good reason). Yes, fifteen lines, with a set rhyme scheme and a set metrical scheme. I use it loosely in different places. It occurs first in a poem called "Asylum," then in "Contra Mortem," then in those paragraphs, and then in *The Sleeping Beauty,* and I've written a few since then.

Feinstein: It seems in keeping with what you were saying about blues musicians—improvisation within a set structure.

Carruth: Oh yeah. I think so.

Feinstein: The last three sections in "Paragraphs" address jazz most directly. Do you remember writing them, or just the lines, "I druther've bin a-settin there, supernumerary / cockroach i' th' corner, a-listenin, a-listenin,,,,,,, / than be the Prazedint of the Wurrurld"?

Carruth: [Laughs.] I love that—if I say so myself. I can *vaguely* remember writing them. It was a long time ago. The record I was writing about [*Albert Ammons and the Rhythm Kings,* Commodore 1516] is one that I still play from time to time. I think it's a great record, with Dickenson on there doing his thing. I don't know what exactly I had in mind with those final lines, except that I was imagining a voice—I think a woman's voice, maybe Billie Holiday's voice—saying those lines.

Feinstein: It seems to me a jam session is the perfect close when you've taken on as much as you have in "Paragraphs." It brings it all together.

Carruth: The sequence of poems in those paragraphs is pretty rough and ready. I did put those three paragraphs at the end because that's where I wanted them to be. Originally the sequence was longer—quite a bit longer. There were about eighty of them. But various people didn't like them, and I started cutting them out, which may have been a mistake. It's the kind of thing I've done in my life, a number of times. So it got reduced to what's there. I think they do draw things together. The themes in the paragraphs are about suffering and war and deprivation and the defoliation of the world.

I made a mistake in those last three paragraphs, which I've always regretted but never have found a way to change.

Feinstein: Change it now.

Carruth: Can't. [Laughs.] It's built in. There's someplace in there where I say that this is a music of "blacks & jews," but there isn't any Jew on that record. I thought that bass player [Israel Crosby] was a Jew, but he's not. He's a black man. [Laughs.]

Feinstein: Let me ask you about a different ending. Your poem "Mort aux Belges!" originally concluded with references to Bechet and Dickenson and Clayton. This is a poem about crime and punishment, or perhaps criminal punishments. What made you close with jazz?

Carruth: I've always loved the recording that was made in Belgium [Sidney Bechet, *Recorded in Concert at the Brussels Fair, 1958*, Columbia 1410]. Do you know this record?

Feinstein: No, I don't think so.

Carruth: I'll play it for you.

[Carruth finds the LP and tracks it to "Society Blues." After several other solos, Dickenson enters, and soon he infuses his solo with loud, prolonged growls so fart-like in their translation that we both laugh throughout the rest of the tune.]

Feinstein: Man, that was great.

Carruth: It was. And you have to imagine the scene. There are these wonderful exponents of a vital culture on the stage in Brussels, facing a huge audience of affluent Belgians and tourists, and you can bet there wasn't a black person in the whole damn crowd. Then Dickenson did what he did—right at them. In fact, that's what the phrase "in your face" means, isn't it? Moreover, he got paid to do it, which I'm sure delighted him. But the real point is that he did it musically, within the context of the music. Dickenson was a joker and a wry philosopher, but he was never a mugger; he never played Uncle Tom for the white audience the way Armstrong did. Dickenson and the others—Bechet, Clayton, et cetera—were always aware of their dignity as artists and human beings. That's why Armstrong got rich and they were always poor. Give Armstrong all the credit he deserves—he was a fine musician, a great leader, an important influence—but he played the fool, too. He did it over and over, like Stepanfetchit. Dickenson never, never did that.

Feinstein: Do you think Dickenson, then, was a greater figure than Armstrong?

Carruth: No. Anyway, who knows? Let's leave the final judgments to St. Peter. But I do think that Dickenson and musicians like him did more than Armstrong to sustain the artistic integrity of jazz in the long run. They are the ones who made jazz the most important cultural achievement of the twentieth century—which is what some of us predicted would happen fifty or sixty years ago.

Feinstein: Dickenson's having so much fun on that date. What commentary! Perhaps that's why you closed the poem ["Mort aux Belges!"] with that concert—as commentary. But when you reprinted the poem in *Scrambled Eggs & Whiskey,* why did you cut that final stanza?

Carruth: [Looks down, then up again.] That's news to me. [Feinstein laughs.] I don't think I took it out.

Feinstein: It's not there.

Carruth: Huh. I'll have to take it up with those guys out there. [Laughs.] Somebody dropped it, I guess—on proof it just got lost—and I never paid any attention to it. You know, I don't read my own books much. But I have no recollection of deleting those lines, and I don't think I would have.

Feinstein: In your poem "In That Session," you say it would be worth dying just to hear that group play. Did you ever hear Vic Dickenson live?

Carruth: I never heard him live. That's true, in my case, of a great many musicians. As I've said, I have been ill and secluded much of my life, and I feel very uncomfortable in public places. So my listening is mostly on records. You know, there are aspects of technology that all of us deplore, but recording technology has been a lifesaver for me, and for music in general. There are some unfortunate aspects to it: I do think that jazz—taken as a whole span from 1910 to the present—has evolved too fast, and I think in part that's because of recordings. Musicians can listen to what they've done, and listen to what other people have done, too easily. And then the urge for novelty overtakes them.

Feinstein: I never thought of it that way.

Carruth: If you listen to the history of European music from, say, Monteverdi to early Beethoven, it's a nice, slow progression over 150 or 200 years. If that had happened in jazz, I think there would have been more small developments and more filling out of the different modes and styles and movements than there has been.

Feinstein: Let me ask you about a more recent poem, "What a Wonder Among the Instruments Is the Walloping Tramboone!" [Carruth laughs.] Did you make those lines so long so that they would wrap around like trombone slides?

Carruth: I don't know. My practice in writing poems has always been to say things in my mind, to establish a rhythm and a kind of tone or texture. Certainly I was writing about trombones, and maybe I was trying to do something [with the form]—but I don't think [it was done] consciously.

Feinstein: Among the many trombonists in this poem, Dickenson stands out as the most celebrated figure. Here's one line that refers to him: "May these words point to you and your recorded masterwork forever." Is that one function of jazz poetry—to bring more attention to great jazz musicians?

Carruth: It is *a* function, why not? Any kind of writing is a drawing of attention to the topic, whatever that may be. If the topic is jazz, and you can attract some readers to enjoy and appreciate jazz, well, I think that would be great. There is that built-in propagandistic element in any art, and if it becomes too prominent or conspicuous then the art is spoiled. But to deny that it exists would be foolish.

Feinstein: I felt that there was an impulse in this poem to say to the world, "You need to check out Vic Dickenson."

Carruth: I did have that motive. I wanted to draw attention to Dickenson, to jazz—I've tried to do that in all of my jazz poems— though I don't know how successful it was. That poem was published in a very small publication. I doubt if many people read it.

Feinstein: But it also appeared in your *Collected* [*Shorter Poems*], which has been appropriately celebrated and honored.

Carruth: Yeah. It's in that book. Dickenson had just died when I wrote that poem, and partly I just wanted to write an elegy.

Feinstein: Your praise for him seems limitless. Here's another line from that poem: "Never was such range of feeling so integrated in one man or instrument."

Carruth: Well, that's a very sweeping statement, and who knows if it can be supported.

Feinstein: No, but there's real passion. Why does Dickenson do it for you?

Carruth: In the first place, he's a marvelous musician. I don't know anything about his life. I don't know anything about his training. I doubt if he was classically trained on the trombone, but maybe he was. In any case, he taught himself how to exploit the instrument fully, and with great technical virtuosity. He could play very difficult passages, and play them perfectly. But at the same time, he was a man of enormous exuberance and vitality and had the kind of sweetness of emotional fabric that gets into the music, and he was intense about it. And the rest of those guys of his generation were, if they were any good. That's one of the reasons why I like that music—it's fully expressive. It isn't showing off. It isn't simply virtuosity. These guys were playing because they had feelings and wanted to say something.

Music is an integrative force in the human sensibility—much more than poetry. Poetry's always distracted by ideas and abstractions, but music is as concrete as you can get. If you have feelings, it's going to come out in the music as an integrated piece of work. It's one of the things about music that's so wonderful.

Feinstein: In your recent collection of autobiographical essays, *Reluctantly,* I was surprised that Miff Mole was discussed more than Dickenson. In fact, I don't think Dickenson is even mentioned.

Carruth: I don't think he is. That's a book I won't even read . . . [Chuckles.] It is a book about personal reminiscence, and so I write about people I knew, and I knew Miff Mole, a little bit, when I was in Chicago, so I stuck him in there.

One of the things about jazz that makes me so sorrowful is the ending of most musicians' lives. So many of them who did brilliant work ended up in poverty, alone, and suffering in one way or another. And certainly Mole did. I don't think he was a great musician. I think he was a good, capable musician of his time. He was influential, certainly, in white jazz of the '20s and '30s. But when I knew him, he was down and out: old, wandering around the South Side of Chicago like a lost soul.

Feinstein: That's very sad.

Carruth: Yeah.

Feinstein: I agree, too, with what you say about his musicianship. To be fair, Dickenson was a vastly superior player, and he could play in all sorts of settings. He was even on that Langston Hughes record, *Weary Blues.*

Carruth: I've heard that, but I've never owned it, never listened to it properly.

Feinstein: Dickenson primarily plays ensemble work—

Carruth: I think he was a very much admired musician, and he was often used as a sideman. Last night I was listening to that record that Odetta made [*Odetta Sings the Blues*], where she sings with a little band that Panama Francis put together, and Dickenson was on that. He really is a wonderful complement to her. He was a good accompanist as well as a good soloist.

Feinstein: Oh absolutely. The Hughes gig, of course, is a mixed bag of stuff. What's your opinion of jazz and poetry collaborations?

Carruth: Most of them are not successful, and I've always resisted doing it myself. People have wanted me to do it, but I don't know how to do it. The best one I ever heard was Michael Harper playing with Julius Hemphill and the guy on cello was—

Feinstein: Abdul Wadud—

Carruth: Yeah. I heard them down in Wilkes-Barre [PA], a number of years ago, and they had worked out a program ahead of time, which was pretty well rehearsed and pretty well integrated. Of course, Michael is the kind of a guy who could do that, who could fit in well. And Baraka has done a couple of good things, too. But the things that [Kenneth] Rexroth did and people like that I thought were pretty awful. [Laughs.] You know, somebody stands up and reads a poem, and then they play some music—and there's no connection, no thread running through the program.

Feinstein: Your book *Sitting In* [*Selected Writings on Jazz, Blues, and Related Topics*] remains a favorite of mine, and there aren't many like it—that offer both poetry and prose. What inspired that kind of project?

Carruth: It was a miscellaneous book. The essays were written over a period of time. I was living in Pennsylvania at the time, teaching at Bucknell in Lewisburg, and had a lot of time on my hands. I didn't know very many people, but one of the persons I did know down there was Bill Duckworth, a classical composer—quite a good one. (I've written some lyrics in collaboration with him.) He knows jazz, appreciates it a lot, and we used to listen together. So I was thinking about jazz, and a lot of the essays in there were written quickly, spontaneously, but on ideas and feelings and moods and themes that I had been brooding about for years. So it was easy to write about them. But I don't know what I had in mind—I had no audience, and I had no reputation as a jazz writer. I published almost always in literary magazines where I felt, sometimes, they seemed out of place. Some of the essays appeared in *APR* [*American Poetry Review*] and places like that. But the book as a whole was not thought of as a book until later on.

Feinstein: In a few essays, you hit some poets pretty hard, such as William Carlos Williams, for not being able to hear jazz, to understand jazz. Which poets do you admire for their appreciation of the music?

Carruth: None of the older ones. None of them. I don't think there was anyone in Williams' generation, or even the generation following him, that knew how to listen to jazz or had any appreciation of it at all, as far as I know. I never ran into one. It wasn't only Williams who was deaf to jazz; all of them were. Even the guys like [Carl] Van Vechten, who made an effort to understand African American culture in the '20s and '30s, didn't understand the music. I don't know why.

It was like my mother, who hated jazz. She was very musical, she had perfect pitch, she liked opera, she loved to listen to symphonic music. But the idea that jazz came out of the whorehouse and that's where it belonged was so deeply ingrained in her that she literally could not hear what was happening in musical terms. And that was true all through the generation of World War II. Delmore Schwartz couldn't understand jazz. Randall Jarrell couldn't understand jazz. None of those guys could. I think—if I may say so immodestly—I'm just about the oldest poet in the country who does understand jazz. Most of the poets who have written intelligently about jazz are younger than I am—people like yourself, or Yusef [Komunyakaa], or my friend Paul Zimmer. Stephen Dobyns knows jazz and has written about it a little bit. But the older poets, no.

Feinstein: What do you think, in general, about contemporary poetry? Do you think it's too safe?

Carruth: I think it's awful. It's conformist. It's workshoppish. It's governed pretty largely by the politics of literature. The poets themselves have been mistrained and misguided. It's dead. I mean the known, official poets. Some young poets writing in obscurity are doing fine original work.

Feinstein: Do you think the dead ones need to listen to Dickenson?

Carruth: That would be *great.* [Laughs.]

BRIAN HENRY

Freedom and Discipline
Hayden Carruth's Blues

Although many American poets have demonstrated a passion for
jazz, writing about favorite musicians or clubs, sets or songs, most
contemporary poets committed to the music have failed to realize
its potential or to incorporate its possibilities—namely the technique of improvisation within fixed forms. Hayden Carruth has
demonstrated an extraordinary devotion to jazz in relation to poetry, employing its improvisational strategies to express tenderness,
weariness, and political commitment. His attachment to jazz arises
also as an attachment to the blues, which is an especially appropriate
rubric under which to consider Carruth's poetry, concerned as it
has been for half a century with sexual love, politics, suffering, and
injustice. Yet the technical, thematic, and emotional variety in Carruth's poetry has contributed to critics' difficulty in coming to
terms with his work; his poetry has been too flexible to rest comfortably within ideologies or critical frameworks. However, reading
Carruth's poetry through jazz and the blues provides a useful point
from which to assess his career and contribution to American poetry precisely because of the variety of strategies the music makes
available in his work.

While it is generally accepted that the blues arose from the suffering of African-Americans in the South at the end of the nineteenth century, the blues has not been limited to African-Americans.
White and European musicians, artists, and writers have found inspiration in jazz and the blues, and have sought to produce art from
that inspiration in innumerable ways—sometimes honorably, sometimes shamefully. Carruth does not attempt to neutralize—to
bleach—the history of jazz and the blues, as many white writers
have done (however inadvertently). Rather, he seeks to honor and
celebrate "the black part of our consciousness—our thought, vision,
speech, feeling, sensual responsiveness, our whole being" (preface to
Sitting In). His initial attraction to jazz emerged not from any po-

litical stance, but from something deeply personal, even physical: "in intonation, texture, rhythm, and all its sensuous qualities, jazz moved me viscerally from the beginning. The slurred notes and off-the-beat phrasings made me respond autonomically inside as if I were an animal in a mating dance" ("Fragments of Autobiography: Second Series," *Reluctantly* 106).

As Carruth grew older, his relationship to jazz became more intellectual; though still personal, his response to the music was intertwined with his own sensibility as a poet. The elements of jazz that appear in his poetry do so most consistently at the level of technique. Carruth has defined jazz as "spontaneous improvisation within a fixed and simple form" ("Influences: The Formal Idea of Jazz," *SI* 27), and from early in his career, he has embraced improvisation as a poetic mode. Improvisation does not connote carelessness, aimlessness, or formlessness; improvisation, according to Carruth, "is the privilege of the master, the bane of the apprentice. It is the exercise of sensibility in acquired knowledge" ("The Main Thing About Improvisation," *SI* 101). Elsewhere, he has noted that poetry is "locked / in discipline, sworn to / freedom" ("Freedom and Discipline," *Collected Shorter Poems* 61). Some of his own poetry demonstrates the formal techniques of jazz, distinguishing him from other poets who have written *about* jazz rather than *within* it.

Carruth has written that "jazz is original, spontaneous, authentic, and immediate" ("The Spun-Off Independent Dead-End Ten-Star Blast," *SI* 188), whereas poetry tends to have a more studied quality. Dependent upon literary tradition (even if only to react against it) and usually revised toward some ideal form, poetry written for the page is generally more static than performative arts like music. The difficulty for the poet is writing spontaneous and immediate poems that still can be considered poetry that achieves the "fusion of emotion and form" ("Ben Webster," *SI* 176). Form, for Carruth, is hardly a cold medium. On the contrary, in his essay "Ben Webster," he cites "the self-evident verity that artistic function is equivalent to feeling. And the more passionate the feeling, the more complex and unified the form" (*SI* 176). Carruth's oeuvre is characterized by formal complexity—formal restlessness combined with formal mastery—and one could apply his comments about the tenor player Ben Webster to his own poetry: "He played with an enormous dynamic and textural range, from soft purring passages to growls to shrieks; his phrasing was extremely varied, from sequences of staccato blips and bleats to long fluid sentences; his articulation could be lightning fast . . . or so intensely drawn out that it becomes painful; his rhythmic usage was very flexible . . ." ("Ben Webster," *SI* 175). Even a casual look at Carruth's lifework—most of which can be found in *Collected Shorter Poems, Collected Longer Poems, Scrambled Eggs & Whiskey,* and, most recently, *Doctor Jazz*—reveals a poet of "enormous" range and variety. His subject matter stems from his anarchist, ecological, existentialist, realist, and familial concerns as well as from a difficult life. Married three times, Carruth has been an alcoholic, a lifelong sufferer of "extreme insomnia" (*Reluctantly* 144) and "chronic psychiatric disorders" (*Reluctantly* 35), a recluse, a farmer, "a country mechanic, plumber, electrician, and carpenter" (*Reluctantly* 34) as well as a freelance "hack" writer who would turn to his own poetry only after the chores and freelance work were finished.

In the last line of "On the Truistical and Fashionable Eyes of Albert Camus," Carruth paraphrases Walter Pater's statement, but with a twist: "All art aspires to the condition of music. Repeat, aspires" (*TMA* 45). Elsewhere, Carruth acknowledges T. S. Eliot's comment about the difficulty of writing poetry, which originates in the need to communicate a grammatical statement and visual beauty while pursuing the beauty of sound—i.e., music. For Carruth, too many considerations of poetry neglect the music of the language: "In the tedious *ars poetica* which I see being constructed in our literary reviews today, the music of poetry is the last consideration, if indeed it has not been banished altogether" ("Academicism," *SI* 17). When considerations of music have been excised from poetry, he implies, the remains are the brittle shells of grievances and anecdotes that characterize much of American poetry today. Yet Carruth's emphasis on the aspiration in Pater's statement—he chooses to repeat "aspires" in his paraphrase—signals a skepticism about the possibility of poetry attaining "the condition of music." For him, every poem must fail, because "every work struggles willynilly toward the condition of the masterpiece" ("The Defeated Generation," *SI* 91). And when a poet willingly courts improvisation, the masterpiece, even if attained, can never be regained.

This acknowledgment of failure, however, does not have to be viewed negatively. In "Got Those Forever Inadequate Blues," Carruth refers to the blues as "a seeking and a failure" (*SI* 56), and in "The Defeated Generation," he insists on the "affirmative" nature of making art: "Many, many times the words of the blues have made the point that even the slowest, draggiest, saddest, most despairing blues gives a kind of joy to the performer" (*SI* 85). Thus, the artistic—musical, poetic—process contains its own justification. This might explain, at least in part, the extraordinary range of Carruth's poetry. Despite its importance to his work, jazz does not dominate his oeuvre to the exclusion of other concerns; he does not emerge as a "jazz poet." To consider him solely as such would distort and diminish the formal, tonal, and thematic diversity and complexity of his poetry, which represents a lifetime of "a seeking and a failure."

The formal variety of Carruth's poems—including, most notably, the sonnet and sonnet sequence, his "asphalt georgics," haiku, and an invented sonnet-like form called the "paragraph"—represents a substantial achievement in itself. As jazz musicians consistently try to outplay or outperform themselves, as well as those playing with them, pushing themselves to and beyond the creative limit, Carruth frequently presents himself with significant formal challenges in his poems in traditional and invented forms as well as in his poems in free verse. His "asphalt georgics" update the traditionally didactic form by using the colloquial manner reminiscent of Robert Frost's New England monologues, going further in their colloquialism than Frost did while adhering to ABAB quatrains with lines alternating between eight and six syllables. The thirteen-part "Asylum" addresses the poet's time in a mental institution through a strict invented form—based on the sonnet—called the "paragraph." "Saturday at the Border" is an improvised villanelle: "Here I am writing my first villanelle / At seventy-one, and feeling old and tired— / 'Hey, pops, why dontcha just give us the old death-knell?'" (*Scrambled Eggs & Whiskey* 54); because the poem is his first villanelle, and because he is "working from memory and not remembering well / How many stanzas and in what order," he gives the poem two extra tercets before releasing the poem with a final quatrain.

However, some of Carruth's most virtuosic poems explicitly work with jazz and blues techniques while testing the poet's own formal skills. At times, the subject of these poems is jazz itself, as in "An Expatiation on the Combining of Weathers at Thirty-Seventh and Indiana Where the Southern More or Less Crosses the Dog," a thirty-two-line poem that consists of one sentence:

Oh, Ammons rolled the octaves slow
And the piano softened like butter in his hands,

And underward Catlett caught the beat
One sixteenth before the measure with a snip-snap touch on the
    snare
And a feathery brush on the cymbal, and Shapiro
Bowed the bass, half-glissing down past E-flat to A, to D,
And after a while
Berigan tested a limping figure low
In the coronet's baritone and raised it a third and then another
Until he was poised
On the always falling fulcrum of the blues,
And Bechet came in just as the phrase expired
And doubled it and inverted it
In a growl descending, the voice of the reed
Almost protesting, then to be made explicit
On the trombone as O'Brien took it
And raised it again, while Berigan stroked a high tone
Until it quavered and cried,
And Carruth came achingly on, the clarinet's most pure
High C-sharp, and he held it
Over the turn of the twelfth measure
And into the next verse with Bechet a fifth below rumbling
Upward on the back beat powerfully,
And O'Brien downward,
And Catlett press-rolling the slow beat now,
The old, old pattern of call and response unending,
And they felt the stir of the animal's soul in the cave,
And heard the animal's song, indefinable utterance,
And saw
A hot flowing of the eternal, many-colored, essential plasm
As they leaned outward together, away from place, from time,
In one only person, which was the blues.

                                     (*TMA* 7–8)

Elsewhere, music takes a place in the background of the poem. Although Carruth's poems that name specific musicians—several of which, like "An Expatiation," are virtual jam sessions—are his most explicitly jazz-related poems, the poems that evince some of the formal qualities of jazz and some of the subject matter of the blues seem especially relevant to the spirit of the music.

"Michigan Water: A Few Riffs Before Dawn" demonstrates a relatively subtle reliance on jazz and the blues. The poem is highly structured—a sequence with seven sections, each of which consists of seven tercets. Each line works from a base of four beats (there are occasional trimeter and pentameter lines), so each stanza corresponds to twelve beats, as in the blues; and in most stanzas, two of the lines rhyme, with the placement of the caesura shifting from line to line. In the first six sections of "Michigan Water," each stanza is end-stopped, and therefore disciplined:

> Listen, the softly thinking drum
> measures the silence in which the bass
> murmurs to make the meaning come.
>
> Tranquilly my fingers contemplate
> the bone they are, the bone they meet—
> these keys breathing among shadows.
>
> Silence holds the sweetness in the tune.
> But now who cares? Will our affection,
> the great slow sound, tell anything?
>
> (*Collected Longer Poems* 83)

The explicit focus on music—the drum, the bass, the keys, the tune—in part one expands to incorporate politics in part two, aligning the poem gradually with the blues:

> Define. So the drum commands,
> so the bass entreats. Define.
> Ten black men setting out to dine.
>
> Food of heaven had they none,
> food of hell was so damned sweet
> they sought and sought, and they had none.
>
> The rope, the knife, the stone, the gun,
> the train, the door, the cave, the tree,
> the sign, the shutter, the snow, the dead.
>
> . . . .
>
> At one rotten moment of the light
> the room stops, neither day nor night,
> the music falters, neither black nor white.
>
> (*CLP* 83–84)

Here the language of the poem becomes more overtly musical— mainly through repetition ("Define. . . . Define," "food of . . . food of," "they sought and sought," "had they none . . . they had none," "neither . . . nor . . . neither . . . nor") and strict rhyme ("Define"/"dine," "entreats"/"sweet," "none"/"gun," "light"/"night"/"white").

As the sequence progresses, the improvisational atmosphere of the poem becomes more prominent; and in the sixth section, anaphora and carefully employed poetic devices—especially assonance and alliteration—join so that the poem begins to obfuscate the clarity that marks its beginning sections:

In the cage no amnesty
waits in the government of the days,
no behoof, no behest.

In the cage no listener hears
these superb particular concussions
of blood, neither a brother nor a sister.

In the cage the moon is irrelevant,
the sun unintelligible,
and the constellations unrecognizable.

In the cage laughter is courage
and courage is laughter and laughter
is courage is laughter is—*the cage!*

(*CLP* 87)

How strange the last stanza seems, how unexpected in its series of equations. Each of these stanzas arises as a cluster of sounds—linguistic notes—and each stanza is connected to the others by the repetition of "In the cage." The conventional poetic devices establish various threads through each stanza—the long "a" of "cage"/"waits"/"days"; the various "er" sounds of "listener"/"superb"/"particular," "neither"/ "brother"/"sister"; the "l" sounds in "irrelevant"/"unintelligible"/"constellations"/ "unrecognizable"; and others. In the seventh and final section of "Michigan Water," Carruth drops the end-stopped stanzas while keeping to seven tercets and the twelve-beat stanza:

Gray dawn seeping through stone—
see, the room blanches. Let the beat
intensify. Between bone and bone

the little blood aches with rain
and the tones deepen. Music!
Given all to Saint Harmony, all,

the pain, the awareness of the pain.
That is all. Music is heard
in one heart, harmony's great chord

in one conscience only . . .

                    . . . The drum
murmurs against the graylight dawn,

the bass, in unison now, is calm,
the piano descends firmly. Chicago,
city of our music, the long "no,"

listen; the night was a good song;
and we are a true city, rising
in the unjust hour, honorable and strong.

(*CLP* 87–88)

This last section unites many of the formal elements of the earlier sections—repetition, rhyme, enjambment, assonance, alliteration—but no particular strategy dominates the poem's ending.

"Song About Earl Hines" combines the subject matter of "An Expatiation" with the multi-layered technical prowess of "Michigan Water":

"Turn out all the lights
    and call the law
right now." And it's true, it's veridical, he had that raw
    necessary animal spirit and enjoyed a hell of a
good time all those nights

of his life, yet you can't hear and not know
    how he studied to make his left hand do
those rhythmic variations, how he began
    new musics again and again. "Oh Father Hines, you
dirty old man."

(*SI* 32)

The colloquial tone of "Song About Earl Hines" at first masks the poem's craft. The poem has an improvised rhyme scheme—ABBBA

CCDCD, with "a" and "know" as off-rhymes in an otherwise strictly rhyming poem—and impeccable pacing. The cadences of the poem, which seems intended to be read aloud, permit such a construction as "it's true, it's veridical," as if "veridical"—a formal and increasingly rare word for "truthful"—were a part of everyone's daily vocabulary like "a hell of a good time" and "dirty old man" are. The subject of the poem—the coexistence of artistic discipline and personal freedom—seems especially fitting for Carruth. This explicit focus on music and its relationship to poetry and personal and artistic freedom appears throughout Carruth's work.

Couched in the terms of an oral poetry lesson, "How To" is something of a primer on poetry *and* jazz:

> The main
>   element of technique
> is verve, movement, energy, what
>   musicians also seek
>
> under the rubric, *attack*. You
>   have to *hit* and keep on
> *hitting,* sharp, hard, make it crackle,
>   make it brilliant; maun-
>
> dering ain't allowed. Hit each note
>   unmitigatedly
> and just a hair off the beat.
>
> (*CSP* 273)

Openly didactic, "How To" is one of Carruth's georgics from *Asphalt Georgics,* which rhyme and are composed in syllabics so exact that some words are hyphenated across line breaks to achieve the syllabic count. Carruth addresses his reader/audience as "Chillens" and refers to such musicians as Little Jazz, Hawk, Sweets, Pee-Wee, and Mr. Webster. Yet at the same time, he is providing valuable information, teaching his readers how to play/write jazz while playing/writing jazz (and writing about jazz) himself:

> Max-
>
> imum energy is sometimes
>   obtained by restraining
> the inner violence of force,
>   though always with the swing-

ing propulsion that comes from clar-
    ity of phrasing a-
gainst the beat. What you've been told is
    too easy. Listen. *The*

ear is more important than the
    eye. Dass de trooth! So next
week let's have 30 lines, allit-
    erating *m* and *k*.

(*CSP* 273–274)

The violent enjambments—across lines and across stanzas—seem to work against "clarity of phrasing"; but they help the poet generate "maximum energy" and "swinging propulsion." The flippant ending, in which the poet doles out an assignment, does not undercut the wisdom and mastery demonstrated in the poem.

More flexible and lyrical than the georgic, Carruth's "paragraph" demonstrates sonnet-like structure and development. Although an exacting form, the paragraph is also liberating and flexible with a poet as skilled as Carruth. The paragraph's initial innovation occurs in the displacement of the final couplet of the Shakespearean sonnet, placing it instead after the first sestet. (Although a couplet appears before the displaced couplet in the paragraph, the first couplet connects to the first quatrain of the poem and therefore is not disparate.) The full rhyme scheme of the paragraph—ABABAACCDEDEFEF—acknowledges both the Shakespearean and the Petrarchan sonnet while establishing a unique and complex structure. Carruth introduced the form in his thirteen-part sequence "The Asylum" (1957), an ambitious and moving, if occasionally awkward, account of the poet's experience in a mental institution. And he has returned to the paragraph throughout his career, most notably in "Contra Mortem" (1966), *The Sleeping Beauty* (1970–1980), and "Paragraphs" (1978), each of which demonstrates increasing formal improvisation. *The Sleeping Beauty* (a book-length sequence of 125 stylistically diverse yet thematically connected paragraphs) and the twenty-eight-part "Paragraphs" especially illuminate Carruth's ability to improvise within the form.

Of Carruth's many poems in paragraphs, the "Paragraphs" sequence demonstrates the most variation. With unevenly broken lines, unconventional or missing punctuation, lists, brief passages in foreign languages, and typographical/visual displacement, the twenty-eight paragraphs in the sequence represent a powerful advance over Carruth's earlier forays into the form. Despite being composed in the same "form," no paragraph here resembles another paragraph. And after the halfway point in the sequence (paragraph 14), Carruth allows paragraphs to run into each other (he comments on this move with the terse "And so with paragraphics"). Paragraphs 15 and 16, for example, are contained within the same quotation marks despite being distinct from each other on the page. The last three paragraphs in the sequence are especially jazz-like in matter and technique. Paragraph 26 opens onto a "cheerless" February day in 1944 in New York City, when an album is being recorded:

> The cast
> was Albert Ammons, Lips Page, Vic Dickenson,
> Don Byas, Israel
> Crosby, and Big Sid Catlett. (*And* it was Abe Linkhorn's
> birthday.) And Milt Gabler
> presided beyond the glass with a nod, a sign. Ammons
> counted off
> a-waaaan,,, *tu!*
> and went feeling
> his way on the keys gently,
> while Catlett summoned
> 27
>
> the exact beat from—
> say from the sounding depths, the universe . . .
> (*CSP* 196)

The structure of the poem, beyond its paragraph form, is intricately and carefully presented. The exaggerated space between the poet's description of Ammons's counting off and his version of it seems mimetic of the period of silence that precedes Ammons's countdown. The three commas and the additional space before the "*tu!*" also approximate Ammons's actual speech. Carruth enjambs and displaces not only lines but paragraphs, reproducing an even longer pause in his presentation of the session.

The session continues, its lineation enhancing the poem's own music as well as the music it describes:

> When Dickenson came on it was all established,
> no guessing, and he started with a blur

as usual, smears, brays—Christ
the dirtiest noise imaginable
                        belches, farts
                                curses
but it was music
                music now
                        with Ammons trilling in counterpoise.
Byas next, meditative, soft/
                        then Page
with that tone like the torn edge
of reality:
                and so the climax, long dying riffs—
groans, wild with pain—
and Crosby throbbing *and* Catlett riding stiff
yet it was music   music.

(CSP 197)

By this point in "Paragraphs," the rhymes ("established," "Christ,"
"curses," "counterpoise") are nearly undetectable. Aside from attempting to re-create this music in language, Carruth also tries to
convey a musician's feeling of elation during the creative moment,
which is enhanced by the collective nature of a recording or jam
session:

                        And it was done
        and they listened *and* heard themselves
           better than they were, for they had come

        28

high above themselves. Above everything, flux, ooze,
loss, need, shame, improbability/   the awfulness
of gut-wrong, sex-wrack,   horse & booze,
the whole goddamn mess.

(CSP 197)

Carruth's rendition of this session—"a moment ecstatic / in the
history / of creative mind *and* heart"—ends with his own sense of
elation, achieved not only through his imagined eavesdropping but
also through his own final improvisation:

I druther've bin a-settin there, supernumerary
cockroach i' th' corner, a-listenin, a-listenin,,,,,,,,
than be the Prazedint of the Wurrurld.

(*CSP* 198)

Approximating the slurring of jazz as well as its timing with pho-
netic spellings and the unconventional punctuation (the seven
commas create a particularly long pause), Carruth moves beyond
technical achievement to convey the ecstasy that is the creative moment, which is most ecstatic, or affirmative, when "freedom and
discipline concur."

Carruth's determination to express grief, rage, and other emotions
in his poetry remind us that he is much more than a poet of technical skill. When he combines these emotional expressions with formal improvisation and downplays his consciousness of the improvisation itself, his work most resembles the blues. Because he has
suffered acute anxiety and alcoholism, been confined in mental
institutions, attempted suicide, married several times, and lost a
daughter to cancer—mostly while living a life of poverty in rural
northern Vermont—Carruth has ample acquaintance with misfortune. He has earned the blues. Thus, when he writes "I cry out these
lines / without sound. I cry / them out. Listen." ("The Circumstances of Meditation This Morning Led Me to the Cigar of Jo-
hannes Brahms," *TMA* 43), we should listen.
    So closely linked to the blues as to be nearly synonymous with
it, sorrow is the emotion most often expressed in Carruth's blues
poems. And sorrow for Carruth is frequently the result of poverty:

Was I so poor
    in those damned days
that I went in the dark
    in torn shoes
and furtiveness
    to steal fat ears
of cattle corn
    from the good cows
and pound them
    like hard maize
on my worn Aztec
    stone? I was.

("Notes on Poverty," *SEW* 90)

Though accessible and straightforward, this poem is highly formal; every other line ends with the "z" sound and each line has two beats. Other poems are less self-focused, demonstrating Carruth's belief that "Writing is first of all a way of being in the world, a functioning nub of relatedness" ("Suicide," *Reluctantly* 66). From this belief comes Carruth's disdain for "poems formed in the habit of egotism" and his desire for poetry to seek communion and community.

The importance of community—"neighborliness" ("Marshall Washer," *CSP* 173)—often appears in his poems about politics and work (not always two separate subjects), as "Emergency Haying" shows. In the poem, the phrase "Marshall needs help" (*CSP* 89) becomes the only reason necessary to propel the poet into a day of manual labor that exhausts and hurts him. The labor also leads to a meditation on work itself, especially the dehumanizing effects of slave labor: "Hands / too bloodied cannot bear // even the touch of air, even / the touch of love" (*CSP* 90). The poem ends with a condemnation of "you sons of bitches who would drive men and women / to the fields where they can only die" (*CSP* 90). Despite this note of rage at the end of the poem, the poem still recognizes the importance of neighborliness. This community-mindedness links to his affinities with jazz and the blues, for jazz depends upon community for its vitality and the blues builds community around its expressions of sorrow and injustice. Carruth's poems are political even when they are personal. A Carruth poem does not have to be called "On Being Asked to Write a Poem Against the War in Vietnam" to express anti-war sentiment or "The President's Speech" to address political rhetoric. Politics for Carruth is an element of everyday life, not a subject to be cordoned off and dealt with separately. His question in "California"—"How can poetry be written by people who want no change?" (*SEW* 15)—seems sincere, in that his view of poetry inextricably links the art to politics, the artist's temperament to the political imagination (Carruth has written that all true poets are radicals or reactionaries).

More recently for Carruth, sorrow has been the result of growing old, made more poignant by his marriage to a woman much younger than him. Although he says "I am too old to write love songs now" ("Birthday Cake," *SEW* 12), *Scrambled Eggs & Whiskey* includes many love poems: "Yet one young woman lives with me / and is my love . . . // . . . She loves me for / myself, or for what little is left" ("The Best, the Most," *SEW* 65); "I am in love now, /

In it totally all the time" ("Song: Now That She Is Here," *SEW* 91);
"Now / I am almost entirely love" ("Testament," *SEW* 35). These
brief bursts of wonder are counter-weighted in *Scrambled Eggs &
Whiskey* and, especially, *Doctor Jazz* by poems expressing the physical trauma of growing old. "Martha," the long, wrenching elegy for
his daughter who died of cancer, occupies the physical and emotional center in *Doctor Jazz*, which is largely dominated by poems
about (or against) old age. With its relative dearth of jazz-oriented
poems and its emphasis on testimony to human suffering, *Doctor
Jazz* seems mistitled. *Doctor Blues* would be more appropriate, if less
catchy. "Improvising in standard meter on a well-known / Motif"
(*Doctor Jazz* 9), "Because I Am" is the closest that Carruth comes in
this volume to the jazz-like improvisations of his earlier work.

But if we return to the poem "Ecstasy" in *Scrambled Eggs & Whiskey*, Carruth manages to answer in poetry a question he posed and
answered in an essay in 1982. The question—"What happens, sub-
jectively and spiritually, when a musician improvises freely?"—
applies as well to the poet; and his answer—"He transcends the
objective world, including the objectively conditioned ego, and becomes a free, undetermined sensibility in communion with others"
("Influences: The Formal Idea of Jazz," *SI* 27)—moves beyond the
artistic self to encompass others. The poem, like many of Carruth's
poems over the past five decades, improvises its way through "seeking" and "failure" to the state identified by its title:

> For years it was in sex and I thought
> this was the most of it
> so brief
> a moment
> or two of transport out of oneself
> or
> in music which lasted longer and filled me
> with the exquisite wrenching agony
> of the blues
>
> (*SEW* 48)

That "exquisite wrenching agony," of course, is a form of joy, or
ecstasy, and its source for Carruth can be found not only in sex and
the blues, as the poem implies, but also in jazz and poetry. It is this
willingness to pursue ecstasy—*and* community *and* authenticity of
expression—and to seek and fail through improvisation that constitutes one of Carruth's most enduring achievements as a poet.

BARON WORMSER

Harmonic Hayden

My alliterative title points to Hayden Carruth's practice in his masterpiece long poem *The Sleeping Beauty* of focusing individual cantos on subjects whose name begins with the letter *H,* thus alluding, playfully yet thoughtfully, to the letter that begins his first name. This device, located as it is somewhere between fancy and commitment, is a good starting point to consider Hayden Carruth's stature as a writer of poems, for he has managed over the course of his lengthy, accomplished career to combine formal values with improvisational and moral values in ways that place him in very select company.

It is a truism that a poet whose work is valued has forged a recognizable style. The style identifies the poet: we know a Creeley poem or a Wilbur poem or a Plath poem without looking at the author's name. We say that this is how such a poet writes his or her poem. Hayden Carruth is certainly recognizable throughout his many books as a very distinct poet, but the variety of forms and modes in which he has worked stamp him as atypical in the sense that his range is so extraordinary. To read through his books is to find a poet equally adept at meter, syllabics, and free verse; a poet who has adapted, employed, and invented all manner of forms from haiku to terza rima, from "paragraph" to georgic; a poet who in terms of rhythm has never written a slack line. Two poets in whose company I would place Carruth are Auden and Tennyson because they are poets who exemplified a commitment to a dizzyingly full range of poetic expression. As far as American poetry is concerned, I don't think Hayden Carruth has a peer in this regard. This is not to downplay anyone else's achievement, only to point out the particularly ample genius of his accomplishment.

Although this essay emphasizes Carruth's formal achievements, the actualities of rhythm and sound and form, I want to stress at the outset that this achievement is integrally related to the man's outlooks on life and art. Carruth has written that "the artist must not only work but *live* [and that word is italicized by Carruth] in a state of devotion to things greater than him or herself." These "things" include how one lives one's life and how one respects the rudiments, traditions, and challenges of one's art. There is no way to make distinctions between the two and still create an art that aspires to the wholeness that we designate by the word *humane.* Carruth's art is deeply humane in its feeling for both humor and suffering; it is an art that has had a great deal to do with his commitment to necessity, to (in his words) "all the materials of life, not just a selected few." The breadth of the formal achievement is matched by the breadth of the commitment; they are reciprocal. They need one another.

It is important to note that Carruth uses the word *devotion,* a word not very common in the contemporary literary world. He doesn't say "subjugation," "abasement," or even the neutral "participation." The word connotes a species of spiritual allegiance, an acknowledgment that the ego cannot measure those greater things and should not want to measure those greater things, that the wheedling mind is not the arbiter of all things. This makes particular sense in regard to poetry, which is foremost a physical, sensual, and conservative art in the sense that it treasures the primal rhythms of life on earth. Poetry not only creates—it partakes. As Carruth has written, "In art the expressive is the sensual. In poetry the sensual is rhyme and meter, using these terms in the broadest sense. If the sensual is removed, only information or "airy nothing" remains, either of which may be conveyed in computer language without a loss. But the sensual may be apprehended only in the body's privacy."

Poetry is voluntary; though schools with good and not-so-good intentions sometimes push poetry, people cannot be bullied into it. That is one among many reasons why theory is particularly futile in regard to poetry since theory seeks to place the reductionist, explanatory cart before the unclassifiable horse. One comes to poetry with a sense of anticipation; one doesn't know how it will affect one, and that is why one wants it. It is simultaneously an intensification and a release. It is mystery practiced, and to be devoted to poetry is to practice it quite literally by reading, reciting, and memorizing it. Of his growing up Carruth notes that he was touched by "Mother Goose, the songs of Shakespeare . . . Byron, Stephen Foster . . . Longfellow, Whittier, Tennyson, and scores of others, perhaps hundreds of others." This openness, as it is a quality of devotion, an immersion in many traditions—including both high art and folk art, leads to the first poem I wish to consider, "Freedom and Discipline," from *Nothing for Tigers*, published in 1965:

Saint Harmony, many
years I have stript

naked in your service
under the lash. Yes,

I believe the first
I heard (living, there

aloud in the hall) was
Sergei Rachmaninoff

set at the keys like a
great dwarf, a barrel

on three spindles,
megalocephalus, hands

with fourteen fingers,
ugly as Merlin, with whom

I was in love, a boy and
an old man; a boy nodding

and an old man sorrowing
under the bushfire of the

people's heart, until he
coolly knocked out the

Prelude in C Sharp Minor. Second
was Coleman Hawkins

in about 1934 perhaps.
I, stript and bleeding,

leapt to the new touch,
up and over the diminished

in a full-voiced authority
of blue-gold blues. I

would do nothing, locked
in discipline, sworn to

freedom. The years shrieked
and smothered, like billboards

beside a road at night.
I learnt how Catlett

drove the beat without
harming it, how Young

sped between the notes,
how Monk reconstructed

a broken chord to make
my knuckles rattle, and much

from oblivion: Newton,
Fasola, Berigan, my

inconsolable Papa Yancey.
Why I went to verse-making

is unknowable, this
grubbing art. Trying,

Harmony, to fix your beat
in things that have none

and want none—absurdity!
Let that be the answer

to any hope of statecraft.
As Yeats said, *Fol de rol.*

Freedom and discipline concur
only in ecstasy, all else

is shoveling out the muck.
Give me my old hot horn.

Before one gets to the words and sounds in the poem it is crucial to first attend to the rhythmic dimension, the accentual harmony that the poem embodies. The poem is written in what has become one of the most dubious modern forms—the spatial couplet of two lines and a space, two lines and a space, and so on. This form all too often allows the poet to impose a notion of form on material that has no discernible formal inclination and that bestows, due to the frequent spatial pauses, a gravity that feels like portentous concrete. It is a form that can become very boring very quickly.

It can also sing in the hands of a master such as Hayden Carruth. Carruth's lines typically contain three accents, but that observation is only the beginning of what there is to say. In his own words, Carruth has "interfused thematic improvisation and metrical regularity, or, as [he] prefers to say, metrical predictability." Rhythm is based on devotion to beat, and beat is inspired because it is sensual, because it is the pulse and breath music of the body heard aloud. Beat is tonic in the senses that it is invigorating and that it represents the keynote of poetry. Beat is ongoing but changing and thus embodies the feeling of movement. At the same time, the journey—the linear movement through the poem—is how we experience every local texture. Thus, throughout the couplet structure Carruth consistently varies syntax, syllable counts, pauses, mono- and polysyllabic words, and punctuation while all the while honoring the unmitigated accentual nature of the English language. He is improvising in the sense that he is not writing patterned rhythm (strict iambs, for instance), but rather he is working within the strictures of rhythm, strictures that exist to be pushed and shoved and finessed so as to allow for optimum expressiveness and downright beauty. He is playing with rhythm in the true sense of the verb—fooling around in great artistic seriousness. Every lurch or glide from couplet to couplet is an act of rhythmic faith: the beat will go on. Yet the forward movement is existential in the sense that nothing is preordained. The poem is alive because the poet is determinedly blowing—to use a jazz verb. And this is occurring (to quote Carruth) "within the limits of a fixed and simple form, as fixed and simple as the chord changes of the traditional twelve-bar blues." To see those couplets in their formality and elasticity as musical bars does not seem a far-fetched analogy.

Read aloud (as it must be experienced), one can hear the propulsion of the beat, but a listener can also hear the words as words: the spiritual nature of the poet's devotion, the sense of addressing the saint and of considering his own life as part of that address, the expressive actuality of the language ("Yes, / I believe the first / I heard (living, there / aloud in the hall"), the reveling in the weight of a sheer, line-filling name ("Sergei Rachmaninoff"), the varying of mono- and polysyllabic words, the physical empathy (" . . . make / my knuckles rattle"), the casual quoting of other poetry, and the rising at the end of the poem into uncompromising statement. These are gifts of words ever so carefully chosen as they pulsate within the drive of the rhythm. Language and rhythm come together perfectly in the second half of the last couplet. After all the turnings through the couplets the poem ends with a brief request that matches a sentence to a line: "Give me my old hot horn." That the poem ends in the frank, down-home ardor of monosyllables seems appropriate. They are the notes upon which every poem in English is based, and in the final line they are honored in their own right.

Carruth's willingness to hazard statements, to tell rather than show (to reverse a shopworn axiom) speaks to the tradition of poems that invoke the powers of music and poetry. There are many such poems, but I am thinking specifically of John Dryden's seventeenth-century poem "A Song for St. Cecilia's Day, 1687." Here is the second stanza:

> What passion cannot Music raise and quell!
> When Jubal struck the corded shell,
> His list'ning brethren stood around,
> And wond'ring, on their faces fell
> To worship that celestial sound.
> Less than a god they thought there could not dwell
> Within the hollow of that shell
> That spoke so sweetly and so well.
> What passion cannot Music raise and quell!

Across centuries there are bridges between these two poems that go beyond their witnessing the power of music. To choose one example, Dryden's poem as it seeks to embody the variety of musical expression makes use of different length stanzas and especially of different length lines. Thus, a longer line will rhyme with a shorter line within a stanza, and the effect is to slightly challenge the listener's expectations. Thus the various stanzas employ various rhyme schemes; the ear cannot settle in because one feels Dryden wants the reader to really have to listen and attend to the unpredictability of rhyme within the basic predictability of patterned rhythm. As in a classical piece of music, there are large movements that indicate sections (stanzas) and then movements within those sections that rely on longer and shorter lines. We can designate Dryden's poem as participating in the traditions of the ode just as we can designate Carruth's poem as acknowledging the spatial couplet, but that is only to note forms, not to the energy that animates them.

Just as Hayden Carruth draws on a wide range of emotional sources, so does Dryden. He exclaims, quotes, describes, states, and in the final stanza, designated the "Grand Chorus" by the poet, he positively sings: "The Trumpet shall be heard on high, / The dead shall live, the living die, / And Music shall untune the sky." Like Carruth's, his poem is devotional in the sense that it embodies in its art the poet's commitment to the rhythmic resources available to him. Rhythm is inspiration. Dryden chooses, as does Carruth, to infer philosophical consequences from the musical analogy: Dryden writes of "The diapason closing full in Man." The "ecstasy" Carruth invokes seems not far from the crescendo of Dryden's last three lines (quoted above) where he employs a rhymed triplet to end the poem on a passionately conclusive note.

I bring up Dryden's poem not for the purpose of displaying influences but to illustrate how much Hayden Carruth's poetry resides within the rhythmic traditions of English-language verse and how he has worked to expand those traditions. For as much as anyone, Carruth has acknowledged how crucial jazz has been to his art and to the poetic art of modern times. When he locates the improvisational lyric at the heart of the modern achievement, he pinpoints jazz as the exemplar of how the modern lyric proceeds. I quote from his essay on Yeats and Pee Wee Russell, the jazz clarinetist (a unique pairing if there ever was one): "Today the open-ended, random, improvised, indeterminate poem, whatever its length, concluding usually with inconclusion, is our norm. And the transition may be seen with extraordinary clarity in the work of Yeats. Beginning with some of the middle poems . . . and continuing to late poems like . . . 'Lapis Lazuli' . . . the poet evolves a flexible, personal style that permits him to extemporize (no matter how he revised and even if in fact he put his poems through many revisions, just as jazz musicians put their improvisations through many remembered versions) within very simple formal limits, as simple, for instance, as the twelve-bar form of the conventional blues. The endings obviously come where passion has expended itself, not where passion has been crimped to fit a premeditated structure." As Carruth has noted, this improvisational impulse has meant "the final abandonment of the neo-classical idea of structure as a function of form, which the romantics and post-romantics of the nineteenth century had never given up. Instead structure has become a function of feeling."

When one spends an evening reading through poetry journals and letting one slack, randomly lined free-verse poem after another wander across one's rapidly tiring mind, to say nothing of one's rapidly tiring goodwill, one understands that freedom exists in relation to some sense of discipline—the accents want to be managed in some compelling fashion. If they aren't, then what's the point? Carruth's own poetry provides us with many examples of how freedom and discipline can work together to create a poetry that has rhythmic presence that runs deeper than the intoning (and sometimes, for all its putative naturalness, droning) voice of the poet.

Throughout his career Carruth has tended toward writing poems that maintain a consistent number of beats from line to line. At times the lines vary a beat—a line of so many beats, for instance, will veer toward one beat less or one beat more, but the home, so to speak, will be the norm of x number of beats. Whereas many poets never go near the short line, throughout his career Carruth has shown a fondness for the truncated, two-beat line. I think this propensity represents a sort of tuning of the line, a resourcefulness that acknowledges the short line as the ultimate test of making a line sing, of avowing the importance of each accent and celebrating that importance, indeed of reveling in it. The short line, when it is consistently maintained throughout a poem, breaks the accents down and creates a brief, sharp pulse. The artistic challenge is whether the short line enforces the poem's subject matter or is merely decorative, whether structure is expressive or showy—or arbitrary.

Consider the poem entitled "The Poet":

All night his window
shines in the woods
shadowed under the hills
where the gray owl

is hunting. He hears
the woodmouse scream—
so small a sound
in the great darkness

entering his pain.
For he is all and all
of pain, attracting
every new injury

to be taken and borne
as he must take
and bear it. He is
nothing; he is

his admiration. So
they seem almost
to know—the woodmouse
and the roving owl,

the woods and hills.
All night they move
around the stillness
of the poet's light.

At times the beat is very steady; the last stanza, for instance "the woods and hills. / All night they move / around the stillness / of the poet's light." At times, the beat wavers and hovers as in the line "nothing; he is" where accent touches both "he" and "is." This dual touching of accents seems very close to the jazz sense Carruth has written about, for it is analogous to the drummer's brushwork where beats are alluded to rather than enforced. The poem's miniaturism creates a great hush, and Carruth has shown a genius for creating poems that are tautly quiet, that conjure an experience in its smallest aspects. This plainly has a mimetic quality when one thinks about the stillness of the scene, of the light and the tiny scream. The light is steady, but events are occurring; there are "new" injuries. To conjure up a world of timeless, metrically relentless, poetic reverie would be a lie. Rather, the poem delineates beautifully the equation of the poet's psyche, an equation that is balanced precariously but deliberately—"he must take / and bear it." The rhythmic feeling does just what rhythm is supposed to do—create subliminal meaning, create a visceral thrill (almost a chill in this poem) that is below words and that bears the words up. The short lines hone the experience, making of it something pointed yet muted. The short lines provide no refuge; they must move on. The poem is not in the poet's mind but in the world around the poet, a world that exists in its own right. It is a world always undergoing transitions of the starkest sort, a world ever breaking down into predator and prey: "So / they seem almost / to know . . ." The buried rhyme recalls Dryden's use of the hetero-metrical rhyme—off balance yet concordant. The short lines create a modest base, one that barely can anchor the words—yet does.

When one looks at a poem based on a three- to four-beat line, one feels the somewhat broader scope. The poem feels more expansive but only somewhat. There is still a careful pondering of accent, a tuneful wariness. Here is Carruth's well-known lyric, "The Cows at Night":

The moon was like a full cup tonight,
too heavy, and sank in the mist
soon after dark, leaving for light

faint stars and the silver leaves
of milkweed beside the road,
gleaming before my car.

Yet I like driving at night
in summer and in Vermont:
the brown road through the mist

of mountain-dark, among farms
so quiet, and the roadside willows
opening out where I saw

the cows. Always a shock
to remember them there, those
great breathings close in the dark.

I stopped and took my flashlight
to the pasture fence. They turned
to me where they lay, sad

and beautiful faces in the dark,
and I counted them—forty
near and far in the pasture,

turning to me, sad and beautiful
like girls very long ago
who were innocent, and sad

because they were innocent,
and beautiful because they were
sad. I switched off my light.

But I did not want to go,
not yet, nor knew what to do
if I should stay, for how

in that great darkness could I explain
anything, anything at all.
I stood by the fence. And then

very gently it began to rain.

Again, scale seems crucial to rhythm. The poem has a modest narrative intent, and the expanded rhythmic scale allows for a reflective quality. Still it is a long way to a four- to five-beat line. Consider a line such as "the cows. Always a shock . . ." Here Carruth intentionally breaks the rhythm down to basic components; one feels that he doesn't want to natter on—as agreeable as the descriptive component is. Rather, he wants to emphasize the physical reality of the cows, their "great" (to use the poet's word) presence. Their presence must be respected in its own right, and the shorter lines enact that respect. We are made to feel the physical presence as an entity in its own right and not as part of some grander view or commentary—"near and far in the pasture." When the line expands as in "in that great darkness could I explain," one feels the need to expand, to make a statement, to reach for the powers of disquisition. It is, however, only a reaching. The poem ends very close to pure meter "very gently it began to rain." One can hear that line as having one more accented syllable than it has unaccented syllables, and sometimes Carruth does this to create (to my mind and ear) additional presence and gravity. Certainly the last line has a beautiful deliberateness that epitomizes the physicality the poem achieves throughout by means of rhythm, full and half rhymes, the repetition of words, and the quiet jazz of the syntax breaking across the lines, the enjambments that propel, hover, and glide.

At times Carruth has written poems that home in on the four-beat line and are, unlike the two previous poems, composed of one long stanza. Here is "The Ravine":

Stones, brown tufted grass, but no water,
it is dry to the bottom. A seedy eye

of orange hawkweed blinks in sunlight
stupidly, a mink bumbles away,
a ringnecked snake among stones lifts its head
like a spark, a dead young woodcock—
long dead, the mink will not touch it—
sprawls in the hatchment of its soft plumage
and clutches emptiness with drawn talons.
This is the ravine today. But in spring it
cascaded, in winter it filled with snow
until it lay hidden completely. In time,
geologic time, it will melt away
or deepen beyond recognition, a huge
gorge. These are what I remember and foresee.
These are what I see here every day,
not things but relationships of things,
quick changes and slow. These are my sorrow,
for unlike my bright admonitory friends
I see relationships, I do not see things.
These, such as they are, every day, every
unique day, the first in time and the last,
are my thoughts, the sequences of my mind.
I wonder what they mean. Every day,
day after day, I wonder what they mean.

This is a much talkier poem, much closer to the standard English-language, five-beat line. But it isn't fully engaged in its talkiness, and it doesn't want to be. In its spare way it's full of wonder and almost assertively prosy at times, as in "This is the ravine today." One hears an unvarnished voice talking to itself, carefully enumerating. The sort of attentiveness that the shorter-lined, stanzaic poems embodied would be out of place in a poem that emphasizes relationships, that tries to puzzle out what one thing has to do with anything else, that questions itself and the mind's feeling for coherence. All the comma pauses add to the slowness of the poem; it doesn't want the jumpiness from stanza to stanza that, for instance, the spatial couplet form embodies. The pauses, indeed, feel like additional accents, so though the lines refuse a clear pentameter they create the feeling of a soliloquy. This seems in part because the lines don't waver from line to line as to numbers of accents. There are no radically shorter lines. What is present is a variable steadiness: the variability stemming from syntax and punctuation and the steadiness stemming from the commitment to the perception of rhythmic predictability.

The five-beat line has a natural importance given its tradition, and Carruth uses it throughout his body of work to write the full line that is capable, at once, of assertion and description and that we associate with much English-language verse. It's interesting to take a look at a very early poem to see where he was coming from. One place was the carefully written lyric in which the forties and fifties excelled. In a poem such as "The Sound of Snow" from Carruth's first book, one can hear the deliberate, practiced tread of meter. He isn't jazzing it. Throughout his long, rich career he moves, I think, beyond standard meter in the sense of his ability to combine urgency with deliberation. He never sacrifices rhythm to the random importuning of voice, yet he cherishes the nuances of emotion that the tightening and loosening of accents create. In this sense he is much more concerned with rhythmic practice than the, at times, semi-mystical focus on the free verse line. Rhythm accounts for line, and improvisation is accountable to the line as a unit analogous to the bar. The fabled expressiveness of line breaks constitutes a small grace note rather than a series of nanosecond epiphanies. The genius lies in what the poet does within rhythm's promptings, and the extent of Carruth's range is far beyond this essay. Such a commentary would probably be book length. As I noted in the beginning, his corpus bears comparison with Auden and Tennyson, and that means its formal range is extraordinary.

I want to end with two poems. One is the early "The Sound of Snow" to which I have alluded. It is decorous, precise, selfless, and yet here too, even in a poem that stems from the outset of his vocation as a poet, one feels the particular edginess that Carruth's work often touches on, the sense (literally) of the stranger. It is a quiet sense here, existing as it does in a sort of heaven of appositives, but it seems unmistakable:

Snow falls in the dusk of Connecticut. The stranger
Looks up to the glutenous sky, and it is remembrance
That tickles the end of his nose like the fingertips
Of a child and remembrance that touches the end of his
Tongue with the antique purity and coolness of the snow,
As if this were almost the beginning, the first snowstorm
Fluttering between his house and the serious hemlocks.

And best of all is the sound of the snow in the stillness,
A susurration, the minute percussion of settling flakes;
And the stranger listens, intent to the whispering snow
In the fir boughs, earth's most intimate confiding,

And he thinks that this is the time of sweet cognizance
As it was once when the house, graying in old dusk,
Knew him and sang to him, before the house forgot.

In the last moments of day the earth and the sky
Close in the veils of snow that flutter around him,
Shutting him in the sphere of the storm, where he stands
In his elephantine galoshes, peering this way and that
At the trees in their aloofness and the nameless house
Vanishing into the dark; and he stamps his feet urgently,
Turning as if in anger away from an evil companion.

Yet when, like a warning just at the fall of darkness,
Yellow light cries from the window above in the house,
From the boy's room, from the old sixteen-paned window,
The stranger remembers the boy who sits in the light
And turns the glass sphere, watching to see the snowstorm
Whirling inside. And the stranger shivers and listens
To the tranquil and lucid whispering of the snow.

Although this poem has many verbal tics of the era, right down to
the double adjective ending hinged on "and," they are beautiful tics.
Certainly, in terms of rhythm the poem shows how firm yet sensitive a hand Carruth had at the onset of his career. Already, he excelled at marshaling phrases within long sentences to create that
harmonic feeling—a complex chiming of notes and accents—that
is a hallmark of the ample line. When—as is common in the
poem—he pushes lines into six beats, the opportune detailing, both
physical and emotional, makes itself felt with delicate force. When
he relishes the lengthy weight of certain words: "a susurration, the
minute percussion of settling flakes," one feels how rhythm can be
a form of enunciation, both care in speaking and care of speaking.
Dryden would have grasped the integrity of this line in a flash.

The poem I want to end with is a poem of celebration—"A
Little Old Funky Homeric Blues for Herm." It shows how far Carruth can go when he, at once, tightens up and lets it all hang out. In
some ways, this seems the epitome of the jazz poem in the sense of
getting down by means of alliteration, monosyllabic swats, assonance, and consonance and at the same time of goofing, of indulg-
ing rhythmic and verbal energies for the sake of their energies. He
honors the beat while fooling around with it. Here is the opening
stanza:

> Knock off that hincty blowing, you Megarians,
> I got a new beat, mellow and melic, like
> warm, man. I sing of heisty Herm.

One could give a workshop on rhythm on the basis of these mere three lines, for instance, in how Carruth deftly uses monosyllabic words as rhythmic sparks, Gerard-Manley-Hopkins-goes-beatnik— "like / warm, man. . . ." Or how two monosyllables can take a share of stress and lead into the clearly accented first syllable of a two-syllable word—"new beat, mellow. . . ." Or how a poem can lead off with monosyllables and create an imperative sense of rhythmic propulsion that awaits the first, two-syllable word—"Knock off that hincty blowing. . . ." Or how within the ambit of pentameter the variations can fly thick and fast. All these shadings and forces create a poem that for its joyful verbal energy is as delightful as anything any poet has ever put on paper. The grateful word to salute Hayden Carruth's achievement—harmonic and otherwise—is again an *h* word—"Hallelujah!"

SAM HAMILL

Listening In, an Essay-Review of *The Sleeping Beauty*

"The great contribution of the twentieth century to art is the idea of spontaneous improvisation within a determined style, a style comprising equally or inseparably both conventional and personal elements. What does this mean? It means a great deal more than the breakup of traditional prosody or rules of composition, as announced in 1910 by Ezra Pound and Pablo Picasso. It means the final abandonment of the neo-classical idea of structure as a function of form, which the romantics and post-romantics of the nineteenth century had never given up. Instead structure has become a function of feeling." So saith Hayden Carruth in a marvelous essay on Pee Wee Russell and Willie Yeats collected with other poems and essays in *Sitting In: Selected Writings on Jazz, Blues, and Related Topics* (University of Iowa Press, 1986).

"Form," Robert Creeley observes, "is never more than an extension of content." Which Denise Levertov clarifies, "Form is the *revelation* of content." Carruth's idea of structure as a function of feeling (especially in jazz and poetry) enlarges and clarifies something that has been at the center of critical philosophical debate for most of twentieth century.

Picasso's cubism grew out of his study of African art as surely as the blues grew out of African music transplanted in the New World. And the idea of spontaneous improvisation within a determined style or form is at least as old as the *Shih Ching*, the *Classic of Poetry* Confucius compiled 2,500 years ago. Perhaps the greatest literary contribution of the Sung dynasty a thousand years ago is the elevation of *tzu*, a verse form wherein the poet composes new lyrics for a preexisting tune. The form reached its pinnacle in the poetry of Li Ch'ing-chao. But the *structure* of the poem was an externally fixed form based upon musical measure—new lyrics composed for preexisting tunes. Carruth is seeking a structure from within—spontaneous and self-articulating.

"Genius,"William Blake said, opening English poetry to a whole universe found in a grain of sand, "is not lawless." Ezra Pound insisted that the line in poetry be composed "by the musical phrase and not by the metronome." Hayden Carruth, that perennial jazz aficionado and compulsive "woodshedder" with his clarinet, understands Pound's dictum probably as well as anyone presently writing poetry in the U. S. of A.

"Improvisation, "Carruth says elsewhere in the same book, "is the privilege of the master, the bane of the apprentice. It is the exercise of sensibility in acquired knowledge. When it becomes too often repeated, either in the work of the master or later in that of his followers, it loses spontaneity, because nothing of freshness is happening, and then it is over. Done. . . . Improvisation then is composition, but composition impelled by knowledgeable spirit . . ."

And what is the spirit of a master? And how does the poem arise from one's deepest and most sincere practice? A composition impelled by knowledgeable spirit? It might take the form of poetry by Robert Duncan, or by Denise Levertov, the former still read only by a handful of poets, the latter rather grudgingly granted status as a major poet by a fickle, ignorant public. That we prefer the simple and immediately recognizable in all things can be seen perfectly clearly in the rise of the national fast food chain, in best seller lists, in the idiocy of American television and movie-star politicians, in atrocious pop music fads, and in our poetry anthologies.

The "knowledgeable spirit" arises out of long-standing practice of "woodshedding," what Duncan called "the scales of the marvelous," or by seeking what Carruth has called "wisdom that is the ghost of wisdom, otherwise called humility before one's task." One primary major task of the poet is to bring the whole of one's life into the presence of disciplined improvisation within a measure, whether that measure be fixed from within or without, or whether that measure is spontaneously variable, as in the case of William Carlos Williams's "variable foot," which brought Charles Olson to observe that "a foot is for kicking."

> "To break the back of the iamb, that was the first heave."
> (EZRA POUND)

Well . . . It sagged, it bent . . . but it didn't break. And it won't break as long as we choose to place greater stress upon one syllable than upon another with any degree of regularity or identifiable pattern: the iamb is the foundation of English and American English spoken or sung music. Chaucer's natural speech patterns were probably very close to iambic pentameter, as were Shakespeare's. And it is precisely the flexibility of our tongue that makes it one of the finest poetic languages in the world, capable of compression and expansion, capable of working within externally fixed measures like the metronome (based upon the heartbeat?) and more "organic" measures such as the breath or ear alert to vowel weights and the durations of syllables rather than their stresses. As poets, we are invited to learn the Greek resonating vowel scale, the syllabus of elementary linguistics, the regulated syllabic lines that were the foundation upon which our literary ancestors constructed our English heritage, the open motion of "rowing poetry" (as Robert Graves identified it) as opposed to "hammer-and-anvil measures" (which were the source, according to Graves, of that same iambic ancestry). What could be more "hammer-and-anvil" than Rap music?

In brief, our melopoeia is among the most sophisticated, flexible, and most resonant in the world. But, like our most important gift to the arts of the world, North American jazz, its supreme beauty is far more widely understood elsewhere in the world than by the general public (even the literary public) at home.

Graves's research into prosody divides poetry into these two basic measures. But we might also divide poetry into two other categories: 1) the lyric or *sincere* mode; and 2) the bardic or narrative mode. In the latter (as, for instance, in Chaucer), the tale may or may not be formed primarily by the exercise of exterior structure; but in the former, a flexibility is mandatory since feeling or emotion is paramount because the poet is searching out the *structure of articulate feeling*. The flexibility of the classical Greek line accommodated, inspired, a grandly lyrical form—simultaneously with the development of "rowing" narrative. Or as Carruth, a sincere poet, says, "Structure is a *function* of feeling."

In 1982, Carruth published a masterpiece, *The Sleeping Beauty,* an epic of one hundred and twenty-four choruses built upon a fifteen-line movement grounded in pentameter and interior and end rhyme and slant rhyme. It is a form he first began exploring in a suite of thirteen poems, "The Asylum," in his first book, *The Crow and the Heart* (Macmillan, 1959). A quarter-century of woodshedding has transformed this variation on the sonnet into a measure entirely his own. More flexible because of its composition in irregular syllabics, the form is neither as emotionally or melodically confined as the sonnet, the more predetermined form.

The poem itself is a long meditation on the exploitation of woman and the natural world through stubbornly naive romanticism, including the poet's own, since the poem is itself a kind of romance. The "sleeping beauty" of the title is Rose Marie Dorn, the poet's wife, whose dreams insistently involve men with names beginning with the letter *H:* Homer, Hesiod, Hannibal, Hegel, Hitler, and, not incidentally, the historical/philosophical horrors of Hermaphroditism, the Holocaust, and the Hydrogen bomb. Interwoven among her dreams, there is a narrative structure, as much philosophical as literal, often articulated in anecdotal passages narrated by a northeastern backcountry prophet named Amos. The devices are many and sophisticated.

Opening the poem, beginning "out of nothing" (and with a "nothing" carried over from an epigraph from Goethe—"Vanitas! Vanitatum Vanitas!"), Carruth sets his scene and invokes his muse:

> The word is silent . . .
>   Oh, begin
> In all and nothing then, the vision from a name,
> This Rose Marie Dorn,
> Woman alive exactly when the Red Army came
> To that crook of the Oder where she was born,
> Woman who fled and fled in her human duty
> And bore her name, meaning Rose in the Thorn,
> Her name, the mythologos, the Sleeping Beauty. (#3)

But this is no neo-Byronic declaration of eternally adolescent love worship. Carruth's most obvious ancestor is Pound, and it is in the mode of the *Cantos* that the poet seeks to join his narrative with his lyric. "Let the song," he says in the fifth chorus, "Sing, from that inward stress, this world so surely/ Created in her sleep, this beauty in its centuries of wrong."

As the beauty sleeps, the reader awakens to Hesiod, who was "willing to do what nobody else would do," and to the idealized man, the Hero, fashioned out of dreamtime—"And your dream made him./ He was yours and he was wise."—and the real joys and tragedies of love:

> "For fifteen years he never knew I never
> Came. The jerk. I faked, but anyone could have told.

At last, 'Maybe it could be better,'
I said. 'Why don't we go
To one of those counselors?' and we did. Then after
A spell we stopped. That was in '65. It's later
Now. It's goddamn '75, and two years ago
He 'came out,' as he called it, he went gay,
And I'm—so soon, would you believe it?—I'm in menopause,
And I don't feel so good,
And no matter what, the diet, the exercise,
I don't age nicely. Too much droop—
Chin, breast, belly, ass. He said I should forget.
And I said what the hell's the use. I sit on this stoop
In the same old chair where grandmother used to set." (#42)

It is as much this dexterity with complicated abstract images of relationship as his melopoeia that distinguishes the poetry of Hayden Carruth, and has for more than thirty years. This sorting through our own masculine and feminine aspects requires most of a lifetime of knowledgeable spirit, and, try as we might, we cannot forget what we have learned. Our tragedies are comic; our comedies all tragic:

> His name was Husband, his title Herr,
> Noblest denomination, since he came from God
> In the olden tongue.
>   . . .
> He was Herr Husband,
> Householder, Handyman to all your joys,
> And if he stumbled or looked askance
> You had only to think your clever sexual thought
> That brought him to his parfit gentillesse again,
> Your knightly teacher whom none but you had taught. (#63)

The echoes and puns and allusions—Sylvia Plath to Chaucer—are no accident, but are a part of the whole resonance, the intellectual melopoeia of the poem, the "dance of the intellect" which inspires a need to speak. The poet's methods owe something to Pound's so-called "ideogrammic method," to the Latin poets, Catullus and Lucretius, and probably to the Provençal poetry-singers whose Arabic roots brought "Romance" to European literature.

Robert Duncan, in his essay "Ideas of the Meaning of Form," quotes the closure of Williams's masterpiece, "The Asphodel, That Greeny Flower," and says, "The end of masterpieces . . . the beginning of testimony. Having their mastery obedient to the play of forms that makes a path between what is in the language and what is in their lives. In this light that has something to do with all flowering things together, a free association of living things then—for my longing moves beyond governments to a co-operation; that may have seeds of being in free verse or free thought, or in that other free association where Freud led me to re-member [sic] their lives, admitting into the light of the acknowledged and then of meaning what had been sins and guilts, heresies, shames and wounds;/ that may have to do with following the sentence along a line of feeling until the law becomes melody . . ."

Omnia, quae sunt, lumina sunt.

Or as Pound says in Canto 76: "nothing matters but the quality/ of the affection—/ in the end—that has carved the trace in the mind/ dove sta memoria . . ." Pound's own resonance is established by his quote from Guido Cavalcanti's "Donna Mi Prega," which recalls the hieratic triad Pound offers in his famous (and now largely unread) essay on Cavalcanti:

"memory   intelligence   will"

Pound being equally concerned with quality of affection which creates—*carves*—quality of memory.

Identifying *qualitative* measures in "affection" is a very dangerous social undertaking, as any feminist must know. In a society built upon the exploitation of the Social Lie, it is truly revolutionary, threatening the very foundation of social structure. Carruth's poem is in every sense a feminist poem. After making love with a woman in his cabin—refraining from objectifying her through graphic titillation—lying in an eternal moment, he says:

> His being and hers were indistinguishable,
> So intermingled that he could not tell
> Which was man, which woman. Is that
> What Plato meant by the reunited
> Soul? Or his own sex-whelmed mind defecting?
> Neither hypothesis
> Appeals to him. He knows his feminine aspect,
> Always his, deeply and dearly his.
> He wonders: necessarily so are we all

And why is it hidden? Without this synthesis
How could we be, alone or together, whole? (#76)

He is filled with self-doubts and mistrusts, even his own mind, which may be "defecting"—a fascinating choice of word—telling him that his qualities of affection may be delusionary, a self-beguilement. But he also recognizes that only a complete synthesis of masculine and feminine within each of us can ever make us "whole" again. Two verses later, he thinks of classical women, "Helen, Julia, Amarintha," and others:

Julia had no wart? Or
Cynthia no straggling yellow tooth?
Then they were mere conceptions, youth
Feminized, sexual but eternal, held
In the long access of rhyme
That you, dear dreamer, are inventing,
                                    romance unwilled
And unrelenting.

        And yet that time,
He thinks, was actual: they lived, unknown women,
Flawed and misnamed, their soft rank bodies prime
For idealization. Convention is also human. (#78)

And later, in another verse, "No love without hurt? No lovesong without distortion?/ . . .We must love humanly, no debasement. We must sing/ Our passion, as ineluctable as breath,/ Without distortion, yet still this wondrous thing." Even in his rejection of most—not all, but most—of the conventions of the romantic tradition, Carruth composes a romance in the act of composing himself.

Aristotle divided poetry into lyric, elegiac, epic, and dramatic; his categories were clearly conceived, and his organization is, at an elementary level, effective. But, much to the chagrin of our unifarcity departments of Literature, all such classification remains ultimately false.

The drama, the epic, in Sophokles and Euripedes, unfolds—is spoken—in lyric lines. Even the concerns of poetry themselves defy classification as they seek out truths as ancient as human knowledge. Near the end of *Philoktetes,* Sophokles has Neoptolemos tell Philoktetes, "And those who choose to clutch their miseries/ and not release them deserve no pity./ You have become a savage through your anger;/ you refuse good advice and hate him who offers it . . ."

Ugolino tells Dante in the depths of Hell, "Io no piangeva; si dentro impietrai," or "Because I did not speak, I turned to stone inside." Hesiod believed "Angels deliver light; the Muse delivers form."

Obeying the need to make music, the poem reveals itself in the act of being made. Carruth explores improvisation within a form in order to confront the demons of history that have traditionally punished woman for being woman, thereby separating (arbitrarily and irrationally) the masculine from the feminine within each of us, and, by dividing, rendering each impotent. The "meaning" of his long poem is inseparable from the sounds of the poem.

All criticism, Eugenio Montale observes, is after the fact of the poem itself. The poet speaks from a deep need to *make music*. The one who has not courage to speak and the will and courage to wrestle with his or her own angel/muse is condemned to a silence that turns one to stone inside, that delivers one into the bowels of Hell. Valéry says, "An epic poem is a poem that can be told. When one *tells* it, one has a bilingual text." The poetry, of course, is *in the telling*. In verse 120, Carruth says,

> The border is what creates illegal aliens,
> Dividing what one knows from what one knows,
> This called an "imaginary line,"
> Not even drawn on the snow,
> With a huge officious multilingual sign . . .
> Action and knowledge are one, free, far in the depths
>   of consciousness.

It is not the poet's intention to cross borders, but to demolish them. And by the 124th chorus, he tells his awakening Beauty,

> The sun
> Will rise on the snowy firs and set on the sleeping
> Lavender mountain as always, and no one
> Will possess or command or defile you where you belong,
> Here in the authentic world.
> The work is done.
> My name is Hayden and I have made this song.

Beginning his song with a loose pentameter, and having played in and with its tenets and variations for one hundred and twenty-four choruses, all but one restricted to fifteen lines, he closes his poem on a pentameter. It is a song that includes resonant quotes and echoes from history, mythology and philosophy, literature, music (especially jazz), The Arts in general—but not as though they were different things. They are not other than the dance of the intellect, the life of the imagination. Nor are they more or less important than the "nine little birds" of chorus 27. They are resonances which are what music is, their sounds heard clearly only by those who have learned to listen, by the knowledgeable spirit.

The Sleeping Beauty is perhaps Hayden Carruth's grandest achievement. It is astonishingly inclusive, making use of his enormous narrative skills as revealed in *Brothers, I Loved You All;* formal without being metronomically heavy-handed, predictable, awkward or self-conscious; lyrical in its execution and epic in its proportion; sweeping in its broad affections and horrors. Squarely in the American romantic-mythopoeic tradition, *The Sleeping Beauty* is a sustained visionary icon of our culture. It returns to us a spirit now too often missing in our poetry, one that dares the sustained experience, a spirit which encourages as many literary lions as housecats.

There was a time when we still believed in classics—not only the ancient classics, but the modern and the contemporary as well—no matter that the list was and is constantly changing. *The Sleeping Beauty* is a classic. And because it is a contemporary classic written in the purr and roar of a lion, it has been read almost exclusively by Carruth's fellow poets.

It is time for a little lyrical genius to trickle down into the economy of our communal souls.

O the thought of what America would be like if the classics had a wide circulation!

3. *Survivor—writing through poverty, personal chaos, and literary isolation*

survivor, N. 3. A person who continues to function or prosper despite: one who withstands.

> . . . I know when I walk out out-of-doors
> I have a sorrow not wholly mine, but another's.
>
> —HC, "On a Certain Engagement South of Seoul"

Let his breath come
                    hard
                         let his shoulders

kill him
        these late afternoons
                after his long illness

still he climbs
        the long hill out back
                    through snow
                        to his absent son's trailer

where he will sit for awhile
                    with the old cat who gets
                        lonely up there.

(What else?—with his son on the road
        week-in
            week-out.)

To change her water,
to clean her box
if needed, humbly, on all fours,
to feed her treats—in substance
no different from thousands
of manuscripts edited,
hundreds of blurbs written, letters
answered, hungers appeased . . .

He will remove his boots
                    just inside the door
                        taking care

as always
        not to make a mess
                        then
        as always
            steady his nerves
with a cigarette.

"Envy of the placid beasts
is a very widespread affliction

in this type of sadness,"
William James wrote in *The Varieties*
of Religious Experience.

                    Poetry? The old
cat's pleasure will warm him
                              halfway like heat
                                   cast by an open
fireplace in a drafty hall
                    which falls
short
        which cannot quite
                         reach around
no matter how
    radiant—even at home
            in bed with his wife.

                         Snow
will have melted through
    his jeans to his calves. He will
                    remember then before
he leaves he must water his son's plants

            Or at the windbreak
halfway down
        how he will count five

                              no six

male cardinals lighting
    on a wild choke cherry
        (getting it right   exactly)
                    this image he will carry

home for his wife
    who will be watching
        for him down there

in the little red house
    with its huge bird feeder
                         and neatly

stacked half-cord
    at which he will be stopping first
        to gather more wood
            while there's still light.
                    —Joe-Anne McLaughlin, *Jam,* 2001

DONALD HALL

Text As Test, an Excerpt from an Essay-Review of *The Sleeping Beauty* and Galway Kinnell's *Selected Poems*

Poets make long poems to contain what they have learned and to set the parts of their knowledge in order. The *Odyssey* is the model—that moves a many-minded hero among islands and underworld to home. Long poems need not be epics; the anecdotes and *fabliaux* of *The Canterbury Tales* organize a life's understanding. On the other hand, some long poems are merely short ones blown up, like the *Idylls of the King.* (I cherish doubts about *The Changing Light at Sandoval.* Order is serious only when it rules extreme multiplicity and diversity; a structure of glued toothpicks, however artfully constructed, remains trivial because the units are repetitive.) In recent years, poets have made something like long poems from sequences of related short poems. In Berryman's *Dream Songs* and Lowell's *Histories,* we find diversity and chaos enough, each an *omnium gatherum,* insatiable of experience and the world—the day's headlines and the deaths of friends. . . . But in these works coherence relies on voice, which can degenerate into mannerism, and on stanza-form, which alone is insufficient. The net's holes are wide and big fish escape: each collapses into anthological snippets. . . . In the unavoidable paradox of art, manyness requires singularity and variety needs sameness.

Hayden Carruth's *The Sleeping Beauty* is a life's knowledge set in order. It consists of one hundred and twenty-four stanzas of fifteen lines each, sonnet-like, rhymed and off-rhymed *ababaaudedefef.* The form has a history. Carruth made it up, in 1955 or thereabouts, for "The Asylum," which turns up in his first book; ten years later the stanza reappears in *For You;* ten years later again, he used it in "Paragraphs" in the excellent book he published before this one: *Brothers, I Loved You All.* Beginning with direct rhyme and strict meter, he gradually loosened the stanza and allowed it visual variety, kept the rhyme scheme but searched out distant off-rhymes; by the time the stanza reaches *The Sleeping Beauty,* one can read stanzas through without noticing the rhymes—but the rhymes are there all the same. Unity of stanza finds antithesis in variety of off-rhymes, broken lines, and visual detachments. . . . Carruth has it both ways—which in poetry as in life is the only way to have it.

The form is one of many unities in *The Sleeping Beauty*—unities which double as varieties. The poem explores romance through the image of the sleeping beauty, and meditates on the romantic exploitation of women and the natural world. It meditates on its subject and, having it both ways, participates in it—for this poem that attacks romance is also romantic. Although the poem contains and develops an idea—its intellectual unity is greater than that of most modern long poems—it is romantic not only in its elegy for the Beauty but in its implicit poetics. The poem presents itself for judgment by the standard of intensity—not of doctrinal correctness nor of faultlessness, but intensity of feeling. By necessity it must use formal devices as a grid against which the feelings deploy themselves. One more such device is the letter *H,* which allows Carruth to "include history," by inserting the Beauty's dreams of Heraclitus, Hydrogen Bomb, Hamlet, Heliopolis, Heathcliff, Harlequin, Honeywell—not to mention an omnipresent He—and end with: "My name is Hayden and I have made this song." Again, this unity exhibits diversity *and* multiplicity: using the gap between the figure from the commedia dell'arte and the corporation that sounds like a fountain of sweetness, between the daydreamed lover and the world-killing engine, Carruth creates a universe inside an initial.

This long poem contains what Carruth has learned, some intellectual history and much experience—more Vermont than Provence. A dead voice named Amos, Vermonter and Old Testament prophet, talks sound morals in an accurate Yankee dialect. Amos allows Carruth to speak the ethics of an adopted place—the Tiresias of this poem, made wise by death and endurance. The old ghost tells about pulling a beautiful woman's Mercedes out of the ditch; she tries to reward him, to buy what was freely given, and we have in the same anecdote anarchist politics and Vermont manners and Yankee talk and the sleeping beauty raised alive from the deep.

What we don't have, I suppose, is what usually passes for poetry. Now I admire the sheer *writerliness* of James Wright, Louis Simpson, Galway Kinnell, W. S. Merwin . . . but if we demand the sweetness—if we will not read the poem that will not display this credential—we miss the rough excellence of poets who either cannot do

it or who can but refuse to—for whom the writerly seems ingrati-
ating. . . . We may also fall prey to the minor aestheticians of poetry,
who can coordinate colors or frame a print but who cannot distinguish a hangnail from heart-cancer or a missed train from a lost
love; makers of toothpick structures.

Here is a stanza from *The Sleeping Beauty* in which Carruth identifies capitalism and romance.

> Your dream:
> > Its name apparently is Honeywell,
> But what is it? A tree of thorns, a bush, a vine
> Tangled with many others, a wall
> Encircling you, entwined
> Twig to twig, thorn to thorn, like fire?
> > Hell
> Hath such fires, burning and consuming, themselves
> Never consumed.
> > Out of the circle
> Come voices corporate and low:
> > "Oh darling,
> Thank you, thank you, we are eternally yours. Only
> Stay as you are and we'll burn.
> We'll consume forever, and we promise there'll be hotels
> On Boardwalk and Park, and champagne, furs.
> Weekends in Spain, anything you want,
> > you won't be forsaken.
> But we'll love and protect you as long as the world is ours,
> As long as we burn, as long as you never waken."

The allusiveness is casual, speech-like, ironic—confounding Milton
and Monopoly. The stanza-form on the one hand (without meaning, purely numbers and order) and the myth on the other hand
(narrative and interpretation) confer such unity that the diction can
sustain (may even require?) great diversity of level and of allusion.
(Amos says things like, "I mind one time down to the Grange/
Sucking up them venison meatballs. . . .") This unity allows Carruth
to travel as far as China for his testifying voices:

> "My mother did it. She had to, she said. She took
> Ten yards of binding cloth and wrapped my toes
> Backward underneath like a broken book.
> Then came the embroidered shoes,
> Smaller and smaller for two years, and so I forsook

My childhood, which was my only life. Now look—
You see a Chinese lady, sixteen,
Stylish and sexy and properly constrained
For her bridegroom, who has never seen my feet
And never will, just my pretty
Three-inch shoes. Inside are pain and heat
Perpetual. They never stop. Well, I totter
In this garden, snipping carnations. Is there another
System, do you think, where girls run and a daughter
Smiles? You smile. Yes, in a year I shall be a mother."

These stanzas show the poem's variety *and* its inclusiveness—for the
space between them is also filled. I speak in these formal terms because the poem's formal coherence amazes me. But it also amazes
me in its spooky, obsessive, guilty *import*. If it is not Carruth's best
work, it is surpassed only by certain shorter poems in *Brothers, I
Loved You All,* which appeared in 1978.

What are we to make of a poet, author of many volumes beginning with *The Crow and the Heart* in 1955, who writes his best work
as he approaches sixty? We remember his long struggles with madness, the courage to survive. . . . The recent work is no mere example of courage but of excellence.

WENDELL BERRY

My Friend Hayden

When I was in college and had become certain that Anonymous was not the name of a prolific medieval poet, I began to read the "little magazines" to try to learn about the poetry of my own time. That was in the early fifties. And so I must have known the name "Hayden Carruth" for a good many years of such scattered reading before it meant much to me.

It began to mean much to me in May of 1964. My family and I had been living as neighbors to Denise Levertov and Mitchell Goodman on Greenwich Street in New York City. Denise and Mitch had bought an old farm in Temple, Maine, where they spent their summers. They invited us to come up for a visit, and in that May we did so. It was a good visit in a good place. The weather was fine, the landscape beautiful, the talk warm-hearted. The voice of that time in my memory is that of the white-throated sparrow, who is mostly silent when he winters with us in Kentucky.

While we were there, Denise handed me a sheaf of poems, a carbon copy on yellow paper. The poems were the sequence entitled *North Winter*, by her friend Hayden Carruth. Denise was an ardent and generous friend to the poetry and the poets she liked, and she just as ardently wanted the poets she liked to like each other's poems. She wanted to know if I wouldn't love those poems by Hayden Carruth as much as she did.

To disagree with Denise on such a matter was not invariably cost-free. And so I took the poems in hand with some anxiety, wanting very much to love them as much as she did and very much afraid I wouldn't. But I did, I think, love those poems as much as Denise did. I could see their mastery and their beauty. I could see how entirely the poet loved the place and the creatures he was writing about. Beyond that, those poems were a revelation to me, one I greatly needed at the time.

I was then finishing up two years I had spent in New York, and was about to return to take a job at the University of Kentucky, where, a few years before, I had been a student. Understandably, as I now see, most of my literary friends were upset with me for this choice. They thought I was ruining myself. There I was, with a good job in the great cultural center, getting to know other writers, attending literary events, visiting the museums, in general having a good time—and was I going to turn my back on all that to return to, of all places, Kentucky?

Well, for all I know, they may have been right, for I certainly can't prove them wrong. There are no control plots in one's life. I can't compare the life I've had with the life I might have had. All I can say with certainty, after forty-three years, is that I am glad I chose as I did, I am grateful for the life I have had, and I can see some advantages in living outside the great cultural centers.

But in the spring of 1964 I had not lived the life I was going to live any more than the life I might have lived. I did not, in truth, know what I was doing. I was returning to Kentucky merely because I wanted to; beyond that, I had no reason or argument. And so the admonitions of my friends had affected me strongly.

My first reading of *North Winter*, then, had this context of uncertainty and uneasiness. I did, after all, want to be a good writer. I wanted my life to be sustained in part by the intelligence of reading and writing. If I had forestalled or deformed that possibility I would have been diminished, and of course sorry.

I don't think I could have said then why that carbon copy of Hayden's poems meant as much to me as it did. But the poems sank deeply into me, and they consoled me. By now I can say why.

Those poems, in addition to the much else they were, clearly did not come from any great center of culture, not from New York or Boston or even Concord. They came from Johnson, Vermont, a place not central to the culture even of Vermont, and yet a place obviously central to the consciousness and imagination of a fine poet. It was a place that, on the scale of grandeur, might have been any place, except that by the use of his senses, his wits, and his art, the poet had given standing to its unique life, first in his own imagination, then in Denise's, then in mine, and eventually in the imaginations of many others. In those poems I was seeing, though I could not then have said so, the virtue that William Carlos Williams attributed to the work of Poe: a "scrupulous originality, *not* 'originality' in the bastard sense, but in its legitimate sense of solidity which goes back to the ground," a "burst through to expressions of a re-awakened genius of *place.*"

The poems of *North Winter* are poems of praise, lamentation, humor, and exuberant technical inventiveness. And they are in a curious way didactic. They are poems of survival. They tell how to be fully and eagerly alive all the way through a cold northern winter.

There is, as Blake rightly said, no competition among true poets, and I agree, despite the current trade in prizes, grants, and teaching jobs. *North Winter* is not necessarily better or worse than a book of poems from New York or Boston or San Francisco, but it is necessarily different from any book from any of those places or from any other place. It belongs uniquely to the place it came from. But in its fullness of imagination and realization, it belongs also to all of us in our own places. This is not something that one dopes out, or can dope out, by a critical method. It is merely something that one knows, or does not know.

To me, *North Winter* will always speak of the way one poet by his work can help another—or, to put it more truly, of the way a poet by his work can help a fellow human. It told me, at a time when I greatly needed to hear it, that one writer may do life-sustaining work in a place that, to others, would be "nowhere." It told me that somebody rural by predilection, like me, could be a good writer. Soon after I returned to Kentucky *North Winter* was beautifully printed by Carroll Coleman at The Prairie Press in Iowa City. I ordered a copy that I still have and still love, and that still delights and consoles me every time I read it. And so before I became Hayden's friend, I had become his debtor. And my debt to him has steadily grown. I have been mindful of his work and example, and under his influence, for forty-three years.

I became his friend by surprise several years later. On a cloudy afternoon, I was leading a mare and foal from my place in the river valley to my uncle's farm at the top of the hill. A man passed me in a green pickup truck and then stopped up ahead. The man opened the door, stuck his head out, and called, "Are you Wendell Berry?"

I called back, "Yeah!"

"Well," the man said, "I'm Hayden Carruth."

By then I had read more of the poems of Hayden Carruth, and I believe we had written some letters to each other. But I was not prepared to meet him on the road between Lanes Landing and Port Royal. I could hardly have been more surprised if he had told me he was William Shakespeare or Tu Fu. I called back, "The hell you are!"

Hayden stayed with us a night or two on that visit. I showed him around a little, and of course we talked. Our talk, from the first words, was that of friends between whom much does not have to be explained, but rather is assumed or taken for granted. We did not need to tell each other about the happiness of belonging to a place, of loving neighbors who do not read poetry, of ricked firewood, of a garden, of a rough-carpentered shelter for writing, of silence, of the wildness surrounding and suffusing, of handwork outdoors. There are certain griefs and indignations that we have in common also, and have not needed to elaborate or defend.

We have also understood from the first that Hayden is far better read and better educated than I am. We had to waste no time in settling that. And so I have freely come to Hayden for instruction and correction. And Hayden has freely given the help I have asked for. He has sometimes enjoyed rather extravagantly the authority of his seniority, but then I too have enjoyed it rather extravagantly. In fact there have been moments that have delighted me, and then re-delighted me when I have recounted them to other friends.

Once, for instance, when we were talking on the telephone, I lapsed into the illiteracy I am always tempted to enjoy, and I said something about the need to "lay down" for a nap.

And Hayden said in a split second: "*Lie* down! God damn it!"

That is funny, of course, and I always laugh when I remember it. But it is instructive too. What I took from the instruction, what was instructive about it, was the *force* of it. As it came flying to me through the receiver, I felt and liked and was helped by his un-qualified passion for our poor language and his unrelenting insis-tence that it should be used well.

Talk is different from writing. Good talk is in some ways better and more precious than any writing. That it goes off "into thin air," leaving a few memories that eventually are reduced to thin air also, in no way detracts from its value. I have been lucky to have a few friends with whom my conversation seems never to resume but merely to continue, and Hayden is one of them.

After Hayden's first visit to Lanes Landing, there have been other visits—never enough, but a good many—at his place and mine, and others, in Pennsylvania and New Jersey, where neither of us was at home except in our long, old conversation.

One fall, maybe not long after Hayden was first here, I visited him at his place, "Crow's Mark," near Johnson. We sat and talked in his writing shack, as we had done here in mine, and I helped him put a load of firewood into his woodshed.

Another time I was there in the winter and Hayden took me on my first (and, so far, my only) walk on snowshoes. I had come partly to write an article for *The Draft Horse Journal,* and Hayden drove with me over quite a lot of Vermont and New Hampshire, visiting horse people. I daresay we both remember Anne Harper on a brilliant afternoon running in the snow beside her great Belgian stallion, Babar de Wolvertem.

In the summer (I believe) of 1975, Hayden and Rose Marie and their son David visited us here, in weather so much like our own and so little like Vermont's that I was embarrassed. Activity so strenuous as standing still made you sweat through your shirt.

But whatever the circumstances, when we have been together we have talked, and when we have not been together I often have had a book of his poems or essays at hand, and I have read him, as I have listened to him, with respect for his probity, with admiration for his artistry and knowledge, with pleasure, and always with a sense of companionship and consolation.

What I have been trying to prepare myself to say and now will have to say without preparation—for I can see that I am not writing "criticism"—is that, to me, there is an extraordinary continuousness between listening to Hayden and reading him. Some poets seem to me to go to their work as to something removed from themselves, like an office, but Hayden seems to be at his work, or in it, as it seems to be in him, all the time. His poems are not spoken by "the speaker," that suppositional personage of critical convention. When a poem by Hayden is not spoken by a person designated as different from himself, then Hayden is speaking it. When I am talking with him, he is entirely present to me as the poet he is. When I am reading him, I am hearing his voice.

This seamlessness cannot be the result of any sort of idealism. It is the result, I think, of a thought or a hope of a livable life. Hayden's thought, his expectation, starts from and is ever qualified by a careful, deliberate, strictly limited resignation. His work does not arise from a false expectation of ideal causes or effects. He assumes absolutely that our life begins and ends on the everyday, the real, the mortal, the "losing" side of the ideal. In the too-quick view this may seem pessimistic, but it is never that, or never programmatically that:

The point is, there's a losing kind of man
who still will save this world if anybody
can save it, who believes . . . oh, many things,
that horses, say, are fundamentally preferable
to tractors, that small is more likeable than big,
and that human beings work better and last longer
when they're free.

There is a certain darkness in Hayden's affirmation of "the loser, the forlorn believer, the passer on," but it is nevertheless an affirmation. It is a darkness readily lighted by announcements of great happiness and great joy.

I think that Hayden's idea of a livable life is a life that has affection in it—a life, to give it the fullest scope of his art, in which the things you love are properly praised and properly mourned. What I most value Hayden for and most thank him for (in this age of deniability, when the merest public honesty is made doctrinally tentative) is his wholehearted, unabashed, unapologetic affection: affection for women and men, for neighbors, friends, other poets, jazz musicians, wild creatures, beloved places, the weather. If you know his work, you know you can find dislike in it, and anger too. Even so, he is a poet of affection. If he dislikes, that is because he likes. If he is angry, that is because of damage to what he loves. His affection is capacious and generous; everything worthy is at home in it. As he knows, everything worthy is fragile and under threat, is prey to time and invisible to power, and yet affection keeps the accounting in the black. Worthy things, invested with affection, pass into "the now / which is eternal." I don't know how this can be, and I don't think Hayden knows. And yet I believe that it is so; I believe that Hayden believes that it is so.

Affection is the motive force also of his literary essays and reviews, which characteristically are written in tribute to people or work he admires. Maybe therefore he is not a critic, for he doesn't practice the "objectivity" that gives with one hand and takes back with the other and never makes up its mind in favor of anything. And certainly therefore I am not a critic, for I confess that I can't see why anybody would write anything, even the harshest criticism, that doesn't come ultimately from affection. I don't admire poetry that values its subject only as a subject of poetry.

Nobody has been a better servant and teacher of the art of poetry than Hayden has been in his essays and reviews. And there can be no doubt that these have come from his affection, affection that sometimes necessarily requires a passionate discrimination between what is worthy and what is not.

In his essay of 1966, "Ezra Pound and the Great Style," for example, Hayden's affection for what is best in Pound carries him past the rote condemnation of Pound for his obvious faults, with a bare notice that it exists, and goes straight on to a question of real interest: Why, in spite of all Pound's faults, do we still read him? And Hayden answers: Because Pound's work, preeminently among the poets of our time, reveals "a great and splendid light" that we recognize in all great works of art. And Hayden then devotes his care to that revelation. He speaks of Pound's "vision of the good" ("meaning proportion, plenty, the spirit of the earth at work in man's heart"), and of his belief that "nothing matters but the quality of the affection."

But what most impresses me in that essay, what seems to me most characteristic of Hayden, is the way he treats four lines quoted from an ancient Chinese ode translated by Pound. The lines are "quite good," though "a long way . . . from Pound's best." But Hayden proceeds to surround those lines with knowledge and insight, not as explanation but as a way of cherishing them, showing, by the articulation of his respect, precisely what their quality is. The passage that I am talking about is in *Selected Essays and Reviews,* pages 50 and 51.

And now I want to consider a poem that, in exactly the same way, summons knowledge and insight into the service of affection. The poem is entitled simply "Marshall Washer." It is from Hayden's beautiful book of 1978, *Brothers, I Loved You All.* This poem is immensely important to me—and, I think, to our time—for reasons I hope will come clear. But I want to write about it now because, in doing so, I may be able to signify my great indebtedness to Hayden and my gratitude.

Marshall Washer was Hayden's neighbor and friend in Johnson, Vermont. They exchanged work and other goods, as rural neighbors once did, and now do less and less. On one of my visits to his place, Hayden took me to meet Marshall, who showed me with pride his milking barn and his cows, and with greater pride, because they were his fellow workers, his team of Belgian horses. He was a man I recognized and honored according to his kind (as Hayden had trusted I would do): an excellent farmer and an excellent man. His own generation included many like him on small farms all over the eastern United States. We talked a long time on Marshall's hilltop that afternoon. Our visit included several moments of fine hilarity, courtesy of Marshall's brother-in-law, Wesley, a gifted teller of scandalous tales about himself.

In my copy of Hayden's *Collected Shorter Poems,* I have kept a picture of Hayden in the State House of Vermont on the day in November of 2002 when he was made that state's poet laureate. Standing immediately behind him, wearing a suit and tie, is Marshall Washer. And with that picture I have kept, from the next year, Hayden's eulogy for Marshall, dead at the age of eighty-eight, who "represented, and still does, the finest element of the culture and civilization of northern New England" and who was "the consummate small farmer."

The poem "Marshall Washer" takes up more than six pages in the *Collected Shorter Poems.* It begins with what may seem a sort of wisecrack—"They are cowshit farmers"—but is actually a trap cunningly set, which is sprung about forty lines later, and the snap of it reverberates to the final lines.

The first of the poem's six parts is a small essay on the lives of New England dairy farmers, who sometimes in self-derogation call themselves "cowshit farmers," and whose lives in fact do revolve around the manure that the cows deposit daily in the milking barns and that must be returned to the fields. By their production of milk these farmers make a living. By their handling of the manure they are involved in the fertility cycle, which is the continuity of farming and of the living world. Hayden depends on us to know, as we certainly should, that "manure" means not just excrement but also the handwork and the handcare, by which it is returned to the fields, by which the fields are cultivated, by which, and only by which, we will continue to eat:

> Notice how many times
> I have said "manure"? It is serious business.
> It breaks the farmers' backs. It makes their land.
> It is the link eternal, binding man and beast
> and earth.

"Cowshit," then, has an eternal value. A "cowshit farmer" is an artist whose art makes of cowshit "the link eternal."

The poem then shifts from this description of the kind of man Marshall is to Marshall himself. It is concerned from then on specifically with him—a depiction, an act of understanding and affection, a tribute—though his story clearly also is that of farmers of his kind in the age of industry and urbanization. Part 2 shows us Marshall at work on his place and in his time:

I see a man notching a cedar post
with a double-blade axe, rolling the post
under his foot in the grass: quick strokes and there
is a ringed groove one inch across, as clean
as if cut with the router blade down at the mill.
I see a man who drags a dead calf or watches
a barn roaring with fire and thirteen heifers
inside, I see his helpless eyes. He has stood
helpless often, of course: when his wife died
from congenital heart disease a few months before
open-heart surgery came to Vermont, when his sons
departed, caring little for the farm because
he had educated them . . .

My quotations by now should have given an idea of the kind of artifact this poem is. Hayden is a poet of extraordinary technical resourcefulness. He is capable of an exacting and refined lyrical beauty. But this poem is built by the gathering in of knowledge. Somewhere not too far in its background are the catalogues of Whitman and their long, accumulating rhythms. But this poem is as far from Whitman's rhetoric as it is from Hayden's own precise lyricism. Its knowledge is more particular, more characterizing, and more exactly compassionate too, than most of Whitman's. The lines of "Marshall Washer" have a certain rough energy that draws specifically personal knowledge into the reach of comprehension and affection. The knowledge is clarified and ordered by the same means that orders the verse: a strictly maintained integrity and clarity of line, a rhythm precisely inflected and perfectly continuous, a sustained impetus of remembrance and reflection that is never overburdened. The lines are not meant to be lyrical, but they are often as prosodically astute as anybody could wish. Look again at that line about manure: "It breaks the farmers' backs. It makes their land."

Because the poem, its language and its prosody, is so nearly at one with its knowledge, it has a quietness that permits accuracy. The poem's story is so fully imagined, is so clearly seen as belonging to its time and place and character, that it can be set down almost casually—"his sons / departed, caring little for the farm because / he had educated them"—though it carries to the heart a mostly unregarded modern tragedy, necessarily personal, but also national and international. That force is not fully released or felt until it is elaborated, with the same quietness of accuracy at the end of the poem:

> No doubt
> Marshall's sorrow is the same as human
> sorrow generally, but there is this
> difference. To live in a doomed city, a doomed
> nation, a doomed world is desolating, and we all
> are desolated. But to live on a doomed farm
> is worse. It must be worse. There the exact
> point of connection, gate of conversion, is –
> mind and life. The hilltop farms are going.
> . . . .
>
> . . . the link
> of the manure, that had seemed eternal, is broken.

As you read this poem, a terrible beauty leaps from it into your consciousness—if your consciousness has been at all prepared to receive it. The terribleness is in the story of the breaking of "the link / of the manure"—the work and the care, the fertility cycle in agriculture—which "seemed eternal" perhaps because it was, and because it was, and is, necessary if survival is to be a part of our intention. The beauty is in the verse, which is to say in the poet's enactment in verse-making of his intelligent love and regard for Marshall Washer.

Marshall's farming, by which he maintained "the link eternal" of the manure, we must see as an enactment of reverence. And here it is necessary to distinguish the reverence that is enacted from that which is merely felt. Our survival, our culture, and our civilization if they are to be even worthy of survival, depend on our ability to supply to the feeling of reverence the arts necessary for its enactment. Poetry and farming have to be counted equally as two of the necessary arts; and we must understand at last that Hayden's poem is an appreciation of one fine artist by another: reverent men, both of them.

I am a reverent man myself, a farmer and a poet, and I am therefore party to this poem of Hayden's about his friend Marshall Washer, as I was one afternoon, by Hayden's hospitality, party to their friendship and conversation. I am party, moreover, to their fate as rural people. When I read *North Winter* for the first time I was on my way back to my own rural place and life. But I was also going back, as I half knew even then, as I know more completely now, to take up the fate of country people in my time. I was going back to help bury a lot of good men and women who had replaced their predecessors well enough, but who themselves would not be succeeded or replaced. I was going back to witness many times the breaking of the old link and the old reverence of the manuring of the fields.

Near the end of his essay on Ezra Pound that I quoted earlier, Hayden wrote:

> . . . How shall our children live in a world from which first the spirit, then history, and finally nature have fled, leaving only the mindless mechanics of process and chance? Will any place exist for a humane art in a society from which the last trace of reverence—any reverence—has been rubbed out? As a matter of fact I think a place will exist, will be made. . . .

Hayden wrote those sentences more than forty years ago, and yet when I read them now, in spite of the troubles and discouragements of those years, I still feel spoken for. It is the right thought, the right faith, whatever happens.

Can modern Americans conceive of a reverence for "the eternal link" of manure? Well, Hayden can, and I can. And I could quickly fill this page with the names of people I didn't know forty years ago, people in America and in other countries, who can conceive of such reverence, who in various ways practice it, and who could fill pages of their own with the names of others who do—a cowshit sodality making places for reverence, still faithful to the old linkage, its knowledge and its work.

Selected Correspondence

From *The Letters of Robert Duncan and Denise Levertov*

Dear Robert & Jess   Feb. 22, 1970
                                      177 Webster
                                      E Boston, Mass. 02128

The longer it gets the harder it is to write because I feel as if I owe explanations of why I *haven't* written & that paralyzes me. I'll try to make them brief.

We moved to Boston in Sept & I began teaching at MIT &, just as at Berkeley, immediately became very much involved with my students and with various political actions. Under these circumstances I find the only way to not get exhausted & despondent (from fatigue) is to deal with each day's people & events as they come up & more or less ignore letter writing. I manage to get an enormous amount of work done this way, i.e., I do not neglect my own work, even including some lectures & other prose commitments. I also manage to keep cooking pretty imaginative meals (good Italian groceries here) & to give my students all the attention they deserve (which is plenty) but at the price of neglecting my distant friends. It's not an ideal solution but it's the only one I've been able to work out for myself. I do write some letters—answers to people who really need (or are asking for) answers to specific questions, & letters to people in jail, & to my mother. But that's about it, except for "business" letters & I'm not too efficient about that.

However, there's an additional reason why I haven't written to you lately & that is that since the last *Stony Brook* came out with your (Robert) attack on Hayden Carruth I've felt I had to write about it & haven't until now mustered time & energy to do so.[1] Since you know how much I love & admire you (& *for how long*), dear Robert, I hope I can speak to you about this without incurring your wrath. I feel it was an attack not only factually unjustified and quite disproportionately contentious, but humanly a very thoughtless & cruel act. If you listened more attentively than you sometimes do (you *can* listen wonderfully, but often you don't) you wd. have recalled, I think, things that I had told you about Hayden—that he had had a long illness—some of it spent in a mental hospital & most in a room alone in his parents' house from which he was only able to emerge at night occasionally for a solitary walk—that then he came slowly back into the world, Jay L{aughlin}. providing a sort of 1/2-way house for him, where he met Rose Marie (who was working as a nursemaid to Ann Laughlin's sisters' kids) & they married & went on live in Vermont. He has never since his breakdown been able to face groups of people (for instance when I read at Middlebury in Jan. & they drove over, he had to leave the auditorium almost at once) but he manages to make a living one way & another, sometimes by manual labor & sometimes by writing—scientific ghost-writing, reviews, etc. Rose Marie used to work in the diner. Now that little David is in school, R-M is going to school so that she can eventually teach handicapped children. All this has little to do with your attack, you'll say—but what I'm trying to do is remind you of things I know I have mentioned before, so you know *who* it is you were attacking instead of Hayden being an abstraction to you. It was the Carruths who were to have moved to Temple to the house up the road to be our neighbors, except that the damage to the house & then some other circumstances squashed that plan. Hayden was also the guy who wrote a really beautiful piece about your work in *The Hudson Review* a couple of years back.[2] Now, if I read what seemed to me to be a put-down or something of William Carlos Williams or E P by someone I knew to be a dear & trusted friend of *yours*, & whom I knew to be someone who had had a severe breakdown & who therefore might be more sensitive to angry criticism than average, I believe I would at least take the trouble to document that person's critical record in regard to Williams, etc., ask you "What gives with this guy?" and write to him personally to begin with—not just launch out into a public attack on him without warning. In fact as J. can tell you (with ample evidence) Hayden has always cared deeply for Wms & Pound & knows a lot more than average about their work. I don't have *Stony Brook* here (I lent it out) so I can't remember what exactly it was that you picked on but when I read it I was convinced that it was almost certainly a misunderstanding, misinterpretation on your part and in any case was the kind of thing one writes personally about, to argue, not makes a strident public issue out of (as one cd. very justifiably do—with some unequivocally sneering, ignorant comment). I don't mind yr picking on Adrienne Rich because she's a tough woman & perhaps actually deserves it anyway—my point is that if you'd paid any heed when I spoke (many times) about Hayden, you'd have guessed how much it might have hurt him, & wd have refrained. Moreover, I think to pretend you don't know who he is & refer to him as "Mr. Carruth" (or something like that) in a sort of "whoever this upstart chap may be" tone, when you knew perfectly well he was a close friend of ours & that he had reviewed your books so warmly, was just silly. I *don't* mean I think the right hand shd wash the left & that you (or any of us) shd refrain from adverse criticism of our favorable critics! What I *do* mean is that whole thing was unnecessary and insensitive. I'll enclose Hayden's response. He is a courageous man who wages a continual battle with depression & insomnia—he has humor & vigor & persistence, & most of the time he wins—but it is hard, he lives more than most of us on a knife edge.

Now Robert, I am risking a great deal in writing you this letter. You know you are a major person in my life & I cannot endure the thought of your being angry with me—but I cannot *not* write it & keep my self-respect, and I must trust that your friendship, our friendship, can admit this reproach. I was about to write to you when I heard of Olson's illness (when you called me) & of course I could not speak of it at a time of such sorrow for you.

Jess, this letter is so largely addressed to Robert but I think you'll want to discuss with him what I am saying. I think there are 2 parts to the issue: (1) if a public attack is to be made, its justification shd be more carefully considered & documented, a private letter considered as alternative, & its *tone* be commensurate with the supposed evil being attacked.

(2) If the person whose statement is being attacked is someone you have reason to believe is vulnerable beyond the ordinary, & is a good friend of a friend, the whole project (I believe) shd be discussed first with that friend so that you make sure you're not doing him (the attacked one) a real injury. These seem to me to be principles or guidelines not in this case only but in similar situations. Surely one has to ask oneself, am I doing more personal

harm than pedagogic good by making such an attack? Is it necessary and is it humane?

In a separate envelope I'm sending you *Relearning the Alphabet*—advance copies just arrived. With my love, as ever.

I have quite a few more poems too & will try to xerox & send.

Oh—alas, I think reading at M.I.T. is definitely *not possible* now. I held out funds as long as I could but am not really officially in charge of readings, & other faculty have their own ideas, e.g. Mark Strand (ugh!)—everybody & his uncle. So, I'm really sorry, but it is too late now, all the $ is allocated.

When is yr NY show going to be, Jess? If I possibly can I'll go down to see it. And Robert, please write as soon as you can and don't be angry but come to East Boston if possible if you come E. for the show.

I know you must miss Charles.[3]

> *Love*
> *always—Denise*

dear Denny,   Feb. 26, {19}70
                                                        {March 17–18, 1970
                                                        San Francisco}

Your reproach re. my "Critical Difference of View" is quite justified. In any account I could give of from what my high handed polemic sprang the fact remains that it was "disproportionately contentious"—what must be saddest to relate is that I raised the question with myself as to whether I ought to rewrite the whole eliminating all reference to Carruth or Adrienne Rich (beyond quoting the two passages that had enraged me)—I did not have in mind Hayden Carruth's sensitivities and vulnerabilities (for one thing his tone in the review of Tomlinson set the high-handed tone which I took up with a sledge-hammer) tho I certainly did know and was aware that you and Mitch were fond of him, and I have never had the sense that that friendship did not have very real grounds. It doesn't mitigate my offense here that I was not attacking Hayden in his personal life where I should have had a sense of his vulnerability (for you had told me of his alcoholism and his courage in making a new life for himself) but I was attacking him in his criticism where he, charged by a hostility towards Tomlinson, expanded his charge to say of Dr. Williams's tercets that the form was "his alone,

one hastens to say": well, at that red flag the bull in me faces all over again the fight against those who would allow that Williams had an idiosyncratic style that was O.K. for him; and who would then go on to insist: "I tried, without success, to think of a single self-respecting American poet who had *dared* to copy this form, at least for more than a poem or two." Them was fighting words, and they still rankled so that my rancor in my reply read five years later was still invidiously backed up by my still ready dislike of the concentrated impression of the passage.

I had never read any of Carruth's critical work, except in passing—and certainly I had written him that his review in *Hudson* was most encouraging; my piece reveals my utter ignorance of his other writing on Williams. But even if he had written nothing on Williams, that one not only high-handed but out-of-hand sentence of mine " . . . that neither Mr. Carruth or Miss Rich had or have any great concern for the poetry of Pound or Williams" is indefensible and by that time my scoring points and rescoring points in an imaginary debate had led me to the full wretchedness of the unscrupulous debater's closing remarks.

I can't undo the grievous human situation. That passage of his still gets underneath my skin. The "his alone, one hastens to say" hits on my own fanatical sore-spot about them tercets as a viable form not an individual style; and the following remarks about Williams tending towards the pentameter hits on old wars about the measure—where these come up I am intolerant; and that means not only ungracious but also to some degree deaf and in the refusal to imagine the terms of what is opposed—stupid.

But I can owe it to the truth of the situation {to} criticize myself, calling attention to the distortions and projections that enter along the lines of the polemic address in which one fabricates the enemy and launches the attack. Elements of this certainly enter in to passages I have written on Elizabeth Drew (whom I saw as a particularly prejudiced school-marm), and on Robin in the Nerval essay where I had to imply and project much of his intent.[4]

I'll send on the critique on my polemic as soon as I get it done. Hayden's letter certainly gives me a vivid sense of how hurt he is and when he feels it all is an attack of self-loathing it is terrible and pitiable.

Don't forgive me, Denny, for what I have done in this—that anyway I know is not what you are writing about. Jess says it was in my high blood pressure—. . . . well, that may account for the writing of the piece in 1964, but what is at issue in my mind is that in 1969 I decided on sending it to *Stony Brook*. And the underlying streak of going out for the kill in critical attack has been detected at other times. Evidently I view the arena of criticism as open season.

March 17/

The writing of this letter was so vividly present—and that I wanted to return with a perspective after a few days—that I had no idea almost three weeks had past! This morning at last, other work having cleared (a Preface for Grossinger's *Ecological Sections*, which meant an intensive week of reading all of Grossinger's published work again—except for the poetry;[5] and two readings to present "Passages" to date, with prefaces discussing the form and performance of the poem) I have a morning to write a piece "Reflections on the Mode of Literary Polemics" (or "Beating the Dog"){.} Dahlberg in *The Leafless American* devotes a chapter, "The Malice of Witlings," to the venom of apprentices, hacks, those who cannot write, poeticals, olympian dwarves, who decimate in reviews . . . in which he refers to a sycophant "San Francisco versifier" who attackt him in "several thousand words, shrieking like a mandrake that has just been plucked" "divulging countless gargantuan defects of mine."[6] Well, the Dahlberg review was not an insult but a reflection upon rereading his work and taking thought upon the persistent rancor and the disclaimers of any such rancor. . . .

Hayden Carruth's opening statement that "these poems imitatively shaped" "arouse an immediate hostility" was the challenge that aroused in me the polemic mode. If there is an announced hostility, then I am there fighting mad in the cause of poems "imitatively shaped"—I've had to fight my way clear of the demand of school teachers, literary critics, etc. for originality, and to insist on the derivative art as I have had to be willing to pretend and be pretentious . . . but the major cause was, of course, not the right of the poet to imitatively shape but the question as to whether Dr. Williams's "staggered tercets" were a personal property—"His alone, one hastens to say"—Carruth's "to think of a single self-respecting American poet who had *dared* to copy this form" makes me boiling mad all over again when I read it. That he has read Williams earnestly and extensively, only makes his view the more reprehensible.

It's there that I got caught; for picking up on Carruth's opening declarations of hostility towards poems in staggered tercets after the model of Williams (in back of which lay his attack on "that fake Tomlinson"), I came on with all hostilities flying. And succeeded only in losing all the discussion of *shape* versus *form*, of what is going on potentially in those "tercets," of whether or not a true form can be "his alone," a private property and not a communal resource, of metrics in Williams line . . . for the sake of a series of gratuitous insults. That you can remember nothing of what I was contending with and only the contentious air itself is proof enuf of this.

Meantimes *Relearning the Alphabet* and, from Hawley, *Summer Poems* have arrived.[7] The "Alphabet" reads richer and stronger with the full mixture of magic and moralizing, exclamation and expression—the letters and sounds of letters giving a subtle shadow-wrap on which to weave. And the title "From a Notebook" gives perspective to the Revolution or Death sequence.[8] (Did you separate the word "night" from its first relation to "Mayor Daley"? anyway, as I read it now no pun appears active in "Daley"). There is a haunting sense of one-ness in the composition of the book, poems like "An Interim" that seem to me to have a loose center are realized to be the gathering nexus for persons of the book; Miss de Courcy Squire is solidly there when she stands among the saints of the Revolution:

And the great saints of outrage—
who have no lawyers,
who have no interim
in which to come and go . . .

rings out as a passage. And is itself a feeling, rather than a claim to feeling. It's part of the declared range you make in *Relearning the Alphabet* that there will be "Hammering the word against my breast" and, in occasional poems like "At David's Grave" or "For Paul and Sally Goodman" the responsibility is assumed to be to the appropriate commiseration rather than to the course of the poem. What comes to my mind is how right you were about my "Earth's Winter Song" to question, I take it, the initial claim to taking feeling in the courage of the young. Tho now, returning to that poem I am not sure that that was what raised questions of sincerity in your mind reading. What does seem clear to me is that the center had better be what is happening in the poem and not what we are feeling about what is happening. The "feeling" of the poem might be MacBeths or Lady MacBeths, in that imagined world that "I" is such a person—not a model but a raw origin of feeling. . . . well, but no sooner said than I realize that a cultivated sensibility (not only MacBeths but Prosperos and Hermiones) is also a raw origin of feeling.

But I belabor this disturbance of the poem's feeling and reality center. Remembering a poem from *Summer Poems*, these are troublings of the moonlight reflecting surface. It's in the projected realm of the poem we've to find the Self the poet comes into being to speak for. "Bullfrogs to Fireflies to Moths" concentrates some realization

> They inhabit their heritage
> pluck the twilight
> pleasurably

whose *dump* deepens with the accumulated debris of world and compassions that thickens the section of "Elegies," out of which flashes of unbearable reality flash.[9] "Moaning and stinking inn hospitals three abed" is not colord by special caressive sight. Is— the confusion of persuasions and actualities—that dump our "heritage," . . . And "pleasurably" focuses one's memory to attention to seek out:

> I stretch in luxury; knowledge of the superb badness
> of my memory gives me a sense of having thick fur,
> a tail, and buried somewhere
> a sweet bone, rotten, enticing
>
>   . . .
> the black taste of life . . .

[the stink of burning meat that in "Passages" goes up from Viet Nam, from the Texas barbeque,★ then from the Roman Church with the burning of the Albigensian martyrs, in the enclosed "Passage" mounts from a roast lamb]

I assure you, Denny, I will watch that I do not repeat the grave error of the mode of the attack on Carruth's views—

Love
Robert

*Last night, reading Sauer on New World edible plants and cooking I found this is an Indian (South American) word *barbacoa*.[10]

AN ADDENDUM

Re "A Critical Difference of View" (*Stony Brook*, 3/4), it seems that there were readers for whom my contentious mode was more vivid than my contentions. Indeed, some read the piece as a personal attack on Hayden Carruth (all the more puzzling since he had written an understanding and admiring article on *Bending the Bow*) and Adrienne Rich, savoring or suffering the injuries inflicted and taking the content as fuel to the fire. It does not help the matter that my attack was impersonal (inspired by a Hayden Carruth and an Adrienne Rich imagined in their authorship of the particular passages at which I had taken offense)—malice is malice. I wanted, along with my attack on their views, to make those views so painful to them that they would be disheartened from voicing them abroad again. There are times when my own views regarding the nature of meaning of poetic form flash forth with intolerance that betokens remnants of the Puritan bigot in me, whipping the poor would-be heretic anthologist or critic publicly in the stocks or driving him forth from the covenant of the righteous into the wilderness.

For those for whom the address "Mr." Carruth and "Miss" Rich already carries the smart of contemptuous courtesy, cross out "Mr." (Mr. Carruth, Mr. Tomlinson), "Dr." (Dr. Williams), and "Miss" and replace with their proper names.

I am often likely, as in this "Critical Difference," to take the stance of the debater in for the kill at the rebuttal before the summing up, needling his opponent until all issues are lost in the sense of personal injury—a leftover from high school debating zeal that might well have been let go by the time I was fifty.

In all cases, with a marking pencil so that the full disgrace for me of the excised passage will remain visible for reference, cross out the following: "What is most probably at issue is that neither Mr. Carruth nor Miss Rich had or have any great concern for the poetry of Pound or Williams" thru to the end of the sentence. The above comes in the category of gratuitous injury, and, moreover, is injurious to my own concerns in the article as well as to my intelligence in the reader's eyes: it should be clear that a critical difference of view does not warrant the assumption that the opponent view does not have back of it "any great concern." Likewise, strike from the copy of the sentence "I am unacquainted with their work so I cannot say," which is not only added insult (for I had meant to make them smart with the sense that once they had voiced the views they had, I would not read further), but also, it must be noted, seriously disqualifies the preceding assumption.

[I am trying out in my writing book a section on acting scourge or punishing power which has carried me from the Puritan zealot to the terrible genius of Siva "Life, which can exist only in destroying life," and in which I want to analyze the configuration of the original attack for its content. For one thing, not only do I have a special identification with Zukofsky, whom I see as superior and as having discretion where I lack it, as well as a most subtle music—but I had, I remember, a special recognition that Tomlinson was the only other poet who was openly derivative as an homage to a line of inspiration I too drew on—(it was a poem in honor of Schönberg, I remember). Both Zukofsky and Tomlinson ran risks I saw myself as running (it is not incidental that Hayden's sense that Tomlinson is "that fake" has an echo in many critic's outrage at my charlatanism—and in my own sense of "craft entering the art" or, very early, of a sleight-of-soul going on).

Can it be incidental that Hayden and Adrienne Rich, when we view them as figures in the configuration, stand as male and female—a syzygy of critical adversaries? And, you will remember both had been poets in the series you edited at Norton—I would not have come to read their volumes otherwise; a misfortune, for I have much less tolerance of poetry which does not suit me than most reviewers and critics. I'm not going to revisit their poetries—I have long ago ridded the library of the volumes—; my rereading the offending reviews only churned up my ire again.

But the fact, as fact, of this literary intolerance, that it can be as extreme as it is with me (even with Jim Harrison, whom I am fond of and who almost wins me over in passages) ought to be laid out on the table. [Hayden in his attack on Tomlinson (in which he does not touch upon the important fact that he thinks Tomlinson a fake) knows that he means to stir up important controversy:

Likely these considerations appear as unhappily abstruse. But they lie at the heart of the current dissatisfactions and disagreements in the "world" of poetry.]

Once the analysis is made, I can derive a section to be publisht which will make principles clear without bringing up again the principles of the action.

Love,
Robert

Dear Robert,   April 4th 1970
                                177 Webster St.
                                East Boston,
                                Mass. 02128

I'm sure you must know how *glad* your letter made me feel. You're beautiful. I'd begun to think you weren't going to write to me. . . . No time to answer properly yet, but I will. And will send new poems. Thanks for yours.

Much, much love from
Denny.

NOTES

1. "A Critical Difference of View," *Stony Brook* 3/4 (1969): 360–63.
2. Hayden Carruth, "Making It New," *Hudson Review* 21 (Summer 1968): 399–412.
3. Charles Olson died on January 10, 1970.
4. Robert Duncan wrote about Elizabeth Drew in "Ideas of the Meaning of Form," collected in *Fictive Certainties*, and about Robin Blaser in "Returning to Les Chimères of Gérard de Neval," *Audit/Poetry* 4 (1967): 41–64.
5. Richard Grossinger, *Solar Journal: Oecological Sections* (Los Angeles: Black Sparrow Press, 1970). Robert Duncan's introduction was inserted inside the book as a separate publication.
6. Edward Dahlberg, *The Leafless American*, ed. Harold Billings (Sausalito, CA: R. Beachmam, 1967).
7. Denise Levertov, *Summer Poems* (Berkeley: Oyez Press, 1970).
8. The phrase "revolution or death" is the first line of "From a Notebook," subsequently Part I of "Staying Alive," and recurs as a refrain in the poem and in the subsequent letters of between Duncan and Levertov.
9. "Elegies" is the first section of *Relearning the Alphabet*.
10. Carl Sauer, *Land and Life: Selections from the Writings of Carl Ortwin Sauer*, ed. John Leighly (Berkeley: University of California Press, 1963).

LYNNE SHARON SCHWARTZ

Thriving on Hardship

I met Hayden Carruth one summer in the mid-1980's. We were teaching at a writers' conference at a university in New York State, the kind of conference where lots of workshops and heady talk about literature are crammed into a few days, and teachers are quickly exhausted, while students drift close by, awaiting the magical words, the revelatory secrets, that might be uttered at any moment. Hayden and I were both feeling discontented and estranged from what was going on around us—I jogged through a nearby cemetery each morning for distraction; I don't know what he did—and our friendship germinated from that shared discontent. Fruitful grounds for friendship, as it turned out. We began corresponding—long detailed letters that continued until his death, punctuated by occasional phone calls and visits. Drawers full of letters by that time; sometimes he enclosed new poems. In time the poems would appear in his books—a dozen or so books after I first met him (and almost a dozen before that)—but when I want to reread them I look for the manuscripts because they feel fresher and more intimate and were addressed to me, even if only on their envelopes.

What I relish particularly in Hayden's poems is how they revel in raw misery. At every stage of life his laments, whether raging, witty, or somber, are so succulent, so vivid, so thoroughly and actively engaged in the wretchedness *du jour.* "Yes, William," he writes to an imaginary friend,

> I've been,
> God knows, a complainer. It was
> either that or silence. Poets
> are deprived of stoicism.

They are deprived of stoicism because they must tell the truth as they feel it, emotional and intellectual accuracy, to Hayden, having been a moral imperative, from the proper placement of a comma to the proper exposition of current political reality. ("Let us speak plainly," he addresses the President in "Complaint and Petition": You are/ deviously and corruptly manipulating/ events in order to create war.")

Sorrow and travail attended him faithfully throughout his life, and in return for their companionship he portrayed them with the attentive, obsessive scrutiny that memoirists use for their close friends and relations. In mid-life he reports,

> I am fifty-three going on fifty-four,
> a rotten time of life. My end-of-winter clothes
>> are threadbare, my boots cracked, and how
>>> astonishing to see
>
> my back, like that figure in Rembrandt's drawing,
> bent.

But what time of life has not its own variety of rottenness? "The purposelessness of it all, of existence as such," he tells us in *Reluctantly*, a collection of autobiographical essays, "had struck me at so early an age that I have no idea when it happened or how." He suffered intermittently from mental disorders that had him in and out of institutions, as well as from alcoholism and the more commonplace sorts of anguish. In later years he was devastatingly bitter or amusing, giving us some of his best "loquacious stammering," on the humiliations of old age.

And yet this is the same poet who, in his rotten fifties, writes, "I can't/ help it, I have so loved/ this world." Who, decades later, rediscovering love—genuine this time, he assures us and himself—exults in "the stupendousness/ of life." Who at age 75 writes a poem of gratitude:

> My prayers have been answered, if they were prayers.
>   I live.
>   . . . .
>   I prayed. Then on paper I wrote
> Some of the words I said, which are these poems.

Even after his suicide attempt, recounted in *Reluctantly*, a rare happiness came over him as he returned from the "blackness," death's entryway, a place he found "not at all uncomfortable but quite the contrary: it was happy. . . . in the sense of *blissful*, a replete contentedness. It was a state of mind I had never experienced before. . . .

but it was present in my mind clearly and strongly when I first came to. And it has been present ever since, it has become part of my being. . . . I was high on life, my recovered life."

So he is a poet of contradiction, and a contradiction entirely natural and universal: despair coupled with the will to continue, disgust at what the world offers coupled with curiosity and hope about what it will turn up next, even when he had been at the point of saying farewell. The capacity to feel and acknowledge extremes of pain evidently coexists with—or engenders—the capacity for extremes of joy as well.

At the close of the conference where we met there was a big dinner for students and faculty. Hayden and I sat together, and next to us sat a young man who wrote fiction (and very shortly afterwards died of AIDS). He asked us what percentage of human experience could be expressed in language. Ninety percent, I answered thoughtlessly. Ten percent, said Hayden, grimly. I've always remembered this. When I reread his poems now I think of the ninety percent submerged—all that ineffability, intractable yet somehow evoked by the fraction on the page, like a scent, a vapor or effluvia rising from a few grains of a potent spice.

Over and over in the voluminous work of this self-proclaimed "language-driven" poet, for whom "appearance is nothing until it has been spoken and written," comes the notion of the failure of words: "Insurmountable the uselessness of words." In "On Being Asked to Write a Poem Against the War in Vietnam," he recalls earlier wars he's lived through and earlier poems deploring them,

> and not one
> breath was restored
> to one
>
> shattered throat
> mans womans or childs
> not one not
>
> one
> but death went on and on. . . .

Besides the futility of words, he mourns their incapacity to render what he so desperately wants rendered. That doesn't deter him, though, from attempting the most recalcitrant and necessary subjects, those least likely to yield to language, for example, the death of his mother and the death of his daughter. Near the opening of the poem about the latter, "Dearest M—," a "gush of words, this surging elegy," he frankly admits defeat:

> The immensity of what should be said
>   defeats me. Language
> like a dismasted hulk at sea is overwhelmed
> and founders.

That said, he goes on to conjure up his daughter Martha from the instant of her birth through her years of youth and beauty, her loves and her painting, her triumphs, and the indignities of her illness. Language may be abysmally inadequate, but it is the single thing he securely possesses and inhabits, and so he deploys it not merely with technical skill but with valor: he wrestles with the inaccessible and wins, so far as that is possible.

The pain he feels at the death of his mother is of a different sort. The agony is less pure, less unitary, more tangled in a skein of ancient griefs and grievances, moments of ambiguous intimacy and gaps of misunderstanding. His mother suffered terribly for three years, and his elegy, "Mother," does not neglect the physical details. But what galls him most is her loss of language, the mystery of what she might still know, what form of consciousness might remain in her "half-dead mind." "You in your language broken, stammering, whole aggregates of once-luminous words blown out." Above all, "Was your damaged brain the same as a damaged soul?" This is the mystery whose sting does not relent, the essential riddle whose answer will never come:

> As if you were an animal somehow granted the power to know
>   but not to think,
> Or as if you were a philosopher suddenly deprived of every faculty
>   except
> Original fear and pathos. I cannot surmise a state of being more
>   inconsonant
> With human consciousness.

I like that "surmise," that "inconsonant." In the midst of passionate grief, the poet's indefatigable intellect goes chugging on, prying at the enigma at the center of his own life and work. How much of what we know is in our words? What do we know beyond words and how can we know or say it? How much can a mind without words comprehend? And finally, what is there to know? He brooded on this always: witness an earlier poem, "Cowshed Blues":

in the mystery of the word

is a force
contained but not expressed—
spoken and unexplained

for meaning falls away
as the stars in their spirals
fall from the void of creation

Nevertheless, he was the most prolific and articulate of contemporary poets; in the face of his own pessimism, he never stopped returning to language, the unreliable ally who would not abandon him, whom he could count on for ten percent of what he needed.

Critics have noted the variety of Hayden Carruth's work, in style, form, breadth and range of themes—love, rural life, war, jazz, the idea of community and its assault by the current "sanctification of avarice" are only a few. The work that draws me most, regardless of subject, is that of his last two decades, perhaps because it was written while I knew him. But more, I think, because it has the stamp and tone of ripened experience: a certain ease and confident looseness, a relaxation even when the poems are in a formal mode, as if the rigors of poetry have been so well absorbed that the poet writes effortlessly, rigor already part of his musculature and neural pathways; none of the usual barriers or anxieties interfere with the direct transference of emotion and thought into syllable and rhythm. Or at least they don't seem to: Hayden compared the writing of poetry, on his dark days, to squeezing hardened glue from a tube, though the reader would never know it. Certainly not in "Agenda at 74," a funny catalogue of an old man's fragmented day spent in trivial activities (except maybe for "write President," "write congressmen," and "write letter to the editor") linked by the repetition of "tap barometer," a compulsive futile checking to see what the weather—no doubt inner as well as cosmic—has in store.

Also notably unglue-like is the limpid unfurling of words in "A Few Dilapidated Arias," the last group of poems from his latest collection, *Toward the Distant Islands,* spanning work from 1959 to 2005. Here, with deceptive casualness, the poet unburdens his mind—as active as his physical abilities are curtailed—after a fallow spell. The poems have the nonchalance of cultivated skill associated with the "late style" of the great poets and composers, though not their frequently imputed serenity or resignation. They open with a dazzling image and move from strength to strength like a Brahms sonata, now thundering, now muted, now wistful:

> And thus the morning has descended. Slowly like
> a tremulous lady down the great stairs of the East.
> What I notice is language pressing in my mind,
> surprising me, as in those times when I made poems
> like sweet tarts cooling on the windowsill of a
> studio in the woods. . . .
>
> So let the sentences unfold again, like a measuring rule
> jerked into angled shapes that nevertheless trace
> the line onward toward resolution. Let them be
> a little sonorous, but only a little.

Even earlier, he bemoaned his own "slipping." "Song: Luxury," written in his mere sixties, declares:

> Even to think
> of installing an air-conditioner
> in his car is
> to the old man a
> shame and hurt,
> who throve on hardship.

"Who throve on hardship" becomes the pungent closing refrain of each of the four stanzas; it echoes the life of arduous labor described in *Reluctantly,* when he lived with his wife and son in rural Vermont and did physical work all day, for himself and his neighbors, then various sorts of editorial work-for-hire all night, for extra money, then wrote poems in what time remained. In that essay he urges hardship on young writers, especially graduate students poised to enter the relative ease of the academic world. "If your life is easy, your writing will be slack and purposeless. . . . You need difficulty, you need necessity. And it isn't a paradox that you can choose necessity, can actually create necessity, if you seek the right objectives; not the great metaphysical necessity, but your own personal necessity; and it will be no less inexorable because you have chosen it. Once you are in it, your writing will be in it too." This in opposition to young writers' customary view that the academic life will leave them "time to write." Time, yes, but what intensity? Write out of what urgency, if not the press of practical necessity against passionate desire?

The most poignant and scrupulous poem about old age is "In the Long Hall," from the 1996 collection, *Scrambled Eggs & Whiskey,* an extended metaphor for writing poetry as well as watching one's life ravel and unravel with the passage of time:

> On his knees he was weaving a tapestry
> which was unraveling behind him. At first
> he didn't mind it; the work was flawed,
> loose ends, broken threads, a pattern
> he could not control; but as his skill
> improved he began to resent the way
> his tapestry was undoing itself.
> He resolved not to look back
> but to keep going ahead, as he did
> successfully for a long time. Still
> later, however, he began to notice
> that the part of the tapestry in front
> of him was unraveling too; threads
> he had just knotted became loose.
> He tied them again. But before long
> he could not keep up, his hands
> were too slow, his fingers too weak.
> The unraveling in front pushed
> him toward the unraveling in back
> until he found himself isolated
> on a small part of the tapestry whose
> pattern he could not see because
> it was beneath his own body. He spun
> this way and that. He worked as fast as
> he could with trembling fingers
> in futility, in frenzy, in despair.

But to offset the futility and despair the aged artist feels on contemplating his work, Hayden's late poems introduce an unexpected theme: romantic love. Not new, for he often wrote of love before, in *The Sleeping Beauty* and elsewhere, but now refreshed and revivified. Love has come once more, surprising him, eliciting a self that is new as well. He welcomes love with unabashed gratitude and wonderment, in a series of sonnets from the late 1980's, some colloquial and others highly formal, evoking Wyatt and Donne. "More and more I believe the age demands/ incertitude," and of course he means his own advanced age as well as the age in which we all uneasily reside.

> I am no one. Yet your hands
> touching, word-like, can make a person. Who
> is this strange new myself? Woman, do we know
> the I of love that you in love bestow?

Inevitably, poems written in old age will be about approaching death, but few treat death in the same breath as erotic love, as Hayden does in "Testament," from *Scrambled Eggs & Whiskey*. In fluid language and easeful music, he offers the conventional image of the hourglass to represent life seeping away, then puts that image to entirely original and startling use:

> Yet not only our lives drift down. The stuff
> of ego with which we began, the mass
> in the upper chamber, filters away
> as love accumulates below. Now
> I am almost entirely love.

What can he leave his wife, he wonders, as "the sands/ in the upper glass grow few."

> All our embracings?
> I know millions of these will be still
> unspent when the last grain of sand
> falls with its whisper, its inconsequence
> on the mountain of my love below.

Words may be maddeningly inadequate, and yet the lover's hands that "make a person" are "word-like." Words can make a person; they certainly made this poet. And he in turn made the poems that are "a gift, a bestowal/. . . . what instinct is for animals, a continuing and chiefly unthought corroboration of essence." This is from "The Impossible Indispensability of the Ars Poetica," another love poem, where he muses on what a poem is and is not. In the end, it is the elusive, not the articulated, aspect of poetry that enthralls him:

       . . . it has almost the quality of disappearance
In its cage of visibility. It disperses among the words. It is a fluidity,
    a vapor, of love.

The negative, disappearing quality of poetry returns us to the
ineffable, Hayden Carruth's true habitation, the vast tracts of consciousness that words cannot begin to clarify. This fluidity, this vapor
of love, he hovers over in the extraordinary "Words in a Certain
Appropriate Mode," a poem which in its strategy is as evanescent as
trying to catch a wisp of smoke in the hand, and yet precise in its
limning of the effort. It is about an indefinable locale in consciousness, the nothingness within that contains the fullness of the inexpressible world, perhaps like the blackness of the near-death moment from which he emerged so strangely happy:

In the everywhere that is nowhere
Neither the inside nor the outside
. . . .
Where one is neither alone
Nor not alone, where cognition seeps
Jactatively away like the falling tide
If there were a tide, and what is left
Is nothing, or is the everything that keeps
Its undifferentiated unreality
. . . .
Where there is neither breath nor air
The place without locality, the locality

With neither extension nor intention
But there in the weightless fall
. . . .
Without leaf or star or water or stone
Without light, without sound
                    anywhere, anywhere . . .

CAROLYN KIZER

Others Call It God

In the early sixties, when I was editing *Poetry Northwest,* I received a group of poems from Hayden Carruth, including a sonnet called, "Ontological Episode of the Asylum." Although I had read a number of his poems and some of his criticism with admiration, I did not know Carruth personally. But this group of poems was the beginning of a friendship which has remained steadfast ever since. The sonnet, in particular, moved me then—to the point where I almost instantly memorized it—and moves me now, not only because the form is perfectly subsumed in the subject but because it summed up my own feelings about belief:

> The boobyhatch's bars, the guards, the nurses,
> The illimitable locks and keys are all arranged
> To thwart the hand that continually rehearses
> Its ending stroke and raise a barricade
> Against destruction-seeking resolution.
> Many of us in there would have given all
> (But we had nothing) for one small razor blade
> Or seventy grams of the comforting amytal.
>
> So I went down in the attitude of prayer,
> Yes, to my knees on the cold floor of my cell,
> Humped in a corner, a bird with a broken wing,
> And asked and asked as fervently and well
> As I could guess to do for light in the mists
> Of death, until I learned God doesn't care.
> Not only that, he doesn't care at all,
> One way or the other. That is why he exists.

I am surely not the only person to be reminded of the famous passage in William James's *The Varieties of Religious Experience,* where he speaks in the guise of a Frenchman "in a bad nervous condition." Later, he confessed that this had been his own experience:

While in this state of philosophic pessimism and general depression of spirits about my prospects, I went one evening into a dressing-room in the twilight to procure some article that was there; when suddenly there fell upon me without warning, just as if it came out of the darkness, a horrible fear of my own existence. Simultaneously there arose in my mind the image of an epileptic patient whom I had seen in the asylum, a black-haired youth with greenish skin, entirely idiotic, who used to sit all day on one of the benches, or rather shelves against the wall, with his knees drawn up against his chin. . . . This image and my fear entered into a species of combination with each other. *That shape am I*, I felt, potentially. Nothing that I possess can defend me against that fate, if the hour for it should strike for me as it struck for him. . . . I have always thought that this experience of melancholia of mine had a religious bearing.

On responding to a question of himself by himself, James added, "I mean that the fear was so invasive and powerful that if I had not clung to scripture—texts like 'The eternal God is my refuge,' etc., 'Come unto me, all ye that labor and are heavy laden,' etc., I think I should have grown really insane."

Of course calling on God in extremis is not unique to poets and philosophers, but to pray without any expectation of being heard or being helped is perhaps more unusual. It could even be considered an act of heroism, as indeed Carruth calls it in another poem, "Once and Again," written more than a dozen years later, in a situation similar to that of the sonnet:

> To believe in the God
> who does not exist is a heroism of faith, much needed in these
>   times,
> I agree, I know, especially since the hero is and must always be
> unrecognized. But to love the God that does not exist, to love the
>   love
> that does not exist, this is more than heroism, it is perhaps almost
> saintliness, such as we can know it. To discover and to hold, to
>   resurrect
> an idea for its own sake. . . .

To me, Carruth exaggerates the element of heroism and "perhaps almost saintliness" in this gratuitous love of God, and underestimates the neurotic/creative act of the imagination which makes it possible. Elsewhere in *The Varieties of Religious Experience,* James makes the point that, "Few of us are not in some ways infirm, or even diseased; and our very infirmities help us unexpectedly." "If there were such a thing as inspiration from a higher realm, it might well be that the neurotic temperament would furnish the chief condition of the requisite receptivity." From the pit of our desperation we call out to God, even if we don't believe in him, and in the state of receptivity engendered by fear, particularly fear of the cosmos, we may even dream of a response, although not a personal one, and not a comforting one. The sole comfort comes from the act of prayer itself.

Later, James quotes Sabatier, the "liberal French theologian," perhaps the inspiration for James's imaginary Frenchman, in regard to prayer: "Religion is nothing if it be not the vital act by which the entire mind seeks to save itself by clinging to the principle from which it draws its life. This act is prayer, by which term I understand no vain exercise of words, no mere repetition of certain sacred formulae, but the very movement itself of the soul. . . . Wherever the interior prayer is lacking, there is no religion; wherever, on the other hand, the prayer rises and stirs the soul, even in the absence of forms or doctrines, we have living religion." Sabatier, however, would not agree with Carruth because he believed that prayer was a putting of one's self into a personal relation with a mysterious power, while the prayers of unbelieving believers go out to an indifferent God, a God who may not exist at all except as we pray to It.

At the end of his book, James remarks that the God whom science recognizes "must be a God of universal laws exclusively, a God who does a wholesale, not a retail business. He cannot accommodate his processes to the convenience of individuals." "Convenience" is perhaps too casual a word to describe the emotions of those who, in primal panic, fall on their knees in the desperate hope that God will respond and save. Carruth is harsh in his response to John Berryman's late conversion to belief in a personal God, Berryman, too, an alcoholic and—to use Carruth's own word about himself—"crazy." For most of his life Berryman had believed in a transcendent God—"a formal principle of sorts holding the vast complicated harmony of the universe together." This view is rather like the speculative theology of Empedocles, who spoke of God as "a sacred and unutterable mind, flashing through the whole world with rapid thought." Near his end, in the sixth of his "Eleven Addresses to the Lord," Berryman began:

Under new management, Your majesty:
Thine. I have solo'd mine since childhood, since
my father's suicide when I was twelve
blew out my most bright candle faith, and look at me . . .

My double nature fused in that point of time
three weeks ago day before yesterday.
Now, brooding thro' a history of the early Church
I identify with everybody, even the heresiarchs.

Carruth was infuriated with the precise dating of Berryman's revelation, and refused to believe "this boasting, equivocating secularist," when he reviewed *Love & Fame* in *The Nation*. (Are we least sympathetic with those who share some of our darkest failings?)

Perhaps we might agree with one of James's critics who said that "his need to believe was tantamount to having faith" (but this is an attempt to clarify what James deliberately chose to keep obscure). Or, if we cannot agree, we may at least sympathize with those who feel that, in order to stave off insanity, they require some form of belief. Carruth goes out of his way to deny his own belief, but all the same he turns to God when he is "crazy" and only then.

The following is from *The Bloomingdale Papers,* the poems of his craziness, published after the fact in 1975:

Save me, O God; for the waters are come in
    unto my soul.

I sink in deep mire, where there is no standing:
I am come into deep waters, where the floods
    overflow me.
I am weary of my crying: my throat is dried:
    mine eyes fail . . .

Deliver me out of the mire, and let me not sink:
let me be delivered from them that hate me,
and out of the deep waters.

Let not the waterflood overflow me, neither
    let the deep swallow me up,
    and let not the pit
    shut her mouth upon me.

(Carruth's own version of the 69th Psalm,
verses 1–3, 14–16)

In a review in *Harper's* in 1976, Carruth says that "the answer to grief is God, but God does not answer." What then are we to make of his denial of belief coupled with his cries to cold heaven?

In an essay called "Who I Am, 1," he says, speaking of critics, that "they will not consider the work of art as *a transaction between the artist's soul and God*—substitute whatever other two words you like. But that's what it is." (My italics.) I think we must focus on the artist negotiating with his angel—his muse—rather than simply as a man pleading with God, as in the chant of the psalmist quoted above.

In another essay called "The Act of Love: Poetry and Personality," also published in 1976, Carruth restates a position he had taken earlier, in an essay on Robert Lowell: "The poet," he says, "was engaged in the conversion of crude experience into personality through metaphor and the other disciplines of the instrumental imagination," using the term "personality" to mean "the whole individual subjectivity, the spirit-body-soul."

I'm not entirely happy with Carruth's use of the term *personality* (in fact when I first typed the title of this essay I freudianly left off half of it: Poetry and Personality). Of course we are in semantic difficulties, as is almost invariably the case when attempting to talk of matters spiritual and metaphysical. There is no dictionary of personality which includes the entity spirit-body-soul, but it's a question of who is master here, and in this case we must concede that Carruth is. But he does seem to leave out a vital step, *the* vital step of the process, which is the conversion of crude experience into the final product, which is art. I find that a great deal of the poetry being written today is hung up on precisely that hook: personality, whether interpreted narrowly or in the broadest sense; and that the act of transcendence never takes place because the personality intervenes.

But let us go along with Carruth as he expands his definition. He says, further, that personality is universal and relative; it exists in every consciousness. "Personality is a phenomenon of pure existence and occurs in what have been called our existential moments, our moments outside time." The existential moment for the poet occurs when she or he is "intensely engaged in a poem, spontaneously engendering imagery and verbal compounds from the imaginative structures of remembered experience. . . . It is a spiritual happening—at least I do not know what else to call it." Nor do I.

Carruth asserts again that he is not a religious person. He cannot "project this concept of spirit and personality onto any traditional religion that I know, although analogues and affinities occur in many of them." Further, he says that he uses the word "spiritual" to mean "the substance of feeling when personality passes out of time's determinants and into pure essence, which I have called eternity; and in poems I have spoken of meetings there with the holy spirit, though my meaning has not been the same one that Christians use when they refer to the third attribute of the Trinity." "Chiefly I think of the transcendence of personality as a process of innerness, and of the holy spirit as my own." (My own preference would be to use "identity," even spiritual identity, rather than personality. Moreover, I don't see how Carruth can call the holy spirit "my own" when he has supposedly transcended his personality.)

But by now I believe that we have circled back to where we started: with Carruth's poems. In his shying away from the thought that he is a religious man, or a man who can relate to a form of traditional religion, he is in a sense contradicting his own poems, which seem to tell a different story. How many of these defiant rejections of any whiff of traditional faith might have been rendered unnecessary—and conserving of psychic energy—if we, like the American Indians before us, believed in and called upon The Great Spirit, rather than God!

Poetry is not prayer, but it is not not prayer. Prayer is not often poetry, but the greatest prayers are poems. To me, the spiritual is the spiritual, no matter how we quibble over terminology, qualify it or attempt to redefine it. Spirituality is identical with, and achieved through, an act of love. Carruth says as much at the close of his essay: "What I have in mind is what has been called in other places the 'aesthetic emotion,' the feeling that overlies substance and converts substance, whether beautiful or ugly, into something else. Sometimes this 'something else' has been called beauty, but the term is likely to be misunderstood" (like all other terms we have been using). "I prefer to call it spiritual love, the state of being of a pure existence, and the aesthetic emotion is the experience of that state."

However, none of these aesthetic impulses, no matter what their degree of spirituality, can succeed in warding off that cosmic fear. When, in the night, it overtakes us, we turn instinctively to prayer, to the great spirit who is within us. As for me, I pray a good deal, even when I'm not scared or miserable. And one of the people I pray for, nearly every day, is my dear friend, Hayden Carruth. God may not listen or care, one way or the other. But it exists.

4. *Innovator—creator of multiple poetic forms like the "paragraphs," the "georgics," the Vermont poems, and the epic poems*

innovator, N. One who introduces novelties, or who makes changes by introducing something new.

        . . . but Im no Christian
and first becomes last coherence fails
connections cherished 50 years and alls
lost no art more Ill write what I want how I want
dont bug me about my words
the vision is cold chaos and I need what warmth
my old mind knows . . .

        —HC, "Paragraphs, 6"

Been reading your book, thinking
T'aint what you say, it's
the way you say it. Been readin
your book, hearin your say.

Heard Oliver write that when I was young.
Never got over the way his horn sang.

I been seekin and failin all these last years.
I been seekin and failin all these last years.
Failin to give up, to give up old fears.
Seekin to wake up with true words to say,
wakin all night and sleepin all day.

Been reading your book, thinkin
it's good. Every note yours.
Been hearin you jam. Not
just good, plain better than.

T'aint just what you say, it's
the how that you say it:
the slow and the lonely, the hot
and the glad. Hayd, lemme tell you,
you got it bad. You hit right notes
and still make 'em want,
when you hit a wrong note
you let it go sad.

Though a while back I had it made.
Though I'd made it quite a while back.
Know now I never. Not even ever.
Only now startin, over and over.

You're in B flat in a world off key,
playin your sound, you say what you hear,
the cool and the hot notes, the slurred
and the held, the music
of being: old blues getting old.

With all of the All-Stars,
you're *Downbeat*'s main man.

After you've gone
you'll still be around.

—Philip Booth, *Seneca Review,* 1990

MARILYN HACKER

Hayden Carruth

> *Where I am is the cosmic individual. Nothing grand, nothing ro-*
> *mantic. A duck blown out to sea and still squawking.*
> —HC, "FRAGMENTS OF AN AUTOBIOGRAPHY"

In many ways, Hayden Carruth is a quintessentially American poet,
his work precisely what an exacting European reader would expect
or wish an American poet to have written. Or at least, that is my
inference as a transatlantic American. Carruth is rooted in particular
American landscapes, specifically Vermont and upstate New York
(he was born in Connecticut in 1921) and these locations have not
only been central to (and productive of) his work; they have been
the subjects of his most profound poetic analyses and meditations—as well as the necessary settings of dramatic monologues and
narratives. Whereas Robert Frost gave his readers New England in
a kind of fixed, trans-historical and almost theatrical present (that of
the early twentieth century), Carruth's excavations examine the
sociopolitical, literary, even geological histories of his locales, and
project them into a very contemporary present and, by implication,
into a pessimistically-viewed future. The implications of Carruth's
poetry are never limited by a locale: its specificity is its point of
departure for a humanist universality; its accessibility and its creation of complex personae, engaging or rebarbative, are the basis for
the lyrical complexity of its deployment of words, syntax, and metrical music.

Though Carruth has never been an urban poet, jazz, that most
urban and American of art forms, informs his work from myriad
directions, whether that be the re-creation of a legendary but historical jam session in 1944 (at which he was not present), a comic-
bawdy neo-Greek myth of the newborn Hermes inventing the
saxophone in Harlem, or in the application of jazz's techniques of
improvisation upon received melodies/forms to numerous and varied poems. He has been an enthusiastic amateur jazz and classical
clarinetist. *Suicides and Jazzers* is one of his books of critical essays;

Doctor Jazz is his most recent book of poems, and the title of *Scrambled Eggs & Whiskey,* his 1996 National Book Award–winning collection, refers to a jazz group's five AM breakfast after an all-night set.

For a variety of reasons, including agoraphobia, Carruth, except for his Army stint in World War II, has remained almost consistently in the United States, in his corner of it—unlike his near-contemporaries of the previous decade, Lowell and Bishop, and his coevals James Wright, Carolyn Kizer, and James Merrill, all of whose "cosmopolitanism" counterpoints their American identities (and Bishop was Canadian by birth) at many turns. Nor did Carruth emerge from an "Ivy League" university. Yet the polymath breadth and depth of his knowledge, whether it be of prosody, the Napoleonic wars, the techniques of small farming, the influence of the troubadours and the Lingua d'Oc on Western civilization, geology, classical Chinese poetry or, again, jazz, is everywhere evident in his poems and essays, without ever assuming the boys' club preciosity I sometimes associate with Pound or Lowell. Whatever information is imparted by Carruth is there as part of the flesh and bones of the poem.

Carruth gives us ample facts about his own life and intellectual history in his poems, and in several of his essay collections, notably *Suicides and Jazzers* and *Reluctantly* (Copper Canyon Press, 1998): from childhood in Connecticut, a journalist grandfather, precocity in a state school accompanied by a creditable performance as an ordinary small boy, to a vivid description of the converted Vermont cowshed that was his studio for decades, his experience of fatherhood, and the explicit details of a 1988 suicide attempt. Yet even if the "confessional" school actually existed (a fact I'd question) his work in poetry, at least after the 1950s, is of another vein, in which the individual persona is primarily the vehicle of observation and transformation. The opening of "Essay on Stone" (1978) is typical of Carruth: the title indicating some exposition, the modified alcaic stanza, the solid location, the gruff and local speaker letting us know quickly enough that there will be a counterpoint between a fixed place and season and the mental traveler's departures:

> April abomination, that's what I call
> this wet snow sneaking down day after day,
>   down the edges of air, when we
>   were primed for spring.

> The flowers of May will come next week—in theory.
> And I suppose that witty sentimentalist,
>   Heine, saw the same snow falling
>   in the North Sea

Carruth has always been, among his many other attributes, a "nature poet," that is, a poet who observes the natural world around him keenly, and makes use of that fine observation—which is of the same order as his observation of the interworkings of a jazz quintet, or of a the body of a woman standing in his bedroom's moonlight. He knows the way light in his meadow changes daily with the mutable seasons, the names of its wildflowers, the lives of its trees, as well as the precise actions and physical stresses required to split a cord of wood with an axe—the subject or occasion of several poems. But the observation of nature rendered into a lyric is rarely the goal of his poems. It is the intersection of human consciousness (another aspect of "nature," after all, upon which the idea of "Nature" depends) with tree, stone, rock, river, meadow: the human mind observing its own divagations—whether it's the interrogation of Heine in the poem above, or a reflection on the processes that lead to the beauty, formality, and strangeness of the "natural."

> The snow sculpts this object,
> a snow-tree, and does it
> neither by carving nor
> by molding, for there is
> a third way nature knows
> and a few men besides
> (who will not give themselves
> to the controversies
> of theorists) . . .
>
>   ("Loneliness, an Outburst of Hexasyllables")

Carruth is one of the most prolific poets of his generation. Writing this I think of another poet, eight years his senior, Muriel Rukeyser, equally polymath, equally prolific, equally political, and equally out of the "mainstream" critical eye. While they were marked, as is any American poet born after 1910, by the seismic shock of Modernism, their work cannot be placed easily either in any of its currents or in the counter-current represented by lyricists like Millay or Randall Jarrell. This may have something to do with the paucity of criticism devoted to their work: in Rukeyser's case, a silence that lasted through the McCarthy era and the ascendance of the New Criticism till the women's movement; in Carruth's case, an inadequacy of response that seems to continue today. Rukeyser was a democratic socialist and urban as Carruth is rural; Carruth, the countryman, is a self-proclaimed anarchist. She was an activist and, I believe, an optimist about human possibility. He, prevented by agoraphobia and temperament from extra-literary political action other than sheltering draft resisters in the 1960s, thinks otherwise:

Now tell me if we don't need a revolution! Black
is the color of my only flag/
                                        and of man's hope.
Will revolution bring the farms back?
Gone, gone. The only crop
this valley will grow now is the great landwrack,
breakage, erosion, garbage, trash, gimcrack.
We burn it. The stink trails in the air . . .
. . . .
. . . . .his fate
a need without a hope: the will to resist.
The State is universal, the Universe is a state.
Now ask me if I am really an anarchist.

This is from the twenty-second of a series of twenty-eight "Paragraphs" written in the late 1970s (which, I might amend, finishes with the apotheosis of the five-man jazz recording session in 1944 that could be taken to contradict the implications of the above). The "paragraph" is one of Carruth's many prosodic inventions, one of which he has made use frequently over some forty-five years in four significant sequences.

Carruth is the author of, by my count, twenty-three books of poems, not counting Selected or Collected volumes, a novel, and six collections of essays. These last include a thoroughly idiosyncratic "meditation" on Camus' *The Stranger,* published in 1965, which resembles a contemporary French "autofiction" more than a critical essay, in which a surrogate of the writer interacts with fictional and fictionalized characters—here, Camus himself and characters from Camus' other novels. (Again as a point of reference Rukeyser's books on Wendell Wilkie and the physicist Willard Gibbs: these are two poets for whom encounters, on the page, with minds and ways of thinking different from their own have been essential.)

Carruth is a virtuoso of English prosody and all those metrics and strategies which can be transposed to English. Unlike some of his friends and contemporaries, he does not seem to have had a "conversion experience" moving him from fixed to open forms (I notice now that his compendium collections do not include much work written before his mid-thirties), but has used both fluently and to the strongest effect from the outset. Furthermore, though he is an accomplished sonneteer and has frequently worked with terza rima, nonce forms, from the simplest to the most complex, have been the instrument and source of much of his strongest work. "Loneliness: An Outburst of Hexasyllables," quoted above, is an up-country dark night of the soul following the speaker from dusk till dawn in deepest winter in seventy-odd six-syllable lines. I've also mentioned the "paragraph." This is a form Carruth devised in 1957 during internment in a mental hospital, to keep himself sane, one gathers, and the first sequence he produced in the form, on that occasion, is called "The Asylum." The "paragraph" is a fifteen-line poem, which, like a sonnet, can most often either stand alone or work in sequence. It has a fixed rhyme scheme, and a fixed variation in the number of stresses per line (it is accentual rather than accentual-syllabic, though there is quite a bit of not-necessarily inadvertent iambic pentameter in most of them). With the letter representing rhyme and the numeral the number of stresses, the template would look like this:

5A A carpet raveling on the loom a girl
5B with a widowspeak and misty legs a moon
4A like a fisheye rising from a pool
3B a black longwinging loon
5A bursting afire in the sunset a torn sail
5A groveling in a wave a whisper in a stairwell
4C a helmet upturned in the black rain
4C and later a star reflected on a coin
5D glimmering on seastones a sound of motors
3E and machineguns
5D in the dawn a kiss and candleflame a sonata
4E for clarinet a bone cracking a woman
5F wearing a blue veil and in kashan a room
5E where the little darkeyed weaving girls lay down
5F and died a carpet raveling on a loom.

The poem I've used to illustrate the template is from "Contra Mortem," a sequence of thirty paragraphs written in 1966, in which

Carruth "loosened" his own strict form somewhat (one could read lines 8 and 12 as having five stresses) as well as being freer with punctuation, which here follows the trajectory of a free-associative but directed thought-and-image process.

The apotheosis of the paragraph as form and as the fueling energy of a book-length poem came with *The Sleeping Beauty,* written between 1970 and 1980 (reissued by Copper Canyon Press in 1990). This 125-poem sequence uses the fairy/folktale figure, connected to Carruth initially by the name of his third wife, Rose Marie Dorn (the *Dornröschen,* Briar Rose, is the Sleeping Beauty in German) as a focal point for a meditation on history, here not-entirely aleatorically embodied by a series of emblematic *H*-initialed figures, including Heraclitus, Hermes, Hector, Hölderlin, Hegel, Hitler—and of course Hayden—all episodes in the Beauty-persona's dream. But there are several other fugal, contrapuntal themes threading the sequence: the narrator's dialogue with a probably-revenant old Vermont farmer named Amos; and a series of monologues in female voices—Lilith; a foot-bound Chinese lady of sixteen; a Puritan poet whose husband burns her writings; Bessie Smith. *The Sleeping Beauty* is in fact also a profound consideration of gender and its permutations, its wounds, in each human being, in particular in the Jungian sense of anima/animus, response of and to the "opposite" within each of us, whatever our sexuality. It is perhaps not accidental that the sequence was written during the rise of the "second wave" of the American and British feminist movement (feminist poets Carolyn Kizer and Adrienne Rich are among Carruth's oldest friends). Yet I have never seen it analyzed in that context: a male poet's response to and attempt to integrate the damages of gender polarity—except by Kizer, who wrote of it, upon its publication in 1982, "Those two great contemporary issues, recognition of women and respect for our fragile world, are bound together in profound unity."

Another of Carruth's tours de force is the eminently readable *Asphalt Georgics* (New Directions, 1985). These are poems about the lower-middle-class white inhabitants of the prefabricated towns clustered around strip malls in upstate New York, largely dramatic monologues. Again Carruth invents a form: in this case quatrains of alternating eight- and six-syllable lines, with the second and fourth rhyming, often deliberately using hyphenations in the rhyme lines. At times the poet-persona intervenes; in the opening, longest "georgic," "Names," there's a constant metamorphosis. A husband driving to the mall:

. . . Friendly and Ponderosa
looked o.k., but Carvel
was dilapidated, and Mis-
ter Donut had a hell

of a big jagged hole through both
sides of its glass sign. I
saw the killdeer running that has
her nest next to the high-

way on the gravel strip . . .

is eventually a political prisoner caged in a steel box in Latin America:

My name was Julio. But now
by enormous effort
I have transformed my consciousness
to the gleam of consort-

ed light that scintillates round the
dome of gold on the ca-
thedral all day at the top of
the capital plaza.

My name is Santa Julia.

his/her out-of the body state

. . . . attainable by
all those who must forget

themselves completely and absolutely in order to
pass through and beyond the pain that
surpasses knowing . . .

In "Marge," Carruth makes a different kind of audacious narrative move. In this monologue, an isolated sixty-year-old ex-alcoholic recounts the story of a lively friendship between the speaker and an older woman, his "landlady," whose death at eighty-five has left him desolate and destitute. But the woman, from her name, and the account of her illness and death, is Carruth's mother (her own life and prolonged death elegized in a long poem written in 1981) who died when the poet was sixty. The details of "Charlie Spaid's" recovery are congruent with Carruth's, though the rest of the persona's life is presumably invented. Does the poem incorporate Margery Carruth's death in a fiction, or posthumously bestow upon her a fifteen-year quotidian companionship, never qualified as filial? The poem, like Carruth's Camus book, skates on the edge of two different modes of narrative, and is the more effective for it; it is also a hub around which the created community of the "georgics" revolves. It's evident that in Carruth's poems, the "local" is never merely parochial, and the personal may be either or at once political, fictional, and universal.

Carruth has published two new collections since the *Collected Shorter* and *Collected Longer Poems* of 1992 and 1994: *Scrambled Eggs & Whiskey* (1996) and *Doctor Jazz* (2001), whose appearance marked his eightieth birthday. Carruth has explored innumerable modes and forms in his career, and these books pursue many of them—historical permutations (Timor the Lame; Waterloo), erotic lyrics to his wife, new paragraphs, a memorial poem for the trumpet-player Sidney Bechet. Central to the last book is a sixteen-page elegy for Carruth's daughter Martha, dead of liver cancer in her forties. This seems, at first approach, like an expression of unmediated grief and fury, the almost unapproachable raging of a contemporary Lear. But it is no more unmediated than (as much *written* as) Lear's soliloquies, or than the existential solos of Coltrane or Charlie Parker, whose artistry and discipline are such that they inform and form any "free flight" under the pressure of extremity.

Carruth has had lengthy and fruitful relationships with two editors, unusual in these days of corporate editorial anonymity: James Laughlin of New Directions, upon the occasion of whose death Carruth wrote a book-length memoir-tribute; and Sam Hamill of Copper Canyon Press. The two were or are poet-editors; Hamill is, as well, a scholar and translator of Chinese poetry. Carruth has frequently held dialogue with other writers in his poems: Heine, Ovid, Paul Goodman. Camus, Levertov, Laughlin himself. A new mode in this dialogue perhaps comes to Carruth via Hamill: two sequences that engage classical Chinese poets, "A Summer with Tu Fu" and "Bashō." As in all his interrogations of other aesthetics, Carruth grounds his persona firmly in his own landscape and particularities—which bear a certain relationship to those of the exiled Tu Fu, in the sixth century, and the eccentric haiku master Bashō in the seventeenth. The Bashō sequence is cemented by quizzical haiku:

After the setbacks
          of Chicago and New York,
                    he went to Vermont

to a cowshed nine
          feet square. Was he proud to
                    learn that Chomei's hut

in the mountains near
          Kyoto had been "ten feet
                    square"? Maybe. Who knows.
                                        ("The Matter of Huts")

Carruth in his curmudgeon persona grouses or exults that, at eighty, he has another fifteen-hundred-year poetic tradition about which to learn—in which he is already immersed and engaged.

BEN HOWARD

Being Human

The Art of Hayden Carruth

I.

In *Reluctantly* (1998), his collection of autobiographical essays, Hayden Carruth recalls a moment when a woman friend came up to him unexpectedly, embraced him, and kissed him on the mouth "in an unmistakably sexual manner." Caught by surprise, Carruth also felt affirmed:

> It was, in fact, a great gift, or rather a great prize, at least for Carruth, awarded for no reason, out of the blue, by a power whose name and nature were unknown to him. He was astounded. All his hunger sprang into focus immediately.

In the wake of this experience, Carruth realized that "in spite of everything he possessed some singular virtue hidden from everyone, even from himself."

Something similar might be said of the poetry of Hayden Carruth, which possesses its own singular virtue, its own peculiar power. Yet that power is more readily sensed than identified, more easily felt than defined. In Carruth's poems Wendell Berry finds "in rare degree, the quality of trustworthiness." Galway Kinnell perceives a hunger for reality, which "forces [Carruth's] poems into being." Carruth himself lists passion, honesty, and "a radical attitude" as the salient attributes of his work. All of these perceptions seem to me accurate, but they focus primarily on moral attributes, and they don't quite capture the quality aesthetic or moral—which sets Carruth's poems apart from those of other honest, passionate writers. Nor do they describe his distinguishing vision.

A clue, if not a key, to the nature of that vision may be found in *Reluctantly*, where Carruth reflects on the "purposelessness" and the consequent sadness of existence. From a very early age, he sensed that "the most beautiful things in [the Universe], a flower or a song, as well as the most compelling, a desire or a thought, were pointless." All were subject to extinction. Over the years, Carruth's acute awareness of impermanence ripened into a philosophical outlook:

> What is the difference between a "natural object" and a "manmade object." None. In ultimate terms . . . all things in reality are part of reality, and hence are equal; they all plunge equally into transitoriness and nonexistence. The only meaning, such as men and women pretend to find in mathematical or poetic statements, is the meaning of obliteration. . . . And long before I came intellectually to the realization that the notion of relative value implies inescapably a hierarchal structure . . . I knew that everything is equivalent, every pebble and masterpiece, every atom and thought of love: they are *precisely* the same in value. The idea of value is an invention—at its best a sick joke and at its worst an inexpressible sorrow.

Elsewhere Carruth identifies this outlook as "radical relativism" or "equivalentism." And he sets it against its polar opposite: the will to dominate, exploit, and subjugate the natural world. "We must acknowledge the equivalence of all identities," he asserts, "our own included. We must execrate the capitalist bastards who urge otherwise."

Forcefully stated and frequently reiterated, Carruth's conviction commands attention, but it also raises many questions. In ultimate, ontological terms, the concept of equivalence may be tenable, but what currency does it have in the contingent, practical world where Carruth the editor selects poems for an anthology or Carruth the critic values one poem or author over another? More broadly, how can such an outlook survive, much less prevail, in a world where hierarchal values and the will to dominate reside not only in the economic structures of capitalism but in the fabric of language and thought? As Carruth readily acknowledges, his radical relativism demands a "total inversion of attitudes and values."

Entertained as a philosophical idea, Carruth's "equivalentism" gives pause. Perceived as a felt conviction, however, it appears in quite another light. "This is not philosophical idea-spinning," he insists. "It is practical in the most immediate sense: we cannot survive without it . . ." A passionately held belief, pervading his most recent as well as his earlier poems, Carruth's principle of equivalence has shaped the forms and informed the content of his art. And the most fruitful line of inquiry, it seems to me, is not to question the empirical truth of his view but to ask how it has found embodiment in the formal elements of his work, creating a distinctive voice and texture. If a belief in the equivalence of all things lies at the center of Carruth's art, how has it shaped his style, particularly his diction, imagery, and poetic structures? And how has it colored his personal vision?

II.

In "Upon Which to Rejoice" (1965), an essay on T. S. Eliot, Carruth praises Eliot's "willingness to experiment" and his challenge to conventional poetic diction. Eliot, argues Carruth, has "enlarged our poetic diction enormously and made it consonant with the whole range of contemporary experience . . ." What is true, in this instance, of Eliot is no less true of Carruth, whose range of diction is as expansive as it is inclusive. Like Eliot's early poems, Carruth's incorporate the lingoes of multiple social classes and walks of life, while also admitting literary, archaic, and learned speech. Unlike Eliot, however, Carruth has accomplished his purpose without resorting to irony or condescension. On the contrary, his integration of demotic and literary, plain and Latinate diction reflects a generous awareness of American social pluralities. And his adoption of multiple voices and *personae,* ranging from Vermont farmers to urban jazz musicians to a curmudgeonly retiree named Sam, bespeaks an effort to accommodate—indeed, to inhabit—lives very different from his own.

Even a cursory reading of Carruth's *Collected Shorter Poems* (1992) discloses a poet of many idioms and tones of voice. "November Jeans Song," for example, effects a synthesis of jazzy dialect and rural New England speech:

Hey, hey, daddio,
Them old jeans is
   Going to go!

Rose Marie done put in a new
   Valve cover gasket,
Them jeans good for a whole nother
   10,000 mile.

Man the wood them jeans cut,
And split and trucked and stacked,
  No wonder the axe
Been yearning and drooping
Like the poor lone gander
  For them old jeans.

Look out, get set, let
  The woods take warning.
Come six in the morning
  Me and them jeans is back,
What I mean *ready,*
We going to go
And don't care nothing for nobody,
      baby,
Not even the snow.

Mary Kinzie (in *A Poet's Guide to Poetry*) defines *diction* as "style viewed from the perspective of word formation (morphology), word length, and suggestive complexity." Although Kinzie's definition strikes me as overly subtle, it sheds some light on "November Jeans Song," which is, among other things, an exercise in style. Employing disjunctive syntax, nonstandard usage, and a high concentration of monosyllabic words, the poem's style evokes a grounded, undaunted personality, who accepts imperfection and embraces adversity. His patched jeans match his jaunty verbal style.

In other poems, Carruth enlists a plainspoken idiom, rural in inflection and salted with regional dialect. "Marvin McCabe" presents the interior monologue of a fifty-year-old invalid, who long ago lost the power of speech in a car accident and now leads a life of mute despair:

I knew the words but couldn't say them—do you
know what that means? No one knew who I was.
It was like those people who believe your soul
can pass into another body when you die.
I was in the wrong body, but I hadn't died.
Can jail be worse than that? I wanted to die.

Here the plain style, framed in pentameters, gives access to a mind that can no longer speak for itself. An affecting vignette, the poem is also an act of imaginative empathy.

"Marvin McCabe" is one of several vignettes of neighbors and friends, dating from Carruth's years in Lamoille County, Vermont. Although most of Carruth's subjects are downtrodden men, the most vivid is a woman known as "Lady," who owns a "nice old house now, big barn and the shed, / a first-rate meadow, some fair hill pasture, / and a woodlot that's good enough for what I need." Lady recalls the day when she encountered an "old she bear" in the woods, "big / as a spruce-oil kiln." Terrified, she came back to her barn with "more manure than [she] started out with," having "shit [her] britches." When she recounts her adventure to her neighbor Jasper, he sympathizes, admitting that under the circumstances, he would have done the same. "'Twas me, / "he remarks, "I believe I'd of shatten too."

Is "shatten" a solecism? A neologism? A word from another time? In *Reluctantly,* Carruth recalls how he learned to listen to the speech of his neighbors—and to respect regional variants. In one instance, he heard the word *dreen* and thought that he was either mishearing the word or the speaker was being idiosyncratic. But when he consulted his dictionary, he found *dreen* to be an archaic form of *drain.* That experience taught him to trust his ears, "and even more to trust what the people were saying."

Receptive and respectful, Carruth's attitude toward indigenous usage also informs the poems he wrote after his move from Vermont to a town near Syracuse, New York. Collected in *Asphalt Georgics* (1985), these poems feature a variety of speakers, including a disbarred lawyer, an alcoholic named Charlie Spaid, and, most memorably, the sharp-tongued retiree Sam, who has moved from the heartless suburbs to a racially mixed neighborhood in the city. In so doing, he has shed most of his racial prejudice, finding that black people "talk / like poetry," behave "as if everything's sex- // y for them, but nice sexy," and show greater humor, warmth, and generosity than the ethnics in the suburbs, the "Krauts, Harps, Hunkies, Wops going at / each other with no mer- // cy every weekend . . ." Although some of the black folks are "boozed // or zonky half the time," their culture has won Sam over:

> And by
> God, they laugh, they're always
> laughing, joking around. Hang out
> for a month of Sundays

up at the Northlight, you won't hear
  anything like that. Well,
  it means something to me and Poll,
    a whole lot, muscatel

for your ears like. Then say when you
  need a hand, like Poll's bat-
  tery that pooped out the other
    night, here's where help is at,

right here in the old neighborhood.

Playing the colloquial energies of an upstate Archie Bunker against
the constraints of rhymed syllabic verse, these stanzas resurrect cli-
chés ("a month of Sundays") and release the energies of American
speech.

   Carruth's ear for colloquial speech and his artful use of personae
are, in my judgment, two of his most conspicuous strengths. But for
Carruth himself, both are deeply suspect. In *Reluctantly,* Carruth
takes himself to task for his use of masks and his tendency to speak
in "languages not [his] own." The roots of that tendency, he suggests,
lie in a sense of inferiority and in his early upbringing, which taught
him to fear himself and "the least promotion" of himself. Some of
the best work of his middle years, *Asphalt Georgics* included, was
"written in this fear and hence in common or colloquial speech."
And even in the poems which employ archaic diction, literary conventions, and "the guises of history," he detects a drive to subordi-
nate his ego in "camouflage, fronts, deceptions of all kinds." Against
these charges he offers the defense that his use of such deceptions
was usually unconscious. And he expresses the hope that his work is
"honest fundamentally."

   As the scruples of a puritanical temperament, Carruth's comments have the ring of truth, but as a description of his art they are
demonstrably partial. They apply to less than half of Carruth's voluminous oeuvre; and they pertain to his dramatic, as distinguished
from his lyric, poems. In the latter, the speaker is or appears to be
the poet Carruth, stripped of masks and literary guises:

At home the fire has died,
the stove is cold. I touch
the estranging metal.
I pour tea, cold and dark,

in a cup. The clock strikes,
but I forget, until
too late, to count the hours.
I sit by the cold stove
in a stillness broken
by the clock ticking there
in the other room, by
clapboards creaking, and I
begin to shiver, cold,
at home in my own house.

Here (in "Loneliness: An Outburst of Hexasyllables"), as often in
Carruth's lyric poems, the speaker seems at home in his own, plain
voice as well as his own house. Although his speech adheres to a
syllabic norm, it bears few signs of literary artifice.

With respect to voice and diction, it would be fair to say that up
until the past decade or so, Carruth's poems have fallen into two
general categories. In the first are poems like "Marvin McCabe" and
the *Asphalt Georgics,* which employ numerous personae, dialects, and
vernaculars. In the second are poems like "Loneliness," which speak
as directly as possible in the author's own voice. If the first kind of
poem reflects Carruth's inclusiveness, the second expresses his integrity. And if the first affords the pleasures of variety, the second com-
mends itself as evidence of centeredness and wholeness.

But can the two modes be joined in a single poem? In a single,
comprehensive voice? One of the most striking developments in
Carruth's recent work has been his explorations of a diction
which encompasses the many dimensions of his experience and
the many elements of his sensibility, including the scholarly and
the erotic, the literary and physical, the philosophical and the visceral. Although Carruth's poems have always admitted arcane
terms, the range of his diction increases markedly in *Tell Me Again
How the White Heron Rises and Flies Across the Nacreous River at
Twilight Toward the Distant Islands* (1989), where words as rare as
nacreous keep company with blunt locutions and earthy slang. The
mix can be jarring or heady, and it doesn't always work. But it can
also be exhilarating:

Now I remember Lucinda de Ciella who drank a pony of Strega
    every morning before breakfast
And was sober and beautiful for ninety years, I remember her
    saying how peaceful

Were the Atlantic crossings by dirigible in the 1930's when her
    husband was Ecuardorian ambassador to Brussels.
Such a magnificent, polychronogeneous idea, flight by craft that
    are lighter than air!
I am sure it will be revived.

("The Incorrigible Dirigible")

In another context the word *polychronogeneous,* which does not
appear in desktop dictionaries, might seem hopelessly stilted. Here,
in the company of *sober, pony, drank,* and the resonant closing line,
the word contributes to an air of artistic and linguistic freedom. The
long line opens to accommodate it.

Carruth's synthesis of abstract and concrete diction calls to mind
T.S. Eliot's description of the poet's mind as a place where Spinoza
joins with the smell of cooking. But in Carruth's most recent poems, collected in *Scrambled Eggs & Whiskey* (1996), the fusion is not
so much one of philosophy and sensation as one of rationality and
passion, articulate intelligence and acutely felt emotion:

What does it mean, master,
that across fifteen centuries
I make my profoundest and so fatally

inadequate obeisance to your
monarchic presence in the kingdom
of poetry? What does it mean

that two old guys speak to one another
from the sadnesses of exile,
confronting their final

futility after years of futile awkwardness
in the world of doing? We look,
you and I, at the heron in the sunset.

Addressed to the Chinese poet Tu Fu (A.D. 712–770), these lines
open an epistolary sequence on the themes of aging, social violence,
exile, and erotic love. The sharp drop from the Latinate texture of
the second stanza to the colloquial realism of the third ("two old
guys speak to one another") might well have been bathetic, but
here it integrates lofty thought with grounded feeling. In similar
fashion, the abstraction "futile awkwardness" is matched, two lines

later, by the concrete simplicity of "the heron in the sunset." If Carruth's earlier poems incorporated the many voices of his neighbors, his most recent balance the components of a many-sided self.

III.

In his essay "What Does Organic Mean?" Carruth reflects on a statement attributed to Chuang-Tzu: "To have an environment and not treat it as an object, is Tao." After considering what it might mean to treat the natural world as a subject, or "subjectivity," rather than an object, Carruth rejects notions of transcendence and mystical communion, opting for an aesthetic rather than religious vocabulary:

> Instead we should speak of art, of esthetics, the way of the spiritual imagination, for this is a transaction among equals, or at least among equivalents—poet and stone. And for me . . . this is very important. It comes as close as anything can do to dispelling my fear of the human species and its lust for domination. But is art still a mode of forcing, however slight? Is the simplest, loveliest poem flawed by an unappeasable human will to intervene?

Carruth's questions are, I think, rhetorical. The lust for dominion is unappeasable. In any event, Carruth's view of the poet and the stone as equivalents has deeply informed his poetic practice, as has his fear of imposing human will on the natural environment. "Pull down thy vanity," wrote Pound in his *Pisan Cantos* (LXXXI); "Learn of the green world what can be thy place." And to turn from Carruth's diction to his way with the image is to see how consistently he has followed Pound's lead, portraying human figures as parts of nature rather than lords and ladies of the universe. If Carruth's diction reflects a principle of inclusiveness, his imagery projects a vision of interrelatedness, in which the poet and the stone—the human and the non-human subjectivity—co-exist as equivalents in close proximity.

But how may a "transaction among equals" be enacted on the page? And how may the will to intervene be subdued, concretely and convincingly, in lines of verse? "Rummage," a short poem from *Brothers, I Loved You All,* offers a case in point:

Growing old in shabby clothes
is a bewilderment for someone
who wanted all his life
to wear something handsome
under the handsome sun.

In darkness under the bent
moon I bend
to pick from the frozen road
a shred of birch bark
blowing in the wind.

The two stanzas of this lovely poem create a call and response, or, if you like, a thesis and antithesis. The first presents an ego-centered vision, that of a poet-hero conscious of his appearance and desirous of admiration. The second portrays an aging figure, who is, at most, an element of the landscape, the human equivalent of the shred of bark. The repetition of *handsome* and the echo of *bent* in *bend* draw parallels between the human and natural worlds, while also distributing emphasis. Like the moon, the narrator is bent. Neither is more important than the other. Each reflects the other.

"Twilight Comes" offers a similar picture of the poet in his natural environment, but in this instance the two are even more closely interwoven. Set in Vermont, the poem opens with an image of the changing season:

Twilight comes to the little farm
At winter's end. The snowbanks
High as the eaves, which melted
And became pitted during the day,
Are freezing again, and crunch
Under the dog's foot. The mountains
From their place behind our shoulders
Lean close a moment, as if for a
Final inspection, but with kindness,
A benediction as the darkness
Falls. It is my fiftieth year.

Cast in relaxed tetrameters, with frequent medial caesurae, these lines enact an alert receptivity, an openness not only to the natural world but also to the reality of aging. Tensions and parallels between the incipience of spring, the approach of night, and the encroachment of old age are recognized but not insisted upon. And though the anthropomorphic figure—rare in Carruth—of leaning, solicitous mountains introduces a human frame of reference, what the mountains are inspecting is the landscape rather than the poet's personal life.

Subsequent lines develop the parallels between events in the natural and human worlds. "Stars / Come out . . . like the first flowers / Of spring." The brook stirs, "[t]rying its music beneath the ice." Aware of natural and man-made phenomena, the speaker listens and interprets:

> I hear—almost, I am not certain—
> Remote tinklings; perhaps sheepbells
> On the green side of a juniper hill
> Or wineglasses on a summer night.

Reminiscent of the opening of Gray's "Elegy," these lines chronicle a moment of perception. The "remote tinklings" heard by the speaker focus his attention. Misperceiving them as sheepbells, then as wineglasses, he struggles to identify the sounds. A moment later, he discerns their source:

> But no. My wife is at her work,
> There behind yellow windows. Supper
> Will be soon. I crunch the icy snow
> And tilt my head to study the last
> Silvery light of the western sky
> In the pine boughs. I smile. Then
> I smile again, just because I can.
> I am not an old man. Not yet.

If the yellow windows of his home suggest security, the parallels between frozen snow, failing light, and the speaker's advancing age evince its opposite. Like the natural phenomena summoning his awareness, the speaker himself is impermanent. Yet there is blood in his veins—and music stirring beneath the ice. His smile acknowledges as much, as does the musicality—the interior and end rhymes (*then, again, can, man*)—of his closing lines.

The poet and the stone: in Carruth's imagery, these often strike a harmonious balance. But do the larger spheres of matter and mind, "every atom and thought of love," also strike a balance? Can consciousness, however receptive, escape its "lust for dominion"?

Although these questions could apply to most of Carruth's work, they are, I think, most pertinent in relation to his verse essays, where discursive language and analytic intelligence play prominent roles. Carruth's *Collected Shorter Poems* contains five verse essays: "Essay on Marriage," "Essay," "Essay on Stone," "Essay on Love," and "Essay on Death." In these poems the hypothetical equivalency of consciousness and nature, of the mind and the physical world, confronts its severest test, as thoughts of love—or death, or marriage—seek out a just relation with the things of this world.

Here, for example, are the opening stanzas of "Essay on Love":

Years. Many years. Friends laugh, including
even my best friend, Rose Marie, but they all
    are younger, and I might laugh as well
    to think how they will

come to know. Or tears might be as easy.
I used to drive this wedge in the maple blocks
    with pleasure; now I wouldn't care
    if I never saw another.

Yet the air is so clear, utterly clear, and the blue
September sky arching the forest's bright crown
    so very deep; come, lean the sledge
    on its maple block

and walk away, slow, stepping by the little brook
where shad leaves turn coral and the turtlehead
    blooms, late this year, its petals
    still perfect and white.

These four stanzas establish a nearly perfect symmetry: a balance of the thinking mind and the radiant natural world. In the first two stanzas, the vexed speaker pities himself, complaining of lost youth and strength. But in the next two stanzas, he renounces his self-centered worries, surrendering to the beauty of his natural surroundings.

The fifteen remaining stanzas reinforce the rhythm established in the opening four, moving back and forth between human-centered concern and selfless contemplation. Closely observing ladies' tresses, goldenrod, asters, and blue gentians, the speaker forgets his afflictions. But soon enough his pain returns:

the maple leaves if you can. Or those bluebirds
   perched, one by one, apart, on the wire
   over there, seven,

blue in the sunlight: are they a rarity? Then
count too, as one always must, the "rare" pains,
   hernia raving, bladder and penis
   in an acid flame,

arthritic hip—was it Plato said a man
is finished at fifty-five? And Rose Marie,
   my dear friend, whose spine is a pain
   that I see marching

often enough in her young eyes. What do
the bluebirds say? They don't know why they wear
   that rare color, or why they gather now
   on that wire to fly

tomorrow to Guatemala; they don't know,
   nor do I.

In these stanzas, the speaker's "rare" pains and the rare color of the bluebirds receive equal emphasis. They are equal parts of a larger whole, as is the spinal pain of Rose Marie. But as the poem advances to its conclusion, human concerns and the human hunger for meaning assume the foreground. The speaker sees "with the keen / eyes of dispassion, / the trees, flowers, birds, all colors and forms," but he asks "what good is such seeing in this chaos / we used to call order." In the end, as he resumes his wood splitting, he concludes that such labor "is the only meaning." He is doing it for love of Rose Marie, "to keep her warm and give her stovewood / for her kitchen." He will "count / no further, except these firesticks / counted for her."

    Dialectical and in its way dramatic, "Essay on Love" balances the claims of existentialist thought and pure contemplation. The lines are clearly drawn. In other poems, however, mind and nature join in an intricate dance, as the "will to intervene" vies with the desire to let things be. Of the many poems which perform this dance, one of the most beautiful is "Almanach du Printemps Vivarois," set in the Ardèche in southern France. Described by its author as a "lazy song

/ about stones," this expansive meditation depicts the aging poet and a young female companion enjoying an April morning outdoors. While the poet basks in the sun, composing his poem, the young woman sits in her underwear and sunhat, working on a drawing:

> She draws. She is young,
> she has a right to be serious. Finches
>   are serious in the oak-bushes,
> chittering, chattering, gathering gray grass
>   and gray lichen for their nests. Finches?
> They look more or less like finches. Ignorance—
>   how it invades a petulant mind
> aging in laziness and lust. And the sun,
>   higher now, stronger, a radiance
> in the sky and a blaze in the valley's faint
>   blue mist, burning on the stone, turning
> our Ibie white, our river so greenly fresh
>   three weeks ago, now a slow seepage,
> is hot, hot, blessedly hot, stirring my blood,
>   warming me through, and also moving
> the summer savory to even greater
>   fragrance, the plant called *sariette,* known
> as an aphrodisiac. Do I need that?
> Not after last night.

Although these lines feature the human figures in the landscape, and though they contain a component of self-analysis, they make ample room for impressions of the natural world, which seems less a backdrop than an integral element of the scene. And in the larger compass of the poem, natural description plays a role equal to that of self-portrayal, as Carruth sketches a nearly barren region, where meager vegetation scarcely covers the stone:

> yes, a sparse surface
> and the stone shows through, flakes, grits, fragments,
>   sharp shards
>   littering the ground, or the outcrop
> of smooth bedrock here and there, and then the huge
>   escarpment across the way, looming
> over the valley. The stone gleams, pale gray. Life
> has worn thin here, washed always down.

Is this stone of interest in itself? Or is it rather a useful metaphor for the poet's age and temperament? Carruth strongly suggests the latter, reminding himself that stone has been "so long my own / life and song." Feeling stirrings of lust, he likens them to "the seed still / sprouting in hot sun from the hill of stone."

Yet if the stony landscape serves as a metaphor for the poet, it also asserts its own identity. Compelling as a mirror for the poet, it is also a presence in its own right. And at the end of "Almanach du Printemps Vivarois," as both the sounds in the environment and the poet's own chatter die down, silent stone plays a role equal to that of the poet and his song:

> Am I deaf now too? Or is silence
> the indispensable analogue
> of brilliance? And stone is silent. Ancient stone,
> glowing stone. Song in its confusions
> is all extraneous, it dies away. Shreds
> of time. In April when the seed sprouts,
> in the Ardèche huge with silence where life is
> thin, an old man and a girl are held
> in stillness, in radiance, in flames of stone,
> for the moment of eternity.

Measuring their syllables (in an alternating pattern of eleven and nine), these lines express the will of their maker. They represent the mind's dominance over nature. But in their imagery they portray that same mind's desire merely to *be*, in the "moment of eternity." By such means, Carruth endeavors to reconcile the contemplative and the analyst, the naturalist and the artist in himself. Or, if you like, the Taoist and the Western intellectual.

IV.

"A poem," writes Carruth in his essay "The Nature of Art," "is an existent; it has the same status as a pebble or a galaxy. It has no relationship to nature, but only to other existents within nature. And what I think is that any work of art not informed by a bold and determined regard for this equivalency and its effects is deficient intellectually, emotionally, and spiritually, and cannot speak to the discerning contemporary sensibility."

Itself bold and determined, Carruth's statement reiterates his principle of equivalency, while also giving it a fresh turn. Placing a poem on an equal footing with a pebble or a galaxy, he prompts reflections on scale and structure. Are all poems themselves to be seen as equivalents? Are *Paradise Lost* and Shakespeare's 73rd sonnet, for example, to be regarded as existents, differing in scale but equivalent in ontological status? And within a single epic or narrative or meditative poem, such as Stevens's "Notes Toward a Supreme Fiction," should each element of structure—each major section—be seen as having a status equivalent to the others'?

Applied to Carruth's own oeuvre, the concept of ontological equivalence is similarly problematical. As should be evident from my earlier remarks, that concept is indeed embodied in Carruth's diction and imagery, with varying degrees of consistency. But can it also be found in Carruth's poetic structures? In his treatment of line, stanza, and section?

These questions might be asked of any of his poems, but they are especially germane in relation to his *Collected Longer Poems* (1994), which contains poems and sequences ranging from ten to seventy-two pages. Of particular interest are the sequences "The Asylum" (1957), "Contra Mortem" (1966), and "The Sleeping Beauty" (1970–1980), which employ a single structural unit: a fifteen-line form that Carruth has chosen to call the "paragraph." As Carruth notes, his critics have sometimes mistaken the "paragraph" (a rhymed pentameter form with an embedded tetrameter couplet in the middle) for a sonnet. But sonnet-writers, he insists, "will see the difference. The paragraph has its own qualities and problems."

"The Sleeping Beauty" consists of 125 "paragraphs," which present multiple perspectives on the Romantic tradition and its influence in Western history. By turns personal and philosophical, Carruth's paragraphs serve as discrete vehicles for various genres, including myth, memoir, historical anecdote, dream narrative, and vernacular monologue. For the most part, the paragraphs are autonomous units, but Carruth also employs a kind of structural enjambment, whose effect is to underscore the arbitrary nature of the "paragraph."

An example may be found in paragraph 60, which tells the story of a man with his chainsaw, who goes out on his snowshoes to cut wood for his stove. As he walks over the deep snow, he thinks of his lover, and of love generally:

And he sings,
My gal's gotta light
Like a lighthouse out to sea.
And oh,
You loves, say,
do you feel him bestow
Loving on you, which is a valuing? It is your beauty
Given to you in his seeing,
Your intelligence in his thought, so that truly
You become, you are becoming, in his being,
As he in yours. For loving is how you create
Each other, all of you, bestowing and believing
Together.
Well, my gal's gotta light like a light-

Thus ends paragraph 60—in mid-sentence. Integrating anecdote, song lyrics, and discursive reflection, the paragraph resembles a sonnet in its meter, rhyme, and scale, but it subverts the sonnet's traditional closure.

In paragraph 61, the speaker's reverie is ruptured by a sudden, dangerous development:

61

House out to sea.
And he has dropped a dead gray birch
In the snow and is limbing it when his left snowshoe
Slips. Snarling, the saw leaps; he lurches;
The saw snags his bootlace—
And the motor stalls. Gasp. He looks at his unsevered
Foot in astonishment. Alone, completely, in the forest.

Stunned by this accident, which could have maimed or killed him, the woodcutter hearkens to the distant calls of "lovers," who cry "He's alive! / Alive!" Returning to his woodcutting, he reflects on what has just occurred:

Alive. Somehow it is important,
Not because he matters, himself there like a tree
Among other trees, but because you have accorded it.

And ever' time she smile she shine her light on me.

225

Assigning equal value to himself and the trees, the speaker invokes an anonymous, collective "you" (presumably the "loves" and "lovers" mentioned in the earlier lines), who shines a protective light on the woodcutter and the trees.

Sections 60 and 61 of "The Sleeping Beauty" cannot represent all of Carruth's work, structurally or otherwise, but in their shape and development they do represent certain general tendencies in Carruth's poetic structures. To begin with, an arbitrary form is established, in this instance the "paragraph." Within that frame, a speaker recounts a story and engages in reflection. Although the lines respect the established meter, they are allowed to run over one frame and into the next. And though the "paragraphs" employ some of the elements of the sonnet, they largely eschew those devices which create internal drama. In form, as in paraphrasable content, paragraph 61 rejects those conventions which place the self and its conflicts at the center of attention. Carruth's woodcutter is not a latter-day pioneer, heroically portrayed. He and his experience are no more important than the trees.

The structural tendencies evident in "The Sleeping Beauty" are even more apparent in *Asphalt Georgics,* where Carruth introduces a rhymed syllabic stanza, strongly enjambed:

> So there
> we drove, past Hiawatha Pla-
> za, Wegman's, Bayberry
> Mall, with all the other pieces
> of the strip strung in be-
>
> tween. Friendly and Ponderosa
> looked o.k., but Carvel
> was dilapidated and Mis-
> ter Donut had a hell
>
> of a big jagged hole through both
> sides of its glass sign. I
> saw the killdeer running that has
> her nest next to the high-
>
> way on the gravel strip between
> Rite-Aid and Sunoco,
> and I heard her cry in the gnash
> of heat at my window,
>
> as once in cool March rain by the
> Hoh River.

In these lines from "Names," the outlets in a strip mall in upstate New York become events in a chronicle of perception. Reminiscent of Dos Passos in its photographic realism, its roving camera eye, Carruth's sentence moves evenly through its syllabic grid, hyphenating words and enjambing lines and stanzas. Whether the minute particulars be a Wegman's, a Friendly's, or a killdeer, they receive equal attention. Line and stanza give shape and symmetry to the narrator's speech but do not impose or reinforce rhetorical emphasis. On the contrary, the effect is one of unfolding thought rather than dramatic speech, a process of discovery rather than a single dramatic action.

Taken together, the passages from "The Sleeping Beauty" and *Asphalt Georgics* illustrate a central, structural tension in Carruth's art. On the one hand, there is Carruth's attraction to the conventional forms of the English lyric tradition. On the other, there is his attraction to those strategies which subvert conventional form. If the first produces the well-made lyric poem, with its elements of tension, release, and closure, the second produces the poem-in-progress, whose stanzas and numbered sections serve mainly to measure an unfolding process of perception. Insofar as the conventions of the English lyric tradition tend to glorify the self's internal dramas, Carruth's subversive strategies do just the opposite, placing each act, event, or moment of perception on an equal footing.

Carruth's ambivalence with respect to the English formalist tradition pervades his criticism as well as his poetry. In his essay "The Question of Poetic Form" (1976), Carruth argues that "[a] form is an effect, not a cause." Inquiring whether a poet might work from the form toward the poem, he roundly rejects that notion:

No, we work from the thing always, from the perception or experience of the thing, and we move thence into feelings and ideas and other cultural associations, and finally into language, where by trial and error we seek what will be expressive of the thing.

Yet in *Reluctantly,* Carruth remarks that an "arbitrary, artificial structure makes composition easier for me." Such a structure gives the work "greater force and fluency." You can't build a house, he adds, "no matter how inventive or fanciful it may be, without a sturdy frame."

The seeming contradiction between these statements may be

resolved if it's assumed that the poet, having found "what will be expressive of the thing," elects an arbitrary structure. But it might be better to let the contradiction stand, not as fatal inconsistency but as a vital tension in Carruth's thought and art. That tension helps to explain the structural contrasts in his *Collected Shorter Poems,* which includes, at one end of the spectrum, a sequence of sixty-three strictly metered sonnets and, at the other, the poems of *Tell Me Again How the Heron Rises,* with their rolling free-verse lines and asymmetrical forms. If an aesthetic quarrel abides in Carruth's psyche, it has enriched the diversity of his oeuvre.

It has also enriched particular poems, among them "A Summer with Tu Fu," where Carruth adopts a style with the virtues of both free and formal verse. Printed originally as a limited edition by the Brooding Heron Press, this elegant sequence consists of titled, nearly autonomous poems cast in unrhymed tercets and couplets. Some are as short as six lines; the longest extends to thirty. Whatever their length, however, the chief effects are those of calligraphic grace and elliptical concision:

OLD SONG

An old song on a hot
midnight patio of summer.
"The House of the Rising Sun."

Look at the hazy stars
so soft in the coal-dark blue.
Cicadas. A woman singing.

DUCK FEATHER

The brook slow in August, murmuring.
White duck feather floating in a pool.

The meaning of a long summer afternoon.
No one can say it. Duck feather, dark water.

Perhaps influenced by the ancient Chinese master to whom they are addressed, these lines leave an impression of poise and precision. Although they conform to no discernible meter, they retain an unmistakable formal dignity. Galway Kinnell aptly describes the style of Carruth's late poems (collected in *Scrambled Eggs & Whiskey*) as that of "highly formalized free verse," but Kinnell's description could, without loss, be reversed. The manner of "A Summer with Tu Fu" might be characterized as unfettered formal verse, freed not only of rhyme and meter but of the anthrocentric conventions of the English lyric tradition. In the lines above, a duck feather is no less and no more important than a human song. And human meaning, seen here as unfathomable, is no more glorious than the murmur of the brook.

V.

Thirty-four years ago, in "Ezra Pound and the Great Style," Carruth posed a searching question:

> How shall our children live in a world from which first the spirit, then history, and finally nature have fled, leaving only the mindless mechanics of process and change? Will any place exist for a humane art in a society from which the last trace of reverence—any reverence—has been rubbed out?

Sweeping though it is, Carruth's generalization has a basis in empirical reality. For many modern and "postmodern" sensibilities, *spirit, history,* and *nature* are problematical abstractions, rather than entities to be respected or revered. And in the wake of Deconstruction and the "death of the author," the future of a "humane art" is less than assured.

But what, exactly, does Carruth mean by a "humane art"? And in what ways can his own art be called humane? In his long poem "Vermont" (1975) Carruth extols

> a losing kind of man
> who still will save this world if anybody
> can save it, who believes . . . oh, many things,
> that horses, say, are fundamentally preferable
> to tractors, that small is more likable than big,
> and that human beings work better and last longer
> when they're free. Call him an anarchist,
> call him what you will, a humanist . . .

Clearly Carruth approves of such a man. But can Carruth's own vision be meaningfully characterized as humanist? Should an art which assigns—or endeavors to assign—equivalent value to the poet and the stone, to "every atom and thought of love," be seen as continuous with the humanist tradition? As Carruth goes on to say in "Vermont," names "are slippery, unreliable things."

In his critical and autobiographical writing Carruth often extols humanist values. Speaking of Harry Duncan, Sam Hamill, and other exemplars of fine printing, who represent a late flowering of the humanist tradition, Carruth recalls that "in the old days . . . printers were among the most literate and intelligent people I encountered." Remembering his conversations with Louise Bogan, he describes her as the "best writer of short book reviews" he has ever known. "No one today can touch her. Alas, no one today wants to touch her; that old ideal has vanished, has been castigated as 'humanistic' or 'belletristic' and thrown away." And in "Poet of Civility," a review of Auden's *Collected Shorter Poems* (1970), he examines the moral and aesthetic values implicit in Auden's art:

> What shall we say about these values of the specific English literary tradition, values of intelligence, decency, literacy, humaneness, civility, responsibility? Even though condescension, complacency, and blindness have often gone along with them, we could use a little more of them in the world of social reality these days, whatever place they may have in the world of poetry.

Questions such as these echo throughout Carruth's writings, bespeaking his affinity with the humanist tradition and his fear that its values are disappearing. Defending the "attention of logical analysis," as exemplified by lexicographers, he finds in such exactitude a "respect for the human mind and hence for humanity in general."

Yet to represent Carruth as a conservative humanist would be to ignore both his anarchist politics and his view of the social reality. An epitome of the latter appears in "The Writer's Situation" (1970), where Carruth addresses the question, posed by the *New American Review,* of whether writing has entered a "postmodern era." Responding affirmatively, Carruth describes a "great movement," usually called existentialism, which began a century ago and has intensified in recent times:

> It is, to my mind, a great shift of human sensibility, comparable to medieval theism or Renaissance humanism, and like them it entails a change in our conception of our own human place in

reality. If theism was anthropomorphic, if humanism was anthropocentric, then our era is anthropo-eccentric; we exist on the edge of reality. This is no intellectualization, but a profound and popular ethologic retooling. The consequent shift of values is immense.

Although he acknowledges that his analysis is "terribly oversimplified," Carruth proceeds to link it with developments in postwar American poetry from Lowell to Olson, Berryman to Ginsberg. A poem is no longer viewed as an autonomous work of art but as "life coming into being on the page, fragment by fragment." The idea of a masterpiece has given way to "the random poem, open-ended and fragmentary."

As I hope my own analysis of Carruth's structures has shown, the idea of the open-ended, fragmentary poem contends, in Carruth's practice, with the more traditional idea of the well-made, autonomous lyric poem. Similarly, the values of philosophical humanism contend, in Carruth's thought, with his existentialist, "anthro-eccentric" sense of reality. To call his vision humanistic, or to align his art with the humanist tradition, is to include only half of a complex equation.

It would be more accurate to describe Carruth's vision as both humane and radically realistic. Charged with human sympathy, it is also informed by a ruthlessly observant eye. In *Reluctantly* Carruth notes a family trait, a "knowledge that we were common folk and that the common values, including those of common suffering, were worth noticing." And in their choice of subjects, as in their inclusion of vernaculars from many social strata, Carruth's poems express their author's humanity and his concept of the poem as an act of love, extended across the boundaries of race and class and gender. Thus in "Homage to John Lyly and Frankie Newton," he remembers two musicians who were "not great, not / among the acerbic / downtowners" but were nonetheless worthy of remembering. Among the "almost lost," they deserve a place beside the "Dizzies / & Bens."

Yet if Carruth's vision is suffused with common humanity, it is seldom sentimental. On the contrary, it is unremittingly realistic. "We're realists," writes Carruth of himself and his fellow Vermonters. "And realism means place, and place means / where we are. We name it, with all its garbage / and slaughter, and its comeliness too . . ." True to his word, Carruth devotes several pages in *Reluc-*

tantly to recounting the week-by-week disintegration of a frozen bobcat carcass he discovered in the woods. Recalling how it turned from "tawny and patterned with stripes" to a "blanket of hair draped over its bones" to a shining skeleton, "intricate and fine and white," he reflects that "the whole process of the cat's demolition had seemed beautiful to me." More urgently, in his long poem "Mother," he remembers his mother's last illness in graphic detail:

> And fear wailed out of you, unintelligible sentences that vanished
>   in rising tremolo,
> As if you were an animal somehow granted the power to know
>   but not to think,
> Or as if you were a philosopher suddenly deprived of every faculty
>   except
> Original fear and pathos. I cannot surmise a state of being more
>   inconsonant
> With human consciousness.
> Oh, many as evil, many and many, God knows, but none essentially
>   worse.
>
> To which was added, of course, humiliation.
> "I am not nice," you repeated in your weeping quaver. "I am not
>   nice,"
> Covered from head to foot with your own shit.

At once figurative and naturalistic, abstract and concrete, this fierce portrait spares neither the author nor the reader.

To attend to the ugly as well as the beautiful, the garbage and slaughter as well as the comeliness in nature and humanity, is a mark of spiritual maturity. And to give nearly equal weight to those opposed elements, seeing them as they are, is a singular virtue of Hayden Carruth. Flowing naturally from his principle of equivalence, Carruth's balanced, compassionate realism owes something to his family and regional heritage, to his omnivorous reading, and to his literary friends, among them Berry, Kinnell, and Adrienne Rich. But in the end his outlook is more an expression of temperament than of influence or literary precedent. Although he portrays himself (in "Une Présence Absolue") as a "poor stupid bastard half-asleep here under this bridge," his poems bespeak an awakened and radically open mind, keenly aware of "what is and is and is and is and is." And, as he reminds us, "[t]he rest is babble and furiosity."

CHARLOTTE MANDEL

Beautiful Dreamers
Helen in Egypt and *The Sleeping Beauty*

Call the muse Mnemosyne or Beatrice, Ewige Frau, Eve, Helen, or Sleeping Beauty—for poets of either sex, the elusive inspirer materializes as a woman. On the game board of poetic quest, she is initiator, chief dice thrower, and the spiritual reality sought. Her image can never be physically possessed—what she represents is the power of the poet's dreaming self. *Helen in Egypt,* H.D.'s mid-century touchstone of woman's self-discovery, revolves around the beautiful dreamer. For a male poet to risk entrance into that feminine energy field requires rare gifts of sensitive awareness. Hayden Carruth, by his long poem *The Sleeping Beauty,* published a generation after H.D.'s death in 1961, marks a significant turn in literary gender evolution.

While H.D. (Hilda Doolittle) delved for transcendence into projections of the self, her contemporary, William Carlos Williams, yanked his imagined woman by the hair. H.D. portrays her beautiful Helen "moving in a dream," and therein lies her ineffable power. Without dream power, the woman is dispossessed of her generative role. Practicing his preachment, "no ideas but in things," Williams depicts his "beautiful thing" as victim of a catalog of graphic beatings. He goes on to say, "The page also is the same beauty: a dry beauty of the page—beaten by whips." Likened to the physical page his mind wishes to dominate, the poet's feminine subject becomes vincible object; significantly, she does not dream any part of his poem.

The bravest of poets vibrate to a dynamic dilemma on twin cables of opposing tension—trustful surrender to the dream pilot against refusal to let go of the wheel. Male poets have often personified the ambivalent state of submission/control as a sexually seductive woman; by submitting to her attractive force, he nonetheless controls her as a device within his poem, a servant-muse who waits upon his poetic purpose. H.D., innovator, personified the muse as an extension or projection of herself, submission as exploration of the self, control as articulation of underlying dream energy.

Carruth's poem resonates, as does *Helen in Egypt,* with a quest for beauty suspended in dream consciousness. Pound's *Cantos* and Williams's *Paterson* operate stylistically according to a masculine sense of conquest—the poems grab, almost hurl their separate parts into agglutinating series of juxtapositions that never form a true whole. These "epics" stop, rather than end. Within their accretions of historical and legendary images, fragments of feminine personae occasionally appear.

In contrast, *Helen in Egypt* and *The Sleeping Beauty* circle in musical changings around a central quest, H.D.'s in free verse lyrics, Carruth's in a variation of sonnet sequence—rhyming poems of fifteen lines he calls "paragraphs" (discussed later in this essay). Both long poems conflate historical or mythological juxtapositions into structural wholeness. And that sense of wholeness, the poems will conclude, emanates from feminine energy at the source.

Must the dreamer be "beautiful"? Yes, because of the abstract working ideal she represents. "Beauty," H.D. wrote in 1927, is "goodness in its Hellenic sense . . . Beauty and Goodness [are] one thing . . . a curse, a blessing, a responsibility." In 1990, Hayden Carruth, defining his own feelings of artistic responsibility in an interview, stated, "To me, poetry and goodness are almost synonymous. They go together . . . to be a poet, you have to have a vision at some point."

Musical flow impels their poetic visions. Although *Helen in Egypt*'s 160 sequences of three-line stanzas vary in length from four to thirteen stanzas, each flows as a single sentence. A prose voice which introduces each sequence becomes another part of the whole, a participant who sounds a different level of consciousness, simultaneously narrating and questioning the story. Nearly all of *The Sleeping Beauty*'s 125 sequences (including one added in the 1990 reissue) follow a fifteen-line sonnet-based rhyming "paragraph" invented by Carruth. In the interview cited above, he explains the "pivot" effect of a rhyming couplet shortened to tetrameter set in the middle to allow "flow through" the rhymed couplet "barrier" effect that would otherwise "break up the poem."

Both long poems germinate in mysterious silence. H.D.'s opening envisions a timeless Egyptian tomb where Helen, alone, moves "as one in a dream." Achilles—or his ghost—appears, his memories differing from hers of "the whole phantasmagoria of Troy." Later, on the Greek island of Leuke, while dying Paris remembers/ relives his passion for Helen, Theseus, a wise father-guide, leads a younger

Helen through shifting labyrinths of myth. "Eidolon," the final portion of the long poem, carves the image of Thetis, the "Sea-mother," a compelling, feminine generative figure. H.D.'s language continually absorbs and alters the myths received by the poem's personae—and by the reader. Divine and legendary figures superimpose, absorb into new kinships. Through incantatory cinematic word-dissolves, Helen conflates gods of death and war with the name of Achilles, once her lover. "Cypris, Cypria, Amor/ say the word over and over . . . War, Ares, Achilles, Amor." Gradually, the shifting elements resolve: "the assembled host of spirits for the whole arc . . . the circle complete." At the close, Helen, awake, no longer dreaming herself within a dream, believes she has discovered "the innermost/ key or the clue to the rest/ of the mystery."

Carruth's poem opens to the dreamlike silence of invisible snow: "Out of nothing." The poem's silence is attuned to capture "the echo of coincidental voices" in history. Names of poets are called upon, of philosophers, heroes, cities, and even the apocalyptic persona, "Hydrogen Bomb." Within the structural frame, each stanza achieves separate time, diction, and rhythm—from medieval, to rural contemporary Vermont, to insertions of American Jazz wherein the spirit of "Saint Harmonie" is invoked. And yet, with all the differences in voice, plaint, content, and pace, *The Sleeping Beauty,* like *Helen in Egypt,* travels to final cognitive resolution.

Carruth's poet ultimately hears "in the beating universe/ the poem alone and free." Helen as she unravels the cords of bequeathed history that bind her (and the reader's) mind, liberates the poem of herself: as the poem states, "She herself is the writing." The goal is revealed to have been the poem itself—the poems evolving in struggle toward vision embodied and transformed into a living work of art. This sacred grail carries the healing regeneration.

The lyric/narratives of *Helen in Egypt* and *The Sleeping Beauty* offer healing of the original male/female cosmic division within our spiritual identities. By ritual enactment of what has gone before, the poem attains a new state of existence, rhythmically paced to the passage of time coeval with transformation. From silent stirrings of conception, *Helen in Egypt* and *The Sleeping Beauty* grow into life—the poem's ontogeny recapitulating phylogeny through metamorphoses of past images—and come to terms. A new identity is born.

Carruth's poem strives to acknowledge the world's debt to the feminine principle as we may know it in woman, nature, and history.

His axial image, intermittently seen, is a woman's face of stone, visible under a stream, originally sculpted and placed in the brook by a woman who thought it was "flawed." The face in the water, states the poem, is "Our eternity." Carruth brings in a witness who confirms the presence of the stone woman in the water—Amos, ghost of a Vermont farmer. Speaking in twenty-four of the stanzas, Amos functions as guide or teacher, comparable to the character of Theseus in H.D.'s poem. The chiming echo of Dante's Virgil heard in the voices of these guide-figures subtly suggests that H.D. and Carruth are in quest of an ideal. The Vermont farmer says (his words identified in the poem by italics): "I knowed her afore you was thought of . . . Down in the watergrass, just as plain, as calm." The poet asks, "Asleep or awake, Amos?" "Both," replies his guide from the past.

Helen, too, marvels at a sculpted image of a woman linked to water—the carved figure of Thetis upon the prow. "She is the 'sea-mother,'" a goddess who changes embodiment through the ages. "Did her eyes slant in the old way?/ was she Greek or Egyptian?/ had some Phoenician sailor wrought her? . . . had the prow itself been shaped to her mermaid body,/ curved to her mermaid hair?" She is the mother of Achilles, "his childhood's secret idol, the first Thetis-eidolon."

Answering his own question, "Why is the face in the water a woman?" Carruth asserts, " . . . the image is basal,/ From before the beginning of all imagining,/ The a priori of human feeling, ineffaceable/ for good or ill,/ and as such it is, it must be, feminine." He affirms the feminine principle as source of artistic energy for both sexes. Personified as the fairy tale princess, she dreams poems which address societal cruelty to females—binding of feet, accommodations of the harem, mutilations of war. Interspersed are struggles of male persona (sometimes the "prince," awake or dreaming) whose memories include the trauma of institutionalized strapping down for electric shock treatments. The male persona's dream of a menstruating young woman is overturned by a psychoanalyst into a battle between father and son, a castrating anger. But "the prince who is human, driven, and filled with love" recalls the myth of creation as division by divine sword blade, male and female equally wounded; his dream seeks, in fact, wholeness, the healing to be found in loving sexual connection: " . . . for a long (eternal?) moment/ His being and hers were indistinguishable,/ So intermingled that he could not tell/ Which was man, which woman . . . He knows his feminine aspect,/ Always his, deeply and dearly his."

The above passage soars beyond the impression of Solotaroff that *The Sleeping Beauty* calls forth the Provençal troubadour poetic adorations of a woman loved. Provençal tradition treats the woman as an erotic object, generator of a poet's song, and his muse. In her perceptive study of reclamation of the muse by women poets, Mary K. DeShazer states that "muses have typically been portrayed as passive catalysts who stimulate lyricism in the active male poet, helping him 'give birth' to a new entity." Hayden Carruth literalizes the traditional metaphor in one of the prince's dreams: "And his belly is brilliantly broad . . . the birth is easy, a mere gush/ or a happy purging, and behold! in the flash/ Of newborn radiance is a beautiful translucent child . . . and he is wild/ With joy, joy, joy . . . Because he has done it at last,/ the real thing,/ he has done it himself." Carruth, fully conscious of the practice of muse-appropriation, ironically illustrates the male dream with eureka-style shouts of "joy, joy, joy!" The birth dream stanza adds to the catalog of oppressions against women. It is not exploitation of a passive erotic muse, but consonance of masculine-feminine energies that charges *The Sleeping Beauty*.

The initial *H*—an oddly relevant coincidence—suffuses the consciousness of both poets. Hilda Doolittle preferred the use of her initials as her published signature, played upon them in the title of Hermetic Definition, named an autobiographical heroine Hermione/Her, and poetically absorbed the identity of Helen of Troy; Helen was also her mother's name. (See Morris on H.D.'s preoccupation with the letter *H*.) *The Sleeping Beauty* plays variations upon persons and entities whose names begin with the poet's initial, the letter *H:* Homer, Helen, Hero/History, Herod, Holderlin, Heraclitus, Hermes, Herr Husband, Hendryk Hudson, Hitler, Heathcliff, Heliopolis, Hiroshima—personae and things that appear in the princess's dreams, or those of her prince. What cousins to the self may the poet be seeking? In English, these names are initiated by a voiceless exhalation of breath, a sound that evokes the beginning of life and its fragile continuance, just above the border of silence.

At the resolution of *Helen in Egypt,* Helen/H.D. is awake, her consciousness freed by the poem's work of reassembling memories and cultural definitions. Carruth's princess is also awake. The poet has filtered reason and feeling through immersions in past and present literature as well as loves and separations of his own life to an integration of consciousness. The closing stanza speaks with the voice of a mature male poet:

> Princess, the poem is born and you have woken,
>   . . .
>   The sun
> Will rise on the snowy firs and set on the sleeping
> Lavender mountain as always, and no one
> Will possess or command or defile you where you belong,
> Here in the authentic world.
>   The work is done.
> My name is Hayden and I have made this song.

                                                        (125)

The poet is named—he is Hayden, himself. The poem is the song that frees prince and princess who have been entangled in the trance-dreaming and brings into harmonious completion the male and female elements of our natures, an androgyny innate within the universe.

For Helen, harmony breathes within the timeless center of herself: "there is no before and no after,/ there is one finite moment/ that no infinite joy can disperse . . . now I know the best and the worst." A passage in H.D.'s early autobiographical novel, *HERmione,* surprises the moment of awakening/ passing of a winter dawn; "There is a quivering, a slightest infinitesimal shivering. The thing that was is not." *The Sleeping Beauty* envisions the "intricate purity" of invisible snow whitening a branch of pine in a gray world; "Out of nothing . . . or out of a cold November/ Dawn that anyone could see, this grace/ That no one can ever quite remember" (1). The reader, awake within the poems' dreaming visions, hears, in isolated silence, the notes of H.D.'s and Hayden Carruth's questioning/answering. Helen's self-discovery of the dreaming muse reverberates "the seasons evolve around/ a pause in the infinite rhythm/ of the heart and of heaven."

Carruth has said that imagination makes it possible for a poet to become "existentially free, and the same time . . . come into some kind of sympathetic understanding with other imaginations which are also existentially free." Feminist scholars, notably Sandra Gilbert and Susan Gubar, have recorded instances of male/female antagonism in twentieth-century literature as a "war of the words." Nevertheless, *The Sleeping Beauty* comes into existence during a century of imaginative re-vision by women poets. Such re-imagining by a male poet may signal new landscapes. Will it be possible to abstract the dream entirely? Not for H.D. and Carruth, poets whose stance is basically humanistic. Seeking a moral vision, they trust in the terms set by the dreamer. The dreamers within the poems of H.D. and Hayden Carruth envision goodness, a state of healing. By poetry's intellectual and intuitive grace, their visions breathe within the reader's consciousness as well.

At last, at last the night
　　lies down beneath the hill
and the busy city in the sky
　　becomes visible. What
a bustling and confusion of
　　activity up there! I
can see the rape of Helen
　　and hear my own first cry
when I was born, for both
　　of which I feel profoundly
sorry. Somewhere nearby
　　meanwhile a paleolithic
relentless whippoorwill
　　confides his commentary.

—HC, *Scrambled Eggs & Whiskey*

Contributors

Shaun T. Griffin's most recent poetry collection, *This Is What the Desert Surrenders, New and Selected Poems,* came out from Black Rock Press in 2012.

Wendell Berry is a poet, essayist, farmer, and novelist. He is the author of more than forty books.

Philip Booth published ten books of poetry and was one of the founders of Syracuse University's graduate creative writing program.

David Budbill's newest book of poems is *Park Songs: a Poem/Play.* He lives in the mountains of northern Vermont.

Robert Duncan was the author of numerous volumes of poetry and criticism, including *Selected Poems* (1993).

Sascha Feinstein's ten books include *Ajanta's Ledge* (poems), *Black Pearls* (memoir), and *Ask Me Now* (interviews). He edits *Brilliant Corners: A Journal of Jazz & Literature.*

Geoffrey Gardner's poems, essays, and translations of poetry—especially the poetry of Jules Supervielle—have appeared widely over many years.

Marilyn Hacker is the author of twelve books of poems, including *Names,* and of many translations from French.

Donald Hall is a former Poet Laureate of the Library of Congress and New Hampshire.

Sam Hamill is the cofounder of Copper Canyon Press and the author of more than forty books.

Brian Henry is a widely published critic and the author of nine books of poetry.

Ben Howard is the author of eight books, including *Leaf, Sunlight, Asphalt,* the verse novella *Midcentury,* and *The Pressed Melodeon: Essays on Modern Irish Writing.*

Carolyn Kizer has published eight books of poetry, including *YIN,* which won the Pulitzer Prize in 1985.

Stephen Kuusisto teaches at Syracuse University and his latest book is *Letters to Borges.*

Denise Levertov, who was born in England, published over twenty volumes of poetry, including *Freeing the Dust* (1975), which won the Lenore Marshall Poetry Prize.

Charlotte Mandel's eighth book of poetry, *Life Work,* is forthcoming in 2013 from David Robert Books.

Joe-Anne McLaughlin is the author of three collections of poetry, *The Banshee Diaries, Black Irish Blues,* and *Jam.*

Matt Miller is Assistant Professor of English at Yeshiva University in New York City, where he teaches American literature and creative writing.

Adrienne Rich received numerous awards, most recently the National Book Foundation Award for Distinguished Contribution to American Letters.

David Rivard is the author of five poetry books including *Otherwise Elsewhere* and *Sugartown,* and teaches at the University of New Hampshire.

Lynne Sharon Schwartz is the author of twenty-two books, including novels (*Disturbances in the Field* and *Leaving Brooklyn*), short story collections, poetry, essays, and translations from Italian.

Douglas Unger is a novelist and teaches in the master of fine arts program at the University of Nevada, Las Vegas.

David Weiss edits the *Seneca Review* and teaches at Hobart and William Smith Colleges.

Judith Weissman was Professor of English Literature at Syracuse University for more than twenty years.

Baron Wormser is the author or coauthor of twelve books and is former Poet Laureate of Maine.

Also by Shaun T. Griffin

Poetry

This Is What the Desert Surrenders: New and Selected Poems
Winter in Pediatrics
Bathing in the River of Ashes
Snowmelt

Limited Editions

Under Red-Tailed Sky
Words I Lost at Birth

Editions

The River Underground: An Anthology of Nevada Fiction
Torn by Light: Selected Poems of Joanne de Longchamps
Desert Wood: An Anthology of Nevada Poets

Translation

Death to Silence: Poems by Emma Sepúlveda

Printed and bound by CPI Group (UK) Ltd, Croydon, CR0 4YY

09/06/2025

14686096-0001